LIMITING LEGISLATIVE TERMS

LIMITING LEGISLATIVE TERMS

Edited by

Gerald Benjamin
SUNY, New Paltz

Michael J. Malbin
SUNY, Albany

Center for Legislative Studies
Nelson A. Rockefeller Institute of Government
State University of New York
Albany, New York

A Division of Congressional Quarterly, Inc.
Washington, D.C.

Copyright © 1992 Congressional Quarterly Inc.
1414 22nd Street, N.W., Washington, D.C. 20037

Printed in the United States of America

Cover design: Richard Pottern

Limiting legislative terms / edited by Gerald Benjamin and Michael J. Malbin.
    p.   cm.
Includes bibliographical references and index.
ISBN 0-87187-863-1
ISBN 0-87187-740-6 (pbk.)
    1. United States. Congress—Term of office. 2. Legislative bodies—United States—States—Term of office. I. Benjamin, Gerald. II. Malbin, Michael J.
JK1140.L56   1992
328.73'073—dc20   92-16503
                                            CIP

CONTENTS

TABLES AND FIGURE

Tables

Figure

PREFACE

Public opinion in America of Congress and the state legislatures—never very positive—has been sinking to new depths. In response to this downward spiral, the congressional and legislative reform agenda seems to be shifting. No longer content with rearranging power inside these institutions, more people are pushing to alter the character of contemporary representation by focusing on the incentives that shape legislative careers. One mechanism they have chosen is a mandatory limit on the number of consecutive terms a legislator may serve in office.

There should be no surprise about the public's dissatisfaction with their legislative assemblies. American legislatures rarely get collective credit when things go right, but often find themselves the targets of collective blame. And in recent years the opportunities for blame have been rampant. Think about some of the major national headlines of just the past four years: large pay raises adopted without open votes, the resignations of House Speaker Jim Wright and Democratic Whip Tony Coelho under ethical clouds, the savings and loan scandals, sex scandals, drug scandals, illegal gratuities, and overdrawn checks. Combine this drumbeat of stories about Congress with the indictments of several prominent state legislators across the country, a national economic recession, and a general public unhappiness with the government's performance, and no wonder the people seem angry and cynical.

However, even if the public's anger and cynicism have been predictable, the proposals that have moved to the top of the institutional reform agenda have not been. During the late 1980s, many people came to identify legislative failures with the growth of the legislative career. They came to believe—whether correctly or not will be debated in the pages to follow—that political careerism had produced legislators who were so busy protecting their own jobs that they failed to take care of the public's best interest. To remedy the situation, they began pushing for mandatory term limits. In 1990 the voters in three states—Oklahoma, Colorado, and California—passed term-limit initiatives. A similar proposal was defeated narrowly in 1991 in Washington State.

The election of 1992 probably will be a high water mark for such proposals. A dozen or more states (including Washington again) are likely to have term-limit initiatives on their fall ballots. There can be no doubt the issue will be a prominent part of the public debate for at least one more election cycle. And if a reasonable number of the initiatives are successful, the issue could be with us for some time to come.

Unfortunately the debate so far has been conducted with more heat than light, on both sides of the issue. For that reason the Center for Legislative Studies decided to hold a conference in October 1991 to bring people together to think seriously about the politics of term limits, their varieties, and their likely long-range consequences. The event was held at the Rockefeller Institute of Government, the State University of New York's institute for public policy research in Albany, New York. Most of the chapters of this book are revisions of papers presented at that conference. The substantive agenda of the conference, as well as the logic underlying this book, is explained in the book's opening chapter, "Term Limits for Lawmakers."

We have a large number of debts to acknowledge. First of all, our conference, as well as the subsequent research and writing costs, was underwritten in part by a grant from the Harry and Lynde Bradley Foundation of Milwaukee, Wisconsin. We are grateful to the Bradley Foundation for its confidence and support.

The event itself—if we can be excused for the self-praise—worked the way a good conference should. About three dozen people with different experiences and perspectives spent two days around a table, learning from each other. As a result of that discussion, most of the papers in this volume were rewritten substantially over the next several months. In a very real sense, therefore, all of the participants contributed to the efforts you see in this volume.

In addition to the authors, the conference participants (listed alphabetically) included: Carl Carlucci (New York Assembly staff), George Carpinello (Albany Law School), Richard Cohen *(National Journal)*, The Hon. Richard Coombe (New York Assembly), Edward Crane (President, Cato Institute), Len Cutler (Sienna College), Charles Dawson (Center for Legislative Development, SUNY, Albany), Ronald Elving *(Congressional Quarterly)*, Sally Friedman (SUNY, Albany), John Fund *(Wall Street Journal)*, Steven Gold (Center for the Study of the States, Rockefeller Institute), Leon Halpert (Sienna College), Roman Hedges (New York Assembly staff), Karl T. Kurtz (National Conference of State Legislatures), David

Mason (Heritage Foundation), Francesco Mariah (New York Senate staff), Gary Moncrief (Boise State University), Paul Ogle (president, Americans Back in Charge), the Hon. William Proxmire (former U.S. senator) and Rick Scott (American Federation of State, County, and Municipal Employees).

Because this conference was the first major public event of the new Center for Legislative Studies, we would also like to thank the people who were responsible for getting the center off the ground. Richard Nathan wears dual hats as director of the Rockefeller Institute and provost of the university at Albany's Rockefeller College of Public Affairs. In both of these capacities, he has been more than just a supporter of the center. Anyone who has ever worked with Dick knows how his enthusiasm, intelligence, and energy can make the difference between a vague idea and a project that works.

Frank Mauro, the Rockefeller Institute's deputy director, is an action-intellectual who is responsible for helping make the institute an exciting organization almost ideally suited for an event such as this one. The institute's staff—Liz Praetorius, Janet Hall, Maria Augostini, Michael Cooper, Michelle Choiniere, Michelle Kelefant, Charlene Evans, and John Selmer—all had a hand in helping to make the conference and book a success. So, too, did Kenneth Goldfarb, from SUNY central administration's public affairs office, and Peggy Barmore, SUNY, Albany.

At the university we would like to thank Frank Thompson, dean of the Graduate School of Public Affairs, as well as Robert Nakamura and Martin Edelman, the past and current chairpersons, respectively, of the Department of Political Science, for their help with the center's start. The university gave the director released time for his first two years at SUNY, as well as partial support for the research assistants used on this project. The SUNY graduate student who has given the most to this conference and book, over the longest period of time, has been Christopher Grill. Other major help came from Neil Krause and Michael Helm, who are also graduate students in the university at Albany's Political Science Department.

The staff at CQ Press also deserves our thanks for maintaining their editorial quality when we all sought to push deadlines. That includes David Tarr, Shana Wagger, Steve Kennedy, Chris Karlsten, and Kate Quinlin, among others.

And finally, our families deserve special mention. Some time near the end of this project, a friend gave Gerald Benjamin a telling cartoon. It showed a forty-something father in a sweatshirt, slumped in his chair, staring at a computer screen. At the study door was a frustrated-looking boy holding a soccer ball, standing next to his consoling mother. The mother was saying to the boy, "I know, but all promises are off when Daddy's writing his grant proposals." Our colleagues may have to change the facts slightly to fit their own situations. Once they do, they will recognize the bittersweet truth of that cartoon.

GB
MJM

INTRODUCTION

1. TERM LIMITS FOR LAWMAKERS: HOW TO START THINKING ABOUT A PROPOSAL IN PROCESS

Gerald Benjamin and Michael J. Malbin

Limiting lawmakers' terms of office would affect some of the most basic incentives that shape the way legislatures work in the United States. That is the one point on which the supporters and opponents of term limits agree. Beyond that agreement, however, lies a dizzying swarm of irreconcilable assertions. The aim of this volume is to help readers sort through the assertions and begin making sense of the issue for themselves.

The authors approach the task with a sense of urgency. The voters in at least eleven and perhaps as many as eighteen states will be asked in 1992 to vote for or against ballot initiatives imposing mandatory term limits on legislators. If these initiatives are successful, the idea no doubt would gain support in some more of the thirty-six states where initiatives or bills were filed in 1991. Whether one supports or opposes term limits, therefore, it is crucial to begin thinking seriously about the potential consequences of what clearly would be a major change to the political system.

But our interest is not only topical. Any serious examination of the term-limit debate quickly engages some of the most enduring philosophical—and some of the most interesting empirical—issues on the research agenda of legislative scholars. That is because the term-limit debate, at bottom, is about the many-sided relationships among democratic control, personal ambition, and the public good. It is about how members' individual decisions to satisfy personal career goals might help, hinder, or otherwise affect a legislature's collective performance.

Because personal goals and institutional performance are intertwined, we assume that altering legislative career possibilities will also change a great deal about how legislatures work. That is an obvious and safe assumption. However, until we can specify exactly how those relationships will play out, it means we still have a great deal to learn—not only about term limits, but about the underlying causal connections between individual and collective performance. The issues surrounding term limits should help readers think through some of these more general questions.

The Setting

Term limitation involves a simple idea that summarizes and expresses a deep public dissatisfaction with Congress and state legislatures. The American public has a generally low impression of legislative institutions and is quite willing to express that opinion by saying, "Throw the bums out." As a result, when term-limit initiatives began to appear on ballots in the fall of 1990, they captured the public imagination, sweeping to easy victories in Oklahoma (67 percent) and Colorado (71 percent) and to a narrower victory in California (52 percent). Eleven months later, a fourth victory seemed all but assured, as David Olson shows later in this volume. Public opinion surveys in the state of Washington showed the people to be overwhelmingly in favor of term limits. Organized opposition was all but nonexistent.

But this time, the supporters of term limits tried to do too much too quickly. The Washington initiative would have applied retroactively to members of Congress as well as the state legislature. If successful, it would have removed the entire congressional delegation from office by 1994—including the Speaker of the House, Thomas Foley. As a result, the opponents of term limits had a lever they could use to counter the voters' generalized and abstract sense of frustration. In the three weeks before Election Day, Foley and Governor Booth Fowler led a vigorous, last-minute campaign that shifted the public's attention away from Congress as a whole and refocused it on specific incumbents. Faced with a redefined question, the voters rejected the initiative, 54 percent to 46 percent.

The Washington result was important. It showed that a term-limit initiative could be defeated. However, a single defeat hardly means the end of a movement. Both sides have learned from past campaigns and have regrouped for the future. Public disapproval of Congress soared to an all-time high after House members' bank overdrafts became public in March 1992. President Bush supports term limits and shows every sign of trying to run against Congress in his reelection campaign. With so many states voting on the issue in 1992, it would be premature to write the idea off as yesterday's fad. The future of term limits remains very much in doubt.

But to say that an issue will be aired is not the same as to say that it will be aired well. Both sides almost surely will be appealing to emotional symbols. Supporters will talk about entrenched, self-serving incumbents. Opponents will defend the voters' freedom of choice and say that there is adequate turnover already. Good examples of such rhetoric can be seen in the selection in Appendix A-5, a reprint of the arguments distributed to voters by California's secretary of state during the 1990 election campaign.

There are important truths contained in the arguments being put forward on both sides of the political debate. If that were not so, the political battle would not be so hard fought. In favor of term limits, there is no denying how tough it has been to defeat an incumbent member of Congress. In most elections during the past several decades, more than 90 percent of House members who sought reelection have been successful. In the past four elections, that number has been higher than 95 percent—a string unprecedented in American history. (See Appendix B-2, Turnover and Reelection Rates in the U.S. House and Senate, 1790-1990.)

Nor is the incumbency phenomenon confined to the national legislature. While a few state legislatures have shown remarkable electoral volatility—notably New Jersey in 1991—90 percent reelection rates have been common for others. Incumbency advantage was clearly a factor in two of the states that adopted term-limit initiatives. In California, a total of only three incumbent senators have lost in the past three elections. In Colorado, none has lost since 1982.

If the supporters of term limits are right to say that incumbents have an advantage for reelection, the opponents are equally right to point out that there is a much higher degree of turnover from voluntary retirements. More importantly, however, neither set of arguments gets at the underlying issues. After all, there is nothing wrong with a stable membership if the legislature is doing the job it ought to be doing. Stability of membership and incumbency advantage therefore turn out to be surrogates for more basic questions about legislative performance: What are the appropriate standards to use for judging a legislature? How well is the legislature doing against those standards? And would term limits in fact serve to enhance the legislature's performance by the standards laid out? Opponents and proponents in the term-limit debate disagree about standards—about what an effective legislature would look like—and they disagree in their empirical predictions about how term limits in fact would affect legislators' behavior. We shall consider both of these disputes in the pages that follow.

Thinking About Change

Before we turn to the merits of term limits, however, it would be worth spending a moment on the process by which this issue has moved up on the national agenda. There is an old saying in Hollywood that every "overnight sensation" has twenty years of hard work behind it. The same might be said of political reforms, especially reforms of governmental structure or process. Most of these are rediscoveries; few are entirely new. This is an important first lesson in thinking about change.

Term limitations are a good illustration. Mark Petracca's essay in this volume reveals that the idea of rotation in office has had an enduring importance in Western democratic theory and in American history. The exchange reprinted here from the 1788 New York State convention to ratify the U.S. Constitution shows how the long-standing philosophical dispute was translated into a debate over mandatory term limits. Upon reflection, the contemporary resonance produced by this issue is less remarkable than it first might appear. The principles underlying both sides of the current debate have long been a part of our country's unending dialogue about democratic representation.

John Fund and Cleta Deatherage Mitchell support term limits with arguments that parallel the Antifederalist view of representation, in which the most important job of the representative is to reflect the constituents' immediate wishes without distortion (Appendixes A-1 and A-3). In contrast, term-limit opponents Charles R. Kesler (Appendix A-2) and the attorneys for the Clerk of the House of Representatives (Appendix A-3) strike themes self-consciously reminiscent of the Federalist view, in which the representatives' primary responsibility is not to reflect constituents' immediate wishes but to serve their long-term interests. There is no intelligent way to address the current issue without also raising the major historical and philosophical disputes out of which that issue arises.

If a first lesson in thinking about reform is to be aware of history, a second is to be aware of the present. Legislative term limitations might have emerged as the goal of a major movement at other times but did not. They have emerged now. Why?

The answer involves a complex combination of factors. The first, mentioned above, is a receptive public mood—fertile ground in which the idea could grow. There is little doubt that the term-limit movement is linked to a more general public hostility toward legislatures and entrenched power holders. This hostility is shared by citizens of a wide range of social and economic backgrounds and ideological convictions. (See the poll data in Appendix A-1, Table A-1.) There is little doubt, too, that it is tied to a belief, among some, that government is more a source of problems than of solutions and needs to be reined in.

But term limits have not gotten equally far everywhere that the ground has been fertile. A necessary second factor is the availability of an institutional context in which the idea can succeed. If the analogy for a receptive public is fertile ground, that for an accessible institutional context is "good weather."

TABLE 1-1   Term-Limit Bills Introduced in State Legislatures, 1991-92

	Jurisdiction Affected						
	State Only		State and Federal		Federal Only		All
	N	(%)	N	(%)	N	(%)	N	(%)
Partisan origin of bill							
Republican	47	(54)	4	(66.7)	1	(25)	52	(53.6)
Democrat	38	(43.7)	2	(33.3)	3	(75)	43	(44.3)
Independent	2	(2.3)					2	(2.1)
Sponsor's party							
In power	44	(51.8)	4	(66.7)	4	(100)	52	(54.7)
Out of power	41	(48.2)	2	(33.3)	0		43	(45.3)

Source: Let the People Decide, January 7, 1992.

Note: Legislation from 28 states is included in this table: Alabama, Alaska, Arizona, Connecticut, Georgia, Illinois, Iowa, Kansas, Louisiana, Massachusetts, Michigan, Minnesota, Missouri, New Mexico, New York, North Carolina, Ohio, Oklahoma, Pennsylvania, Rhode Island, South Carolina, Tennessee, Utah, Vermont, Virginia, West Virginia, Wisconsin, and Wyoming. Independents (two measures) are counted with the party out of power.

Although the numbers keep shifting as legislation is offered across the nation, one tabulation in early 1992 counted 36 states in which term-limitation initiatives or bills had been introduced. Surprisingly, in the 28 states in which bills had been introduced in the legislature (Table 1-1), the sponsors were only slightly more likely to be Republicans than Democrats, and only slightly more likely to be members of the party out of power. (However, the four bills that applied only to Congress, leaving out the state level, all originated with members of the party in power.)

Few of these bills had a serious chance to pass. In at least one case, however, a legislatively sponsored term-limit proposal was advanced to give the voters a less Draconian alternative than the one being brought up through the initiative process. In January 1992, the Florida house passed a twelve-year limit on consecutive service in the state legislature that was endorsed by the Miami *Herald.* In addition to giving members four more years than the pending "Eight is Enough" initiative, the bill did not apply to members of the U.S. Congress.

Rather than providing conflicting evidence, the Florida experience reinforces the observation that term limitations have their best prospects in states with initiative procedures. These allow established office holders to be bypassed as structural changes not in their interest are advanced. Thus the term-limit movement once again demonstrates that the opportunity for change is clearly affected by "good weather"—the presence of an accessible governmental process.

But fertile ground and "good weather" are still not enough. The seed must be planted and nurtured. For change to occur there must be skilled, effective leadership, motivated by ideology, ambition, partisanship, or the simple belief that the change somehow will make things better. To plant that seed, and nurture it, leaders need resources. This means finding donors, locally or elsewhere. These resource providers will have their own motivations, some of which may be quite different from those of local leaders. As David Olson's case study of the term-limitation movement in Washington State suggests, politics does indeed sometimes make for strange bedfellows.

The fourth and final point is that one single success does not make a movement. Before we think in terms of a "movement," a seed that has taken root and grown in one place should successfully have been transplanted to another, and another. For transplantation to occur, the idea needs to be communicated, from state to state, from state to some central location, from center back to another state, and so on. Some of this might occur spontaneously, the result of the relatively recent emergence of communications media that are truly national in reach. But much transplantation is purposeful, the consequence of national organizations working to spread the idea. Stuart Rothenberg's essay is an effort to examine the role of organizations at the center in advancing the term-limits movement, in the context of what we know about how ideas spread in American politics.

Of course, change must often be achieved in the face of opposition. Both Olson and Rothenberg look at the opponents of term limits—their goals, motivations, and strategies—and question why, until the last days of the campaign in Washington, they were so remarkably unengaged and ineffective. (By comparison, the organized opposition played a crucial role in slowing two other recent grass-roots movements—tax limits and the nuclear freeze.) The organized opposition to term limits may have been weak because the most logical opponents were so clearly self-serving: incumbent office holders and powerful interest groups trying to protect their established relationships with those incumbents. But whatever the explanation for the opponents' failure to organize, the effects were straightforward. There was an asymmetry on the political battleground—that is, until the incumbents began stating their own preferences more forcefully.

Different Proposals, Different Consequences

One major section of this book will be devoted to the process of change. But after all is said and done, the contemporary political debate centers on the intended and unintended *consequences* of change. As we turn to that subject, we quickly come to realize that there is no single term-limitation proposal the potential effects of which we can analyze. Instead, there are several different kinds of proposals, with significant variations. Therefore, if we want to understand the potential effects of a limitation on terms, we have to begin with a close analysis of the proposals advanced in a number of states. Some of the key variations include:

- The length of the limits
- Whether limits last a lifetime or require a break (or discontinuity) in service
- The length of the break, if a break is required
- Whether service in the legislature is governed by a single aggregate limit or by limits that apply separately to separate legislative bodies
- Whether limits apply to service at the national level
- Whether the length of the service to be limited is counted from the dates of the proposals' adoption or retroactively

As of late 1991, sixteen states had either adopted term limits or had initiatives filed and ready for the voters' consideration. Table 1-2 summarizes these initiatives, as well as the one defeated in the state of Washington, and two that were ruled unconstitutional by state authorities before a vote.

State Limits on Service at the National Level

Perhaps the simplest of the variations to understand conceptually is that in which a state proposal would limit federal office holders. Although the constitutionality of such a limitation is controversial, the way it would operate is not complicated. Term-limit advocates are convinced that a Congress filled with members whose terms are not limited will never vote to place limits upon themselves. Therefore, advocates have decided to use state ballot initiatives to put limits on the service of individual state delegations, one at a time. Over time, as an increasing number of members are forced to live with limits for themselves, advocates expect that these members will be willing to vote to impose similar limits on their colleagues.

Twenty of the proposals summarized in Table 1-1 contemplate limiting the length of legislative service in the U.S. Senate and House of

TABLE 1-2   State Term-Limit Initiatives

State	State Limit[a] H	State Limit[a] S	State Limit[a] Combined	U.S. Congress Limit H	U.S. Congress Limit S	Effective Date	Lifetime Limit?[b]	Break in Service?[b]
Passed								
Calif.	6	8	—	—	—	11/90	Yes	—
Colo.	8	8	—	12	12	1/91	No	4
Okla.	12	12	12	—	—	1/91	Yes	—
Failed								
Wash.	6	8	10	6	12	Retro.	No	6
Ruled Unconstitutional before Vote[c]								
Alaska	—	—	8	—	—	Retro.	No	2
Maine	10	10	—	—	—	11/92	No	—
Pending[d]								
Ariz.	8	8	—	—	—	1/93	No	2
	—	—	—	12	12	1/93	No	4
	—	—	—	6/12	12/24	1/93	No	4
	8	8	—	6	12	1/93	No	—
Ark.	6	8	—	6	12	1/93	Yes	—
	12	12	—	—	—	Retro.	Yes	—
Fla.	8	8	—	8	8	11/92	No	—
Mass.	8/9	8/9	—	8	12	1/95	No	Yes
	—	—	—	8	12	1/95	No	—
	8	8	—	8	12	1/95	No	—
	8/9	8/9	—	—	—	1/95	No	Yes
	8	8	—	—	—	1/95	No	—
Mich.	6	8	—	6/12	12/24	1/93	State only	U.S. only
Mo.	8	8	16	—	—	11/92	Yes	—
	—	—	—	8	12	e	Yes	—
Mont.	8/16	6/12	—	6/12	12/24	1/93	Yes	Yes
Nev.	4	8	—	4	12	1/93	No	—
Ohio	8	8	—	8	12	1/92	No	4
Ore.	12/16	12/16	—	—	—	11/92	No	Yes
	4	8	—	4	12	?	No	—
	6	8	12	12	12	1/93	Yes	—
S.D.	8	8	—	12	12	1/93	No	—
Wash.	6	8	—	6	12	f	No	—
Wyo.	6/12	12/24	—	6/12	12/24	1/93	No	Yes

(Continued on next page)

TABLE 1-2 *(Continued)*

Source: Let the People Decide, January 1992.

Notes:

[a] Limits in initiatives presented to the voters may be stated in numbers of terms or numbers of years. For simplicity and ease of comparison, all time lengths in this table are stated in years. Also for simplicity, the larger house in each state is indicated as "H," and the smaller one as "S." Where term limitations are being considered as a number of years or terms over an elapsed period, that is expressed here as "years of service/elapsed period." For example, one proposal in Massachusetts would limit state legislators to eight years service in any nine-year period, presented here as "8/9."

[b] Where limits are not for a lifetime, the length of the break period specified in the proposal is given.

[c] In Alaska, the attorney general ruled that, contrary to assertions by advocates, the term-limits proposal there was a constitutional amendment. It was removed from the ballot because the state constitution cannot be amended by the initiative process. The secretary of state in Maine made a similar determination and took a similar action.

[d] All proposals under consideration in late 1991 are presented here; in several states multiple proposals were pending.

[e] Term limits for Congress would begin in Missouri under this proposal when similar limits are adopted for Congress by one-half of the states.

[f] Term limits for Congress would begin in Washington State under this proposal after ten states have adopted such limits. Term limits would begin for the state legislature on January 1, 1993.

Representatives. Usually the limits are eight years in the House and twelve in the Senate, but the Nevada proposal and one of those in Oregon would limit members of Congress to two terms; six (the one defeated in Washington, the new one in that same state, and those pending in Arizona, Michigan, Montana, and Wyoming) place the limit at three terms. Florida's proposal to limit senators to eight years would effectively prevent them from serving a second term.

These provisions will surely be subject to constitutional challenge. As can be seen from selections later in this volume, proponents of term limits, such as Cleta Mitchell, argue that the states may set term limitations for Congress under Article I, Section 4 of the U.S. Constitution, which establishes their power to regulate federal elections. Opponents, such as Steven Ross and Charles Tiefer, attorneys for the Clerk of the U.S. House of Representatives, argue that such limitations add to the constitutional qualifications for office established in Article I, Sections 2 and 3. This is prohibited, they say, under Supreme Court interpretations of these sections, especially in the 1969 case of *Powell v. McCormack*. This constitutional dispute raises some of the core historical questions of federalism. However, because these issues fit into a framework that is at least somewhat familiar for most readers, we shall let the legal briefs and California Supreme Court opinions speak for themselves. (See Appendixes A-3 and A-4.)

Limit Length

We are on less familiar ground when we begin thinking about the maximum number of terms, and the break in service required once the maximum has been reached. These variations will have a profound effect on whether any particular limit would be likely to promote citizen legislatures or increase electoral competition.

As can be seen from Table 1-1, the most common legislative term limitation now under consideration is eight years, two terms for an office with a four-year term and four for an office with a two-year term. There are six-year limits in California's adopted provision for its assembly, Washington's failed and pending provisions, and proposals in Arkansas, Michigan, Oregon, and Wyoming. The Maine proposal blocked from the ballot would have allowed ten years of service. Three proposals come with twelve-year limits, each slightly different from the others: Oklahoma's adopted provision limits service in each of its houses, and combined service, to twelve years. A proposal in Oregon limits service in each of its legislative houses to twelve years within a sixteen-year span. Wyoming's proposal for its smaller house makes the limit twelve years in twenty-four.

The immediate practical effect on turnover of varying limit lengths is explored by David Everson. Historically, rates of turnover in American legislatures have varied enormously. It stands to reason that the impact of limits on average turnover would vary both with the length of the limits and with the length of an average legislator's service now, without limits. Thus, the impact of any limit would be greatest in the U.S. Congress, and in state legislative bodies where average service tends to be the longest (for example, the New York and California senates or the lower chambers in Arkansas or Illinois). (For tables showing turnover rates in each of the states and in Congress, see Appendixes B-2 and B-5.) Combining the two features—limit length with average tenure—in the three states that have already adopted term limitation, the short limits on service imposed on the highly profes-sionalized California legislature are likely to have a more dramatic effect than the slightly longer limits in Colorado, where voluntary turnover is already high, or the even longer term limits in Oklahoma, whose turnover is roughly equal to Colorado's.

Everson's research also indicates that term limits are most likely to be imposed in places in which they would have the least impact. That is, the states that allow initiative and referendum also tend to be less likely to have large numbers of long-serving state legislators. Here California may be exceptional. (See Appendix B-9 for a table of the states that make provision for citizen initiatives.) Interestingly, an eight- or twelve-year limit might actually increase the average length of service in the legislatures of some states. This would happen if "serving to the limit" were to become the norm in jurisdictions that now have relatively short average periods of service.

Lifetime Limits, "Combined" Limits, and the Break Period

Two of the avowed goals of term-limit supporters are to increase electoral competition and to promote citizen legislatures. It turns out, however, that the two goals are somewhat in conflict and that different kinds of term-limit provisions are likely to have varying impacts on each of the two goals. To understand why this is so, let us consider the effects on political ambition of three different types of term limitation— simple limits on continuous service in one office, lifetime limits, and combined limits that lump together all years of legislative service in either chamber.

A **simple limitation** is one that limits the length of continuous service in one office without placing any restriction—other than reelection—on what the office holder may do after that term of service has ended. Thus, simple limits permit incumbents at the end of their service to compete for another office and thus maintain an active career in politics. Most pending term-limitation proposals are of this variety.

Lifetime limits would place a cap on the number of years a person could serve in a lifetime and thus would prevent political careerism by law. Oklahoma's and California's adopted proposals are for the individual's lifetime. (For California, this was confirmed by that state's supreme court in October 1991, when the court upheld the constitutionality of the state's limitation initiative. For excerpts of the opinion, see Appendix A-4.) Lifetime limits are also included in proposals to be offered to the voters in Arkansas, Missouri, Montana, Oregon, and Michigan.

Finally, **combined limits** would fall midway between simple one-chamber limits and lifetime limits in their effects. They would permit politicians to remain active in politics but might prevent them from running for what might be the most logical next office in a typical political career ladder. Though also not the norm in the proposals presented in Table 1-1, such combined limits are present in the term-limit plans adopted by Oklahoma (twelve years), defeated in Washington (ten years), and offered in Alaska (eight years), Oregon (twelve years) and Missouri (sixteen years).

If we want to think about how these different kinds of limits might affect political competition, we should start with what we already know, or can surmise, from other sources about why competition is so weak today. One key source of incumbency advantage in an age of weak political parties is the use office holders make of their perquisites to increase their name recognition and support among constituents. This is the one advantage of incumbency that usually draws the attention of term-limit supporters. But another side of the equation is too often missed in the political arena: the importance of challengers. As Linda Fowler has argued in her previous publications[1] and in her contribution to this volume, one of the major reasons incumbents win so easily is that they do not have to run against strong challengers. In most districts, the politicians who seem as if they might be the strongest challengers are often incumbents in other offices who have a good deal to lose if they fail. These potentially strong candidates calculate the long odds against winning and choose not to come forward.

But the calculations of such experienced politicians would have to change with term limits. Exactly how they would change cannot be known until term limits are in effect for a while. However, we can begin to get some ideas by looking at the initial impact in states that have already adopted term limits (see the contributions by Charles Price on California and Gary Copeland on Oklahoma) as well as from analogies to other offices with limited terms (see Thad Beyle on governors).

To the extent that staying in one's present office were precluded, a simple limit would, among other things, increase the incentive experienced politicians would have for seeking another office. Experienced lawmakers in any of the 49 bicameral state legislatures might try to continue their legislative careers by running for the "other house." Or office holders might be more willing to move freely between national, state, and local levels of government. In this way, a limit on continuous service in one office could enhance the overall level of competition in the system by setting up a game of musical chairs for professional politicians. Of course, it would do so while permitting professional politicians to remain active in politics. In this way, enhanced competition would conflict with another of the professed aims of term-limit supporters, the citizen legislature.

In contrast, a lifetime limit would effectively end political careers. And combined limits, like lifetime limits, would block not only a career in one office, but a legislative career in general. Thus both kinds of limits would have an effect that was almost the opposite of that of a simple limit. Simple limits would probably increase the pool of experienced challengers; lifetime and combined limits would decrease the pool. Simple limits would increase competition and permit continued political professionalism; conversely, lifetime and combined limits would decrease legislative professionalism but probably would also further depress the level of electoral competition.

The Break Period

Any predictions about the likely effect of a term limit on career politicians would also have to take into account how long politicians would be required to spend in "the private sector" before they were allowed again to stand for election. Most term-limit proposals in Table 1-1 do not specify the length of the break required after an office holder reaches the maximum number of years of continuous service. The clear implication in these states is that the break is to last for one term. Experience shows that a one-term hiatus does not kill political careers; both Michael Dukakis and Bill Clinton were defeated for reelection as governor but returned to win a following election and then became presidential candidates. As Thad Beyle points out in Chapter 8, there are many other examples of governors who returned to office after being defeated or forced out for a term by a term-limitation provision.

Some proposals specify the length of the break but make it fairly short. The adopted Colorado term-limitation provision specifies a four-year break period, as do the proposal for Ohio and one of those for Arizona. The Alaska initiative and another of the Arizona proposals both specify two years. The effect of these should not be dissimilar from that of an implied one-term limit.

However, a few state proposals would require a longer break. The defeated Washington State proposal featured a six-year break period. Montana's proposal would limit service in its larger house to eight years in sixteen and in the smaller house to six years in twelve. Similarly, the proposal pending in neighboring Wyoming would permit six years in twelve for its larger house and twelve of twenty-four years in its smaller house. Finally, a proposal pending in California (not included in Table 1-1) would require a five-year break after nine years of service as a U.S. senator and a three-year break after seven years as a member of the U.S. House.

A long break from service in a single office without a lifetime limit or a prohibition on running for another office could bring about one of two results. For many people, the realities of career planning and the need to earn a living might turn longer break periods into the functional equivalents of lifetime bans. For others, however, the break might simply encourage "back and forth" behavior. Some of these provisions might even occasionally result in job sharing by married couples. The idea would be to keep the job in the family, passing it from wife to husband. This would keep the family name on the ballot and help incumbents' families retain the advantage of voter familiarity while formally meeting the limitation requirements. (To gain the maximum benefit would require, of course, that both spouses use the same family name.) Though this idea may sound farfetched, widows frequently have been candidates to replace their dead husbands, and there is at least one well known example of sequential service in the governorship of Alabama, when Lurleen Wallace was governor in the years between the terms of her husband, George.

Conclusion

Clearly, different kinds of term-limit provisions are likely to have very different kinds of effects on the ambitions of skilled politicians. Some will produce amateur legislatures; others will produce legislatures dominated by itinerant political professionals. It follows from this that they will also have different effects on the internal organization of the legislature, as well as on the relationships between legislators and executives, interest groups and political parties.

In sum, when all of the potential effects are considered, term limits will make a major difference in the policy-making process and therefore in the content of public policy. These effects are likely to be felt in subtle ways. There will be unintended as well as intended consequences; effects we can predict and ones we cannot. Many of these points are addressed in the essays in this volume. All will be revisited in our concluding chapter.

Note

1. See, for example, Linda Fowler and Robert McClure, *Political Ambition* (New Haven: Yale University Press, 1989).

Part I

THE HISTORY AND POLITICAL THEORY
OF TERM LIMITS

2. ROTATION IN OFFICE: THE HISTORY OF AN IDEA

Mark P. Petracca

Term limitation is not a new idea. It is firmly rooted in the idea and historical practice of rotation in office. In 1789, Thomas Jefferson, a devoted advocate and practitioner of rotation in office, defined the concept simply and precisely: [I]n America, . . . by the term rotation in office, then, we mean an obligation on the holder of that office to go out at a certain period."[1] An obligation to leave office after a predetermined term of service by elected or appointed public officials constitutes the action involved in the rotation principle.

Absent from most contemporary discussions and debates about term limitation is a perspective on the history of rotation in office as an idea. Where did the idea come from? Where was it practiced? How is it justified? What sort of experience does America have with it? These are just some of the historical and analytical questions that need to be answered to put the modern controversy about term limitation in proper perspective.

As a principle of political design, rotation in office—along with its modern counterpart, term limitations—is deeply rooted in classical republican political thought. As an idea, it accompanied the emergence of democratic theory in ancient Greece and Rome and the development of representative democracy after the Renaissance. It was popularized and brought to America by the Dutch in "New Amsterdam," and, more significantly, through the influential writings of English Commonwealthmen, oppositionists, and radical Whigs of the seventeenth and eighteenth centuries. From antiquity to eighteenth- and nineteenth-century America, rotation in office was a political principle put into the design of new political institutions in order to prevent the corruption of elected officials, check government tyranny, guarantee liberty, enhance the quality of political representation, and promote widespread service in government.

Today, citizens are looking again to the principle of rotation in office, now dubbed term limitation. Term limits, so advocates claim, are an antidote to the contemporary problems of the permanent government, the advantages of electoral incumbency, bureaucratic excess, the absence of electoral competition, legislative aloofness, institutional deadlock, and the professionalization of American politics.[2] For good or ill, the 1990s may be the decade in which the principle of rotation in office returns to American politics.

There is a remarkable similarity between the contemporary furor over term limitation and historical debates over the wisdom of rotation in office. In many important ways, the contemporary clashes echo earlier debates over the definition of a democratic regime in which rotation was a prominent feature of institutional design.

Just a little more than a century ago, rotation in office was a shibboleth by which people's commitment to democracy and, indeed, their "Americanism" was tested and measured. Today, that relation has been inverted. Over the past few years, politicians, newspaper editors, and political scientists seeking to discredit term limitation have charged that the idea is not only undemocratic, but also un-American.[3] This chapter responds to these claims. Like preceding debates about rotation in office, the contemporary contest over the wisdom of term limitations is squarely within the democratic tradition.

Precedents from Antiquity and the Renaissance

The idea of rotation in office can be traced to political practices in ancient Athens and Rome. During the fourth and fifth centuries B. C. the Athenians selected their council of five hundred annually and by lot, with the provision that no one could serve on it for more than two years in his life. These provisions for representation, unthinkable in a "modern" democracy, were intended to ensure that the views of the council would coincide with those of the people.[4]

The Basics of Democracy

Rotation figured prominently in Aristotle's list of the constitutional features of a democracy. This list included selection to office by lot (the principle of sortition), short terms for officeholders, restrictions on holding the same office twice, and the rule of "all over each and each in turn over all."[5] The principle of rotation was fundamental to Aristotle's understanding of the relation among equal citizens in the polis, relations characterized by the principle of "ruling and being ruled in turn."[6] For Aristotle, democratic citizenship is produced through the exercise of these two different political roles: that of ruler and that of the ruled. Rotation gave more people the opportunity to serve in public office and, in so doing, trained and sensitized a large number of individuals in the art and responsibilities of public life. As a consequence, rotation was good for the development of citizens and good for the state.

Aristotle was also mindful of the limiting effect rotation would have on the use of public office for private gain. Limited tenure in office and the principle of rotation curtailed the possibility that individuals would use their office to acquire positions of leadership and therefore power. For Aristotle, rotation helped to limit the power of the individual as well as to instruct him in the art of democratic rule. As we will see, rotation was also defended as a means to check the power of the state during the seventeenth and eighteenth centuries.

Rotation, coupled with the practice of sortition, kept democracy functioning in Rome and "ensured that power remained at least nominally with the popular Assembly." [7] As practiced in Rome, rotation meant that no citizen should hold any office more than once in his lifetime. Since Rome was admittedly ruled by an oligarchy, rotation had the effect of "ensuring that offices were equitably shared among the comparatively few highly qualified persons who laid claim to them." [8]

Going back as far as the fourth century B. C., anyone who held a magistracy was ineligible for reelection to the same office before ten years had elapsed. As in Athens, terms of office were fixed and brief; indeed, the more exceptional the power of an office, the shorter the term.[9] The practice of rotation was much the same in Cicero's time. Cicero praised rotation in office along much the same lines as Aristotle, saying: "So the man who obeys should have the hope that he will one day command, and he who commands should reflect that in a short time he will have to obey." [10]

Reciprocity of experience made for better representatives, citizens, and policy. A ruler having previously lived as one of the ruled would be more sensitive to their needs. Conversely, those ruled will have a better appreciation of the difficulties faced by rulers if they too have ruled.

The Venetian Experience

The Renaissance city-states of Venice and Florence also adopted the Greco-Roman practice of rotation in office. In *The Classical Republicans,* Zera S. Fink called rotation in office "one of the most striking features of the Venetian constitution." [11] While the Venetian Doge was chosen for life and the Great Council was perpetual, every other aspect of government practiced either full or partial rotation. After 1178, the Ducal Councillors (six in number) generally served for a year, sometimes for six months, and were not eligible for reelection until two years had passed since their prior term.[12] By one estimate, between 1498 and 1524 the Zonta had an annual turnover of 30 percent of its membership.[13] By the principle of rotation, an official was ineligible for reelection until a period equal to the term of his office had passed. Unlike the stricter Roman requirements, Venetian rotation was similar to subsequent American restrictions on holding successive terms, a restriction most commonly applied to state governors.

The Venetian practice of rotation was motivated by ideas similar to those advanced by the Athenians and Romans. Rotation "was motivated also by the idea that in a society of equals it gave many a chance to learn both how to rule and how to be ruled and this supplied the state at all times with a large body of trained and able statesmen." The Venetians added a reason to the defense of rotation based on the assumption that "human nature is such that men cannot be trusted with long continuance in office of great power." [14]

The English Political Heritage

Through the writings of Machiavelli and other political commentators of the sixteenth century, English intellectuals learned about the idea and practice of rotation in antiquity and the Renaissance city-states. In turn, America's colonists and revolutionaries were exposed to the idea of rotation through the writings of so-called Commonwealthmen, oppositionists, and radical Whigs of the seventeenth and eighteenth centuries.[15]

Balancing Public and Private Interests

The seminal work on rotation during this era was *The Commonwealth of Oceana* (1656) by James Harrington. The aim of Harrington's commonwealth was to reconcile public and private interests. To achieve this end, he "declared two institutions to be indispensable, an 'equal Agrarian' and 'equal Rotation.' " By the former he meant "an immutable law preventing the concentration of landed property in the hands of one or few; by the latter, such a law of elections for the magistracies that all qualified persons shall have an equal opportunity to serve their fellow-citizens." [16] Rotation was essential to the electoral dynamics of representative government. "Though rotation may be without the ballot; and the ballot without rotation," the ballot meant little to Harrington unless it included rotation as well. The connection was "not to ensure the supremacy of popular choice," explained J. G. A. Pocock, "so much as to ensure the reality of the individual's participation; he is to take frequent turns at office, and is not to depute or alienate civic functions to others." [17]

Harrington was not only interested in equalizing and increasing the opportunity for individuals to serve in office, he was also concerned with maintaining the balance between public and private interests in the commonwealth. "The contrary," said Harrington, is "Prolongation of Magistracy, which, trashing the wheel of Rotation, destroys the life

or natural motion of a Commonwealth." Rotation prevents officeholders from developing interests separate from those of their constituents
through extended tenure in office and guarantees that such officeholders will behave in a fashion consistent with the knowledge that they will
in a short time return home to the status of a private citizen.[18]
Harrington understood that too much rotation would be dangerous to
the stability of a republic but he was equally concerned that too little
could result in tyranny and oppression.

Harrington was joined in his support for rotation by an impressive
array of seventeenth- and eighteenth-century English intellectuals,
including Sir William Blackstone, Thomas Bradbury, James Burgh,
William Godwin, John Locke, Edmund Ludlow, Catherine Macauley,
Walter Moyle, Henry Neville, Algernon Sidney, Lord John Somers,
and John Trenchard. Each added or confirmed reasons for the
necessity of rotation; all focused attention primarily on the value of
rotation as a protection against tyrannical government and the loss of
individual liberty.[19]

A Rebuke to Tyranny and Corruption

In *Plato Redivivus* (1681), Henry Neville commended the use of
rotation as "excellent" for avoiding the growth of insolence in parlia-
ment and preventing the corruption of its members. Representatives,
said Neville, "should have no other instructions, but to dispose of all
things and act in their several charges for the interest and glory of
England. . . ."[20] Walter Moyle, in *Constitution of the Roman Government* (1726), supported rotation as a means to prevent officials from the
"possession of too much authority," which might "tempt the magistracy
to invade the liberties of the nation."[21] Not only would rotation check a
bad regime, but by systematically sending officials home to feel the
genuine effects of their actions, rotation would promote good government as well. The promise of rotation as a remedy for tyranny and
corruption was eloquently stated by Algernon Sidney in 1698:

> Whatever virtue may be in the first magistrates, many years will not
> pass before they come to be corrupted; and their successors, deflecting
> from their integrity, will seize upon the ill-guarded prey. They will
> then not only govern by will, but by that irregular will, which turns
> the law, that was made for the public good, to the private advantage
> of one or few men. . . . I think I may justly say, that an arbitrary
> power was never well placed in any men, and their successors, who
> were not obliged to obey the laws they should make. This was well
> understood by our Saxon ancestors: they made laws in their
> assemblies and councils of the nation; but all those who proposed or
> assented to those laws, as soon as the assembly was dissolved, were

comprehended under the power of them, as well as other men. They could do nothing to the prejudice of the nation, that would not be as hurtful to those who were present, and their posterity, as to those who by many accidents might be absent.[22]

The last line is crucial to the role played by rotation in office in safeguarding the public interest. With rotation, representatives will not pass laws or take precipitous actions that affect their constituents because they will shortly be returning home to experience those laws and actions directly.

This point was also emphasized by Sir William Blackstone as one of the virtues inherent in the frequent turnover of parliaments: "A legislative assembly also, which is sure to be separated again (whereby its members will themselves become private men, and subject to the full extent of the laws which they have enacted for others) will think themselves bound, in interest as well as duty, to make only such laws as are good." [23] Though not a principal advocate of rotation in office, John Locke also understood the importance of annual parliaments, frequent elections, frequent change in officials, and the need to have representatives "return into the ordinary state of subjects." [24] Absolute arbitrary power could be held in check and the people given the opportunity to secure their peace and tranquility.

Rotation as a check against tyranny and oppression was probably given its most elaborate treatment by James Burgh in *Political Disquisitions,* published in 1774 and 1775, on the eve of the American Revolution, and one of the most widely read works of the era. If a republic was to guard against the "continual danger to liberty," said Burgh, representatives must be chosen for short terms and with frequent rotation.[25] Burgh explained why:

> If the majority of the house be not changed every other year, the same men may be reelected for 20 years together; and if a place-bill should be passed, tricks may be played by riding or splitting of places, unless a rotation bill is likewise passed.... [T]here is no security without exclusion by rotation.... [W]ith that regulation and the others, bribery might easily be rendered impracticable.[26]

Like Neville, Moyle, and Locke, Burgh argued that a lengthy term of office was too much of a temptation to bribery and corruption for even "good men." Rotation was the antidote of choice for corruption and its companion, the usurpation of political power.

Criticism and Response

The idea of rotation was not without its critics, David Hume and Matthew Wren most prominent among them. In *Idea of a Perfect*

Commonwealth (1741), Hume found the inconvenience of rotation to be the "chief defect of the *Oceana*." Without regard to ability or performance, rotation threw men out of office, not only wasting talent, but forcing a new set of office holders to educate themselves in the details of legislative governance. A more thorough critique of Harrington's *Oceana* and the idea of rotation appeared in Wren's *Monarchy Asserted or the State of Monarchicall and Popular Government in Mr. Harrington's Commonwealth of Oceana*, published in 1657. Commonwealths endure "great and dangerous inconveniences" from their rotation, said Wren. Citing examples from Rome and Athens, Wren concluded that rotation did more mischief than good, especially in so far as it sacrificed able public servants to public exigencies.[27]

The criticisms of Hume and Wren presaged contemporary arguments about the impact of legislative turnover on regime stability and the need to retain experienced legislators.

Not surprisingly, the Commonwealthmen had responses to these criticisms. Admitting that some experienced legislators would be lost through a system of rotation, many English thinkers thought it worth the price to prevent an even greater evil. Frances Hutcheson, a Scottish intellectual who claimed Adam Smith as a pupil, explained:

> A rotation in office might deprive the state of the prolonged service of a good man, but it would also be a safeguard against all evil men. New talent would be brought forward. Corruption would be prevented since long continuance in office would be impossible.[28]

Occasionally mentioned as an advocate of rotation, John Milton actually had mixed feelings about the concept. On the one hand, Milton feared the uncertainty and instability generated by rotation. On the other, he feared the danger of unbridled ambition and government tyranny. As a compromise, Milton advocated a mixture of turnover and permanence—a balance of new and experienced office holders brought about by partial rotation. Although hesitant to champion rotation as a key feature of institutional design in a democratic commonwealth, Milton was willing to concede its necessity.[29]

Partial rotation was a way to preserve some legislative experience and yet provide for frequent turnover in office holders. Most of the rotation schemes proposed in Milton's time had one-fourth to one-third of the legislative body returning to private station at a time so that it was never left without a majority of experienced office holders. As a result, seventeenth- and eighteenth-century proponents of rotation in office were much less worried about the loss of experienced representatives than are current opponents of term limitations.[30]

America's Revolutionary Experience

The idea of rotation in office made its way to America through the writings of these seventeenth- and eighteenth-century English intellectuals. America's revolutionary thinkers generally agreed that in a republic "government should be kept as near to the people as possible, chiefly through frequent elections and rotation-in-office." [31] John Adams captured the importance of these two principles on the eve of the American Revolution:

> Elections, especially of representatives and counsellors, should be annual, there not being in the whole circle of the sciences a maxim more infallible than this, "where annual elections end, there slavery begins." These great men . . . should be once a year—Like bubbles on the sea of matter borne, They rise, they break, and to that sea return. This will teach them the great political virtues of humility, patience, and moderation, without which every man in power becomes a ravenous beast of prey. [32]

Before Adams began to popularize Harrington and Burgh for the citizens of Massachusetts, the principle of rotation may have arrived on American shores courtesy of the early Dutch colonists. Rotation of a council by thirds was practiced in the Dutch provincial estates and, according to historian Charles Beard, was introduced in New Amsterdam, where it continued to be practiced in colonial New York. Rotation was also found elsewhere in colonial New England, for instance in the text of the New England Confederation of 1643. The idea made its most significant appearance in William Penn's "Frame of Government" for Pennsylvania, written in 1682. The Frame of Government established annual elections for the provincial council and affirmed the importance of rotation in office for the governor, councillors, and members of the general assembly. [33]

Drawing on lessons from antiquity and the Renaissance and on seventeenth- and eighteenth-century English political theory, America's revolutionaries identified three distinct reasons for incorporating rotation into their new constitutional designs.

Enhanced Participation

Consistent with Athenian practice and the views of Harrington, rotation provided an opportunity for a greater number of individuals to serve in government. Article IV of the "Frame of Government" (1682), for example, stipulated that "after the first seven years, every one of the said third parts, that goeth yearly off, shall be incapable of being chosen again for one whole year following: that so all may be fitted for government, and have experience of the case and burden of it." Not only would more people be able to serve in government through the principle of rotation, but also, as historian Gordon Wood notes, it would compel "mobility in a deferential society where men too often felt obliged to reelect their rulers for fear of dishonoring them." [34]

A Check on Tyranny

Following the views of Sidney, Locke, and Burgh, America's revolutionaries advocated rotation as a check on tyranny and the unbridled usurpation of political power. Fearing abuse of executive power in particular, by 1777 seven of the ten new state constitutions (in Pennsylvania, Delaware, Maryland, Virginia, North Carolina, South Carolina, and Georgia) had limited the number of years that an executive officer could serve in office. Typical of these constitutions is the statement made in Article XXXI of the Maryland constitution of 1776: "That a long continuance, in the first executive departments of power or trust, is dangerous to liberty; a rotation, therefore, in those departments, is one of the best securities of permanent freedom." [35]

One state went much further than the others in adopting the principle of rotation. The Pennsylvania constitution of 1776, considered to be the most radical constitution of the revolutionary era, required rotation in office for all elected officials—executive and legislative—in order to prohibit, as the constitution stated, "the danger of establishing an inconvenient aristocracy." An anonymous publicist in Pennsylvania called rotation "one of the life guards of liberty." [36]

Revolutionary constitutions were particularly influenced by the pamphlets of "Cato," written by the British radical Whigs, John Trenchard and Thomas Gordon. In rather colorful language, Trenchard explained why rotation for representatives was necessary to preserve liberty: "The Possession of Power soon alters and vacillates their Hearts, which are at the same time sure to be leavened, and puffed up to an unnatural size." In what reads very much like the case for term limitations, Trenchard argued that representatives who served too long would grow indifferent to the interests of their constituents, lose their moderation, renounce their commitments and promises, magnify their conceit, and ultimately, become tyrannical. Therefore, said Trenchard, a rotation "in Power and Magistracy, is essentially necessary to a free Government: it is indeed the Thing itself; and constitutes, animates, and informs it, as much as the soul animates the Man." [37]

No other state went as far as Pennsylvania in restricting the reelection of legislators to the lower house. However, three states—

New York, Delaware, and Virginia—required rotation of senators. Six states—New York, New Jersey, Pennsylvania, Delaware, Maryland, and South Carolina—limited the terms of sheriffs, coroners, governors, or members of the governor's council.[38]

Enhanced Representation

Inspired by the Aristotelian principle of "all over each and each in turn over all," America's revolutionaries viewed rotation as way to facilitate and affirm the experiential connection that must necessarily exist between representatives and the represented. The bill of rights contained in the Virginia constitution of 1776 expressed the expectation that the threat of oppression would be diminished and the qualities of representation enhanced if public officials were frequently "reduced to a private station." Section 5 stated:

> That the legislative and executive powers of the State should be separate and distinct from the judiciary; and that the members of the two first may be restrained from oppression, by feeling and participating the burdens of the people, they should at fixed periods, be reduced to a private station, return into that body from which they were originally taken, and the vacancies be supplied by frequent, certain, and regular elections.[39]

The view that the connection between representative and constituent is strengthened and the exuberance of government tamed when representatives know that they must soon return to live in the community they have helped shape through their actions in government was ardently expressed by Thomas Paine in *Common Sense* (1776), one of the most influential tracts of the revolution:

> That the interest of every part of the colony may be attended to, . . . the elected might never form to themselves an interest separate from the electors, prudence will point out the propriety of having elections often, because as the elected might by that means return and mix again with the general body of the electors in a few months, their fidelity to the public will be secured by the prudent reflection of not making a rod for themselves. And as this frequent interchange will establish a common interest with every part of the community, they will mutually and naturally support each other, and on this . . . depends the strength of government and the happiness of the governed.[40]

It is noteworthy that a call for officials to "return to public life" appears in the many bills of rights that served as preambles to almost every state constitution passed during the revolutionary era. Alongside the rights to frequent elections or free speech, rotation in office appeared as a right necessary to preserve liberty and enhance the quality of representative government.[41]

Rotation on Trial: The Articles of Confederation

These republican sentiments influenced the drafting of the Articles of Confederation (1781), which called for the annual appointment of delegates to the national legislature, provided for their recall at any time, and set limits on the length of time a delegate could hold office. Section V of the Articles stated: "No state shall be represented in Congress by less than two, nor by more than seven members; and no person shall be capable of being a delegate for more than three years in any term of six years." [42] Thomas Jefferson praised the principle of rotation "established in the office of President of Congress, who could serve but one year in three." [43] A committee of Congress, consisting of Alexander Hamilton, James Madison, and Thomas Fitzsimmons, reported on the importance of rotation in the design of a representative republic in 1782:

> The truth is, the security intended to the general liberty in the Confederation consists in the frequent election and in the rotation of the members of Congress, by which there is a constant and effective check upon them. This is the security which the people in every state enjoy against the usurpations of their internal government and it is the true source of security in a representative republic.[44]

By the mid-1780s the revolutionary zeal for rotation in office had started to wane due to the disintegration of the Confederation and the forced retirement of six popular and effective state executives. At a meeting of the Pennsylvania Council of Censors in 1784 the Republican Society criticized the principle of rotation for depriving men of an incentive to serve and the state of able servants.[45] Additionally, the Republican Society charged that rotation was antidemocratic, as "the privilege of the people in elections, is so far infringed as they are thereby deprived of the right of choosing those persons whom they would prefer," [46] one of the most frequently heard arguments against contemporary term limitations.

The same year marked the expiration of the first three-year term for delegates to the Continental Congress. A committee was appointed to investigate which members were now serving beyond their terms. Samuel Osgood of Massachusetts, along with two delegates from Delaware and two from Rhode Island, were found to have reached the end of their public service in the Congress. Osgood and the Delaware delegates retired without much of a fuss; not so the Rhode Island contingent. In May of 1784 a battle ensued, with the Rhode Island delegates fighting "tooth and toenail to retain their seats." The recorded debates "were conducted with a good deal of warmth on both sides of the question," remarked Secretary Charles Thomson. James Monroe observed: "I never saw more indecent conduct in any assembly before." Fearing that they would be unable to finish their work before adjourning for the summer, the delegates to Congress simply dropped the controversy.[47]

A New Constitution, without Rotation

Despite such criticisms, the principle of rotation was still popular enough to merit inclusion in the plan presented to the Constitutional Convention in the summer of 1787 by Edmund Randolph of Virginia. Section 4 of the Virginia plan stated that "members of the first branch of the National Legislature" would be "incapable of re-election" for a period of time to be determined by the convention "after the expiration of their term of service." Similarly, the people of Massachusetts were so attached to the principle of rotation that the Massachusetts legislature instructed the state's delegates to the Constitutional Convention "not to depart from the rotation established in the Article." Even after the provision on rotation was eliminated from the Virginia plan by the convention, Rufus King, and Nataniel Gorham of Massachusetts continued to push for a reconsideration of Randolph's proposal. They were not successful. After brief debate on different occasions throughout the summer, neither mandatory rotation nor ineligibility for office was included in subsequent drafts of the constitution for either the House or the Senate.[48]

If rotation in office was such an important part of republican political design, why was it not included in the U.S. Constitution? Most of the convention's discussion about rotation and eligibility for reelection was focused on the executive. Once it was determined that the president's term of office would be relatively short, delegates agreed that a prohibition against reeligibility would not be necessary. Hamilton's critique of rotation in the presidency no doubt helped to persuade other delegates against its inclusion. Rotation, said Hamilton, "would be a diminution of the inducements to good behavior." It would tempt "sordid views" and "peculation," by office holders who think about nothing else but where their next job will be. Finally, echoing the concerns of the Pennsylvania's Council of Censors, rotation would deprive the nation of "the experience and wisdom gained by an incumbent, perhaps just when that experience is needed most." [49]

A number of other reasons help account for why the principle of rotation was not applied to the House or Senate by the Constitutional

Convention. To start, some delegates were convinced that as long as terms were short, mandatory rotation was not needed. Many assumed that frequent elections would mean frequent turnover. Other delegates, such as those from the New England states, were convinced that rotation was not needed where the norm of instruction to representatives prevailed. Because many New England states practiced instruction, most prominently in Massachusetts, delegates may have believed that this norm would bind anyone elected from their state to serve in the new national government.[50]

In addition to short terms and instruction, other constitutional safeguards—most notably the separation of powers and federalism—made rotation appear unnecessary. Both of the latter measures served as a check on ambition and the dangers of tyrannical government so feared by the framers.[51] Given the problems faced by the Congress under the Articles of Confederation, delegates may have wanted to avoid the possibility of unnecessary clash over the enforcement of rotation.

Finally, as the principle of rotation was being practiced on a voluntary basis in many state legislatures, delegates may have rightly assumed that rotation in office would also be the norm in the legislatures of the new national government, even without a constitutional requirement.

The Great Debate over Rotation in Office

The absence of a rotation requirement in the finished Constitution was strongly denounced by the Antifederalists, who viewed the principle as a "truly republican institution." Most of the Antifederalist criticism reflected fear that the Senate would become "a fixed and unchangeable body of men" and the president "a king for life, like the king of Poland." Delegates at the ratification conventions in New York, Virginia, and North Carolina proposed amending the new Constitution to include rotation for the presidency.[52]

The process of ratifying the Constitution was punctuated by great debates over the wisdom of rotation in office, debates every bit as passionate and far more informed than any of the contemporary quarrels over term limitations.

New York's "Brutus" advocated rotation for the Senate on the grounds that it would give more people the opportunity to serve in government: "It would give opportunity to bring forward a greater number of men to serve their country, and would return those, who had served, to their state, and afford them the advantage of becoming better acquainted with the condition and politics of their constituents." [53] This view was shared by Elbridge Gerry of Massachusetts, who criticized the new Constitution at the Massachusetts ratification convention in 1788:

> There is not provision for a rotation, nor anything to prevent the perpetuity of office in the same hands for life; which by a little well timed bribery, will probably be done, to the exclusion of men of the best abilities from their share in the offices of government.[54]

New York's Melancton Smith was the Antifederalist's most articulate and thoughtful advocate of rotation in office. In June of 1788, Smith reaffirmed the potential of rotation to check tyranny and the abuse of power. Calling for a constitutional amendment to remedy the "evil" of the proposed Senate, Smith proposed:

> rotation . . . as the best possible mode of affecting a remedy. The amendment will not only have a tendency to defeat any plots, which may be formed against the liberty and authority of the state governments, but will be the best means to extinguish the factions which often prevail, and which are sometimes so fatal in legislative bodies. . . . We have generally found, that perpetual bodies have either combined in some scheme of usurpation, or have been torn and distracted with cabals—Both have been the source of misfortune to the state. Our Congress would have been a fine field for party spirit to act in—That body would undoubtedly have suffered all the evils of faction, had it not been secured by the rotation established by the articles of the confederation.[55]

Smith and Brutus understood that it would be very difficult to get rid of individuals once they were elected to office. "Every body acquainted with public affairs knows how difficult it is to remove from office a person who is [sic] long been in it. It is seldom except in cases of gross misconduct. It is rare that want of competent ability procures it." Echoing other Antifederalist warnings about the dangers of permanent government, Brutus recommended that "it would be wise to determine that a senator should not be eligible after he had served for the period assigned by the constitution for a certain number of years; perhaps three would be sufficient." [56]

The argument that rotation in office helps to secure fidelity between the representative and the represented, to paraphrase Paine, was made rather simply by James Monroe of Virginia, who argued that "the rotative principle is preserved" for the sake of legislative responsibility "which will I hope never be given up." "Even good men in office," said Virginia's Richard Henry Lee, "in time, imperceptibly lose sight of the people, and gradually fall into measures prejudicial to them." The need for rotation as a means to assure quality representation was also emphasized by John Lansing in New York who urged passage of an amendment to require rotation for senators to "oblige them to return, at certain periods, to their fellow-citizens, that, by mingling with the people, they may recover that knowledge of their interests, and revive that sympathy with their feelings, which power and an exalted station are too apt to efface from the minds of rulers." Elbridge Gerry made the same case to his colleagues in Massachusetts:

> By this neglect [of rotation] we lose the advantages of that check to the overbearing insolence of office which by rendering him ineligible at certain periods, keeps the mind of man in equilibria, and teaches him the feelings of the governed, and better qualifies him to govern in his turn.[57]

The Federalists Strike Back

The Antifederalist critique of the Constitution did not go unchallenged. In New York, Robert R. Livingston provided a scathing response to the rotation proposal of John Lansing and Gilbert Livingston:

> The people are the best judges of who ought to represent them. To dictate and control them, to tell them whom they shall not elect, is to abridge their natural rights. This rotation is an absurd species of ostracism—a mode of proscribing eminent merit, and banishing from stations of trust those who have filled them with the greatest faithfulness. Besides, it takes away the strongest stimulus to public virtue—the hopes of honors and rewards.[58]

Similarly, Roger Sherman lashed out against rotation for the president and senate in "A Citizen of New Haven," printed in 1788:

> It is proposed to make the president and senators ineligible after certain periods. But this would abridge the privilege of the people and remove one great motive to fidelity in office, and render persons incapable of serving in offices, on account of their experience, which would best qualify them for usefulness in office—but if their services are not acceptable they may be left out at any new election.[59]

But the strongest argument against rotation was once again Hamilton's, delivered at the New York ratification convention. Hamilton's final response to Melancton Smith merits attention here as a balance to the case made by the Antifederalists:

> Sir, in contending for a rotation, the gentlemen carry their zeal beyond all reasonable bounds. I am convinced that no government, founded on their feeble principle, can operate well. . . . [R]otation would be productive of many disadvantages: under particular circumstances, it might be extremely inconvenient, *if not fatal to the prosperity of our country.* [Emphasis added.] [60]

Livingston, Sherman, and Hamilton made three arguments which reappear frequently in contemporary clashes about term limitations:

1. The people have a right to judge who they will and will not elect to public office.
2. Rotation reduces the incentives for political accountability.
3. Rotation deprives the polity of experienced public servants.

The Antifederalists Respond

The responses of the Antifederalists to Livingston, Sherman, and Hamilton remain relevant to the current term-limitation debates.

There were two prevalent responses to the argument that the people have a right to choose whom to elect. States imposed many other restrictions on who could be elected to office, including, at the time, property, age, and residence requirements. Furthermore, citizens could not always be relied upon to bring about the degree of electoral turnover necessary to ensure the other values of rotation. Richard Henry Lee explained:

> Were the people always properly attentive, they would at proper periods, call their law makers home, by sending others in their room; but it is not often the case, and therefore, in making constitutions, when the people are attentive, they ought cautiously to provide for these benefits, those advantageous changes in the administration of their affairs, which they are often apt to be inattentive to in practice.[61]

Lee's solution involved frequent elections, a right to recall elected officials (another provision missing from the proposed constitution), and rotation in office.

Melancton Smith and Richard Henry Lee were not moved by the argument that mandatory rotation discouraged accountability, believing that whatever small degree of accountability were lost by rotation would be worth the price to safeguard liberty. Because elected officials would have to return home after stepping down from office, they urged, it was unlikely that they would be inclined while in office to act against the interests of their constituents. In fact, just the opposite would occur, making "a return to private station" an inducement to accountability rather than a distraction from it.

Finally, Smith and Lee believed that objections based on the loss of experience and expertise were specious to the extent that rotation did not require permanent retirement from public life. In some systems of rotation, after "taking a vacation," as it was sometimes called, individuals could run again for the very same office. In others, individuals might be prevented from serving in the same office but could bring their experience and expertise to bear in a different elected position. Rather than squandering experience, the capacity of the individual as a representative and citizen would be enhanced by a period in private station.

To those worried that only a limited number of individuals were qualified to serve in office, Lee responded: "I would not urge the principle of rotation, if I believed the consequence would be an uninformed federal legislature; but I have no apprehension of this in this enlightened country." [62]

In general, the Antifederalists feared that the elimination of annual elections, rotation in office, and recall—together with the extensive powers given to Congress—would make the "federal rulers ... masters, and not servants." [63] Cecelia Kenyon described the Antifederalists as "men of little faith" whose theory of representation reflected a profound distrust of elected officials. While the Antifederalists preferred "actual" to "virtual" representation and instruction to trusteeship, they shared the Federalists' commitment to the close connection that must bind representatives and their constituents. Rotation was considered, and perhaps is, one of the most effective institutions to accomplish this end. [64]

The Early Republic: The Voluntary Norm of Rotation

The Antifederalists were not sufficiently persuasive, and rotation was left out of the Constitution. Nevertheless, it remained a popular principle of republican rule throughout the nineteenth century, a principle with considerable practical effect, albeit much of it voluntary. In August of 1789 Representative Thomas Tucker of South Carolina proposed a constitutional amendment to limit the terms of national elected officials. Although the amendment was never voted upon, rotation became the prevailing norm for presidents, senators, and members of the House of Representatives.

George Washington's voluntary retirement after two terms as president set an important precedent. Like Jefferson, Washington supported rotation and wished others would embrace the idea as well. Toward the end of his first term in office, Washington wrote to Madison: "The spirit of the government may render a rotation in the elected officers of it most congenial with the ideas [the people have] of liberty and safety." [65]

The rotative principle was extended from elected officials to appointed ones following Washington's tenure in office. President Jefferson advocated strict adherence to the principle of rotation in order to prevent the formation of a permanent bureaucracy. [66] The idea of rotation, as Leonard White explains, "gradually spread to appointive positions, at first those from which some danger to public liberties might be apprehended, such as sheriffs and justices of the peace." The principle of rotation was part of the vigorous democratization movement that characterized the early republic. Indeed, as White concludes, the expansion of the rotative principle was "inspired on the whole by devotion to democratic dogma, not to partisan advantage." [67]

For those still concerned about the loss of experience brought about by rotation, John Taylor offered this assurance in 1814: "More talent is lost by long contrivances in office than by the system of rotation." Taylor held that "ability was stimulated by the prospect of future employment and smothered by the monopoly of experiences." [68]

Rotation was further extended to appointive office by federal law through passage of the "Four Year Law," promoted by Secretary of the Treasury William H. Crawford in 1820. The "Tenure of Office Act," as it was widely known, established a fixed term of four years (in place of the previous tenure at the pleasure of the president) for district attorneys, collectors and surveyors of customs, naval officers, money agents, receivers of public money for lands, registers of land offices, paymasters in the army, the apothecary-general, his assistant, and the commissary-general of purchases. [69]

Political practice during the early nineteenth century was generally consistent with the rotative principle. As James Sterling Young discovered, most representatives in Washington during the nation's first four decades viewed their tenure as "splendid misery."

> The thanklessness, the indignity, and the meanness of the political vocation are such recurrent themes of comment in the community record, and the drumfire of self-censure was so constant an accompaniment to the work of governing, as to convey the impression of a community at war with itself.

These were individuals, says Young, "who even as they indulged the urge to power, could not easily turn aside their democratic conscience that instructed them of power's evil." [70] The result, for much of the nineteenth century, was a high rate of resignation from office and high rates of turnover in both the House and Senate. Through the end of the century it was rare for the percentage of first-term members serving in the House of Representatives to be lower than 40 to 45 percent. House members rarely served more than two terms. [71]

Jacksonian Democracy: Rotation and Faith in the Common Citizen

The broadest and most ardent nineteenth-century defense of rotation was made during the presidency of Andrew Jackson. Dedicating a healthy portion of his 1829 inaugural address to a discussion of rotation in office, Jackson gave a new democratic twist to many of the arguments used by the revolutionaries and Antifederalists to defend rotation. Moving beyond the idea that rotation opened up opportunities for citizen involvement in governing, Jackson argued that all men were capable of holding public office: "The duties of all public officers are, or at least admit of being made, so plain and simple that men of intelligence may readily qualify themselves for their performance." [72] If citizens had the opportunity to govern, the quality of governance would be better for it. Jackson observed that "there are, perhaps, few men who can for any great length of time enjoy office and power without being more or less under the influence of feelings unfavorable to the faithful discharge of their public duties." While integrity might suffice to protect the office holder from corruption, the longer the office holder remained in office the more likely he would yield to temptation. "Corruption in some and in others a perversion of correct feelings and principles," said Jackson, "divert government from its legitimate ends and make it an engine for the support of the few at the expense of the many." [73] In short, "the more secure an office holder, the more his interests would diverge from those of his constituents." [74]

In Jacksonian democracy, rotation reduced the chances of corruption borne of familiarity with government and reinstated service on behalf of the public interest as the norm for public officials. No one should "treat public office as a species of property," nor view government "as a means of promoting individual interests," proclaimed Jackson. Government is "an instrument created solely for the service of the people"; rotation in office would keep it that way.[75]

Jackson's defense and extension of rotation was a response to the fervor for democracy brewing in America and "a belief that self-government required wide participation by citizens, not only in legislative halls, but in executive offices." As Leonard White explained, "Rotation was imposed because it was demanded from below, not merely because it was advocated from above." [76]

Nevertheless, strong objection was expressed to Jackson's application of rotation to appointive office. The elderly Madison condemned the application of rotation to administration, as did other political luminaries of the era, such as Daniel Webster, Henry Clay, and John Calhoun. Jackson's Whig opponents contended that rotation applied to administration contributed to the aggrandizement of presidential power, "corrupted public and private morals," and "lowered the competence and impartiality of the public service, reducing it to a mere party agency instead of preserving a status like that of the armed forces—the common servant of the people." [77]

Undaunted by his critics, Jackson used his multifaceted defense of rotation, which Arthur M. Schlesinger, Jr., judged "a sincere measure of reform," to justify creation of the spoils system. In direct response to those who lamented the loss of experience in government that the spoils system produced, Jackson argued, "I can not but believe that more is lost by the long continuance of men in office than is generally to be gained by their experience." To be sure, the spoils system helped Jackson build his power base in the Democratic party, but, in the assessment of Schlesinger, it also helped to "restore faith in government" which had been declining as a reaction to bureaucratic corruption. [78]

In moving beyond the case for rotation made by American revolutionary and Antifederalist theorists, Jackson established the practice "as an essential step in the gradual formulation of a program for democratic America." [79] Under Jackson's tutelage rotation was transformed from a guard against governmental excess into a vehicle for democratic empowerment.

As "a leading principle in the republican creed," rotation in office was also a part of the popular Jacksonian movement against the professionalization of politics and the general expansion of government. "We have no great faith in professional politicians," declared *The Democratic Review* in 1836, "when too long entrusted with too securely established power." [80] This sentiment is reminiscent of charges made against the "Washington establishment" by contemporary critics. Admittedly, there is some irony in Jackson's defense of rotation as a justification for the spoils system. As Max Farrand points out, the spoils system "marks the rise of a class of professional politicians," who, in the terminology of Max Weber, make politics a vocation. In the end, this may say less about the spoils system than it does about the incompatibility of bureaucratic governance (rotation notwithstanding) with the aspirations of traditional republicanism and the demands of representative democracy. [81]

Thus, two ironies may beset Jackson's embrace and extension of the rotative principle. The creation of the spoils system may have contributed to the rise of professional politicians, ultimately leading to the decline of rotation as a popular principle of democratic governance.

The Decline of the Rotative Principle

Jackson's extension of rotation to administrative offices responded to the democratic temper of the time, but it also sowed the seeds of rotation's eventual demise.

Continued Expansion for a Time

For the next three decades (until 1860) rotation remained associated with the democratic creed. By 1830 fifteen states had systems of rotation for the office of governor; nineteen had similar requirements in their constitutions for the rotation of some executive officers. Delegates to an 1837 convention called to amend Pennsylvania's constitution remained committed in word and deed to the principle of rotation placed in the 1776 constitution by Benjamin Franklin and the "patriots of the revolution." [82]

Responding to critics who insisted that rotation squandered the experience of seasoned officials, Frederick Grimke of South Carolina defended the use of the spoils system by the parties as a way to bring "as large a number of citizens as practicable ... into the mode of conducting public affairs." Rotation helped train a greater number of citizens for and about public life, to the betterment of the republic. In 1848 Grimke explained why rotation posed no threat to the quality of government:

> It has been supposed that where these changes are frequent the persons elected must for the most part be inexperienced and incompetent. The fear lest this should be the case is wisely implanted in our nature. It holds us back when we are about to run into an extreme. ... But public office itself creates to a great extent the very ability which is required for the performance of its duties. And it is not at all uncommon when individuals have been snatched up from the walks of private life to fill responsible stations to find that the affairs of society are conducted pretty much upon the same principles and with as much skill and intelligence as before. Habits of order and method are soon imparted to the incumbent, and they constitute the moving spring of all effective exertion, either mental or physical.[83]

Rotation in office continued to receive high marks from politicians through the Civil War. In a long and colorful speech, Senator Allen of Ohio in 1850 extolled rotation in office as constituting the underlying principle of the American political system. Presidents Polk, Buchanan, and Lincoln also celebrated the virtues of rotation in office. However, by failing to turn everyone out of office during his second term, historians hold Lincoln responsible for changing the popularity of rotation. From Lincoln's presidency on, in the judgment of historian Carl Russell Fish, "the popularity of rotation declined. The tide had turned." [84]

It would hardly be accurate or fair to hold Lincoln responsible for the decline of the rotative principle. If ever there was a time to heed Hamilton's call for stability in public service, that time was the Civil War. Furthermore, rotation was avidly defended in many circles well into the second decade of the twentieth century.

Into the 20th Century

The persistent influence of Jacksonian democracy in the 1880s ensured that rotation was often praised as a means to provide an opportunity for the largest number of citizens to serve in public office. In language reminiscent of Aristotle, Theodore Woolsey, president of Yale, commended short service in office so "that the turn of each may come round as often as that of every other." [85] Woolsey agreed that the quality of citizenship in a polity was enhanced when as many people as possible had the opportunity to serve in office. What was good for the individual was also good for political representation. A. Lawrence Lowell, president of Harvard, explained:

> A conviction that everyone in turn has a right to enjoy the sweets of authority had something to do with [the principle of rotation in all offices], but we must not fail to observe also the feeling that a new man, coming fresh from the people, will be in closer touch with popular opinion and will be free from official habits, or in other words, a fairer sample of the public.[86]

Rotation produced better citizens, better representatives, and ultimately better government. An assessment of rotation by James Bryce in *The American Commonwealth* may not have been an overstatement: "Rotation in office was and indeed by most men still is, held to be conformable to the genius of a democracy." [87]

Even as late as 1914, historians R. L. Ashley and Lawrence B. Evans confirmed that rapid rotation in office was an essential ingredient of American democracy and "still finds wide acceptance." [88] This acceptance is captured in an assessment of congressional tenure in 1903 by the noted historian James Albert Woodburn:

> A congressman is elected for two years. Occasionally a man of distinction is continued in service for several consecutive terms, and the most distinguished congressional leaders are those who have sat for long terms by successive re-elections. But the local influences in the States, the ambitions and schemes of the political wire-pullers and workers, and *the practice of rotation in office that has been*

considerably cultivated have tended to limit the average length of service to four to six years. [Emphasis added.][89]

Such an assessment of congressional turnover could not be made in the 1990s.

Rotation's Demise: Spoiled by the Spoils System

Despite these endorsements and positive assessments, support for rotation in office did eventually wane. By the beginning of the First World War, it is difficult to find any authorities, in politics or academe, discussing the principle of rotation. What happened? What went wrong with rotation? What changed in American politics? Complete answers to these questions are well beyond the scope of this essay. But, at the risk of oversimplifying American political development, let us consider five possible explanations.

In the estimation of some historians, the principle of rotation suffered from its association with the spoils system, which came under sharp attack during the second half of the nineteenth century. To discredit the spoils system, journalists and politicos of the last few decades of the nineteenth century attacked the principle of rotation as well. Rotation was blamed for creating a new class of professional politicians. "In practice," said historian Charles Beard, rotation "has been one of the most active agents in debauching political life. The idea of rotation begot the spoils and the large class of professional politicians that has since grown up on it." [90]

By the turn of the century, four additional developments were helping to hasten rotation's demise. First, by the end of the nineteenth century, Washington had become a very different city and the nation was changing. The modernization of the American polity led to the "institutionalization of the House of Representatives," which decentralized power in the House and thus increased the attractiveness of congressional service as a career. By the turn of the century the percentage of first-term members in the House had dropped below 25 percent and the average number of terms served by members prior to the present session came to exceed two, eventually reaching four to five terms by the mid-twentieth century.[91]

Second, the turn of the century also saw the development of the professions and with it the culture and norm of professionalism. This not only made legislative careerism acceptable, it associated careerism with effective governance. Turnover in the U.S. Congress was already declining, as more members of Congress decided to make a career out of legislative service. Turnover in state legislatures, on the other hand, remained high, provoking Charles Hyneman to call in 1938 for the professionalization of state legislatures and a reduction in member turnover in the interest of effective deliberation and good lawmaking.[92]

The third development was the expansion of the American state. A larger state bureaucracy called for greater expertise in the affairs of public administration and for more stability in the halls of Congress. Rotation in office made less sense in the emerging political culture, which valued a more permanent government and the legislative expertise it presumably encouraged.

Finally, the Progressive Movement of the early part of the twentieth century may also be at least partially responsible for the decline of rotation. Progressives were dedicated to taking the politics out of administration and corruption out of politics. Since rotation had been so closely associated with the spoils system—which featured both corrupt and politicized administration—progressive politicians had little use for the principle of rotation in office.

Democratic Recovery: A Return to Government by Amateurs

The principle of rotation in office has been a part of democratic theory and political practice since the time of Aristotle and Cicero and a part of America's experience with representative democracy for more than three hundred years. Reflecting the arguments and justifications from antiquity, Renaissance city-states, and seventeenth- and eighteenth-century English intellectuals, America's experience with rotation in office has been based on a desire to expand the opportunity to hold public office to as many citizens as possible, to check governmental tyranny and the abuse of power, and to build a working representative democracy. Andrew Jackson added a strong democratic flavor to the case for rotation laid down by America's revolutionaries and the Antifederalists.[93]

America's belief in the utility and efficacy of rotation in office reflects a political culture long hostile to the concentration of political power, permanence in government, professional politicians, and bureaucratic power. The principle of rotation embraces the proposition that democracy is properly government by amateurs and that the voices of amateurs in the halls of Congress and in many state legislatures throughout the nation are silenced by a chorus of career legislators and other professional politicians. "The survival of our society," says Daniel Boorstin, "depends on the vitality of the amateur spirit in the United States today and tomorrow." Lamentably, there seems little room left for amateurs in the modern American legislature. "We must find ways to help our representatives preserve their amateur spirit," proposes Boorstin.[94] The rediscovery of America's experience with the republican principle of rotation in office may be one way to restore some semblance of the amateur spirit to the halls of American legislatures and to begin the process of recovering American politics from the professionals.

The idea of rotation in office informs a great deal of American political practice and has much to teach both advocates and opponents of the contemporary term limitation movement. Unfortunately, America's lengthy experience with rotation in office—with its values and potential advantages—has been largely ignored or forgotten during the lengthy debates about constitutional and political reform of the past decade[95] and is even now overlooked by advocates and opponents of the term-limitation movement. Much can be learned about important political values, principles, and behavior by studying America's experience with the principle of rotation. Such study may provide a way to test or evaluate some of the conflicting claims of the contemporary term-limit debate.

Notes

1. John P. Foley, ed., *The Jeffersonian Cyclopedia* (New York: Russel & Russel, 1967), 786.
2. Mark P. Petracca, "The Poison of Professional Politics," *Policy Analysis,* May 10, 1991.
3. Most prominent are a series of editorials published in the *New York Times.* See "The Fearsome Term-Limit Fire," *New York Times,* October 25, 1991, A14; "Why Put Deadlines on Democracy," *New York Times,* December 13, 1990, A14; and "Robbing Voters of Their Rights," *New York Times,* September 10, 1991, A14. Additional examples may be found in Mark P. Petracca, "Rotation in Office: The American Experience," *The Long Term View* 1 (Winter 1992), 33-48.
4. A. H. M. Jones, *Athenian Democracy* [1957] (Baltimore: The Johns Hopkins University Press, 1986), 105. E. S. Staveley, *Greek and Roman Voting and Elections* (Ithaca, N.Y.: Cornell University Press, 1972).
5. R. K. Sinclair, *Democracy and Participation in Athens* (Cambridge: Cambridge University Press, 1988), 21.
6. Quoted in Andrew Lockyet, "Aristotle: *The Politics,*" in *A Guide to the Political Classics,* ed. Murray Forsyth and Maurice Keens-Soper (Oxford: Oxford University Press, 1988), 46. For a more extensive discussion of the Aristotelian prerequisites for democracy, see Sinclair, *Democracy and Participation.*
7. Staveley, *Greek and Roman Voting,* 55. Sortition worked in two ways. In one version, individuals were selected by lot to serve in office. In another, individuals were nominated by lot to run for public office in a competitive election.

8. Staveley, *Greek and Roman Voting*, 241.

9. Frank Frost Abbott, *A History and Description of Roman Political Institutions* [1911] (New York: Biblio and Tannen, 1963), 156. Abbott attributes the downfall of the republic to the failure to strictly observe the principle of rotation.

10. Leon Homo, *Roman Political Institutions* [1929] (New York: Barnes and Noble, 1962), 119.

11. Zera S. Fink, *The Classical Republicans* (Evanston, Ill.: Northwestern University Press, 1962), 31. For information about Florence, see Ferdinand Schevill, *History of Florence* (New York: Harcourt, Brace, 1936). Rotation was also applied to the Doge in Genoa and to the "governors" in the Signiory. See Correa M. Walsh, *The Political Science of John Adams* (New York: G. P. Putnam's Sons, 1915), 246.

12. Frederick C. Lane, *Venice: A Maritime Republic* (Baltimore: The Johns Hopkins University Press, 1973), 96.

13. Robert Finlay, *Politics in Renaissance Venice* (New Brunswick, N.J.: Rutgers University Press, 1980), 67. The Zonta was composed of sixty individuals nominated by the Senate and elected by the Great Council. It was normally made up of the most important senators and played a major role in the Venetian circle of governing groups.

14. Fink, *The Classical Republicans*, 31.

15. Caroline Robbins, *The Eighteenth-Century Commonwealthman* (Cambridge, Mass.: Harvard University Press, 1961); Isaac Kramnick, *Republicanism and Bourgeois Radicalism* (Ithaca, N.Y.: Cornell University Press, 1990); and David L. Jacobson, *The English Libertarian Heritage* (Indianapolis, Ind.: Bobbs-Merrill, 1965).

16. James Harrington, "Oceana [1656]," in *Ideal Commonwealths*, ed. Henry Morley (New York: Collier, 1901), 205. Harrington used examples from Athens, Israel, and Lacadaeman.

17. J. G. A. Pocock, *The Machiavellian Moment* (Princeton, N.J.: Princeton University Press, 1975), 394. According to Pocock, rotation is ultimately about the "constant renewal of virtue in and through action," similar to "Machiavelli's *ridurre ai principii*."

18. William Archibald Dunning, *A History of Political Theories: from Luther to Montesquieu* (New York: Macmillan, 1905), 252. Harrington, "Oceana," in *Ideal Commonwealths*, 205. J. R. Pole, *Political Representation in England and the Origins of the American Republic* (Berkeley: University of California Press, 1966), 12.

19. Robbins, *The Eighteenth-Century Commonwealthman;* Pole, *Political Representation in England;* and Pocock, *The Machiavellian Moment.*

20. In Caroline Robbins, *Two English Republican Tracts* (Cambridge: Cambridge University Press, 1969), 187.

21. Ibid., 239.

22. Algernon Sidney, *Discourses Concerning Government* [1698], 3d ed. (London: A. Miller, 1751), 456.

23. Sir William Blackstone, *Commentaries on the Laws of England* [1765],

rev. ed. (Chicago, Ill.: Callaghan, 1884), 188-189.

24. John Locke, *The Second Treatise on Civil Government* [1690] (Buffalo, N.Y.: Prometheus Books, 1986), 85. By many accounts Locke was one of the most influential English writers in early America.

25. James Burgh, *Political Disquisitions* [1774/1775], 2 vols. (New York: Da Capo Press, 1971). See various references to Burgh's work in Gordon S. Wood, *The Creation of the American Republic 1776-1787* (Chapel Hill, N.C.: University of North Carolina Press, 1969); and an elegant analysis of Burgh and Locke in Kramnick, *Republicanism and Bourgeois Radicalism.*

26. Burgh, *Political Disquisitions,* vol. 1, 175.

27. David Hume, "The Idea of a Perfect Commonwealth [1741]," in *David Hume's Political Essays,* ed. Charles W. Hendel (New York: Liberal Arts Press, 1953), 146. Matthew Wren, *Monarchy Asserted or the State of Monarchicall and Popular Government in Mr. Harrington's Commonwealth of Oceana* (Oxford: W. Hall for F. Bowman, 1657/1659), 161-168.

28. Quoted in Robbins, *The Eighteenth-Century Commonwealthman,* 192. Hutcheson authored *An Inquiry into the Original of Our Ideas of Beauty and Virtue,* printed in 1725.

29. John Milton, "The Readie and Easie Way to Establish a Free Commonwealth [1660]," in *The Complete Prose of John Milton,* vol. 7, 1659-1660, rev. ed. (New Haven: Yale University Press, 1980), 369, 434-438.

30. Burgh and Harrington were both proponents of partial rotation. According to Burgh: "Two thirds of the members must be excluded by rotation . . . and not the whole, because it is pretended by the court-party that it is necessary to keep in the house some of the great officers of the state, and that a whole house of inexperienced members would be at a loss." See Burgh, *Political Disquisitions,* vol. 1, 175. The U.S. Senate is likewise elected in thirds, so that at no time will the Senate be without experienced legislators. Term-limit proponents should consider the advantages of partial rotation as a response to contemporary concerns about the loss of experienced legislators.

31. Clinton Rossiter, *Seedtime of the Republic* (New York: Harcourt, Brace, 1953), 418. For a discussion of contemporary arguments in defense of frequent elections, see Mark P. Petracca and Pamela A. Smith, "How Frequent is Frequent Enough? An Appraisal of the Four-Year Term for House Members," *Congress and the Presidency* 17 (Spring 1990): 45-66.

32. John Adams, *The Political Writing of John Adams,* ed. George A. Peek, Jr. (New York: Macmillan, 1985), 89. This particular selection is from "Thoughts on Government: in a Letter from a Gentleman to his Friend," written by Adams in 1776.

33. Charles E. Beard, "Rotation in Office," in *Cyclopedia of American Government,* ed. Andrew C. McLaughlin and Albert Busnell Hart (New York: D. Appleton, 1914), 235. For a discussion of the New England Confederation of 1643, see Carl Russell Fish, *The Civil Service and the*

Patronage [1904] (New York: Russell and Russell, 1963), 80. On the Pennsylvania "Frame of Government," see Richard L. Perry, ed., *Sources of Our Liberties* (Chicago: American Bar Foundation, 1978), 209-221.

34. Wood, *Creation of the American Republic,* 140.

35. Perry, ed., *Sources of Our Liberties,* 349.

36. Quoted in Rossiter, *Seedtime of the Republic,* 418.

37. John Trenchard, "How free Governments are to be framed so as to last, and how they differ from such as are arbitrary" [January 13, 1721], in *The English Libertarian Heritage,* ed. David L. Jacobson (Indianapolis, Ind.: Bobbs-Merrill, 1965), 126-127. See also Bernard Bailyn, *The Ideological Origins of the American Revolution* (Cambridge, Mass.: Belknap Press, 1967); and Marie P. McMahon, *The Radical Whigs, John Trenchard and Thomas Gordon* (Lanham, Md.: University Press of America, 1990).

38. Even in states without formal requirements for rotation, constitutions still suggested rotation as a norm to be expected by citizens. Massachusetts did not adopt a formal rotation requirement, despite the insistence of Adams and a great many other revolutionaries in the Bay State. However, the Massachusetts constitution of 1780 (part I, article 8) gave citizens the right to expect a frequent turnover of public officials: "In order to prevent those, who are vested with authority, from becoming oppressors, the people have a right, at such periods and in such manner as they shall establish by their frame of government, to cause their public officers to return to private life; and to fill up vacant places by certain and regular elections and appointments." See Ronald M. Peters, Jr., *The Massachusetts Constitution of 1780: A Social Compact* (Amherst, Mass.: University of Massachusetts Press, 1978), 198. Despite the absence of a specific requirement for rotation in office, the Massachusetts constitution of 1780 is an example of how the earliest state constitutions provided for rotation in office. See Beard, "Rotation in Office," 235. The most authoritative discussion of rotation in early state constitutions can be found in Willi Paul Adams, *The First American Constitutions,* trans. Rita and Robert Kimber (Chapel Hill, N.C.: University of North Carolina Press, 1980).

39. Perry, ed., *Sources of Our Liberties,* 311-312.

40. Thomas Paine, *Political Writings,* ed. Bruce Kuklick (Cambridge: Cambridge University Press, 1989), 5.

41. Despite the forcefulness with which the principle of rotation was advocated, the little empirical evidence about rates of turnover suggests that rotation was not as widely practiced as it was espoused. Willi Adams, for example, found: "During the colonial period, short terms of office had not prevented the recurrent reelection of individuals, some of whom retained certain offices for decades at a time, nor had it prevented the growth of dynasties that laid claims to public office." See Adams, *The First American Constitutions,* 251. A similar point is made by Bernard Bailyn, *The Origins of American Politics* (New York: Alfred A. Knopf, 1968), 90.

42. Contained in Ralph Ketcham, ed., *The Anti-Federalist Papers and the Constitutional Convention Debates* (New York: New American Library, 1986), 358.
43. Foley, ed., *The Jeffersonian Cyclopedia*, 786.
44. Quoted in Charles Warren, *The Making of the Constitution* (Cambridge, Mass.: Harvard University Press, 1937), 363.
45. See Jackson Turner Main, *The Sovereign States, 1775-1783* (New York: Franklin Watts, 1973), 194, 219.
46. Quoted in Wood, *Creation of the American Republic*, 439.
47. Edmund C. Burnett, *The Continental Congress* (New York: Macmillan, 1941), 605-606.
48. Ketcham, ed., *The Anti-Federalist Papers and the Constitutional Convention Debates*, 37. Warren, *The Making of the Constitution*, 613. Max Farrand, ed., *The Records of the Federal Convention of 1787* [1911], vol. 1 (New Haven: Yale University Press, 1966), 217 and 421-427.
49. Quoted in Charles R. Kesler, "Bad Housekeeping: The Case Against Congressional Term Limitations," *Policy Review* (Summer 1990): 24-25.
50. Through the principle of instruction elected representatives were obliged to vote in accordance with a clear mandate from the people, or, in the case of U.S. senators, in accordance with the mandate of the respective state legislature. "Binding instructions compelled a legislator to represent in rather explicit terms the people who had elected him," explains Thomas Cronin. "This practice reflects an American belief that the right of the people to participate and be represented in a legislature was the primary means of securing liberty." See Cronin, *Direct Democracy* (Cambridge, Mass.: Harvard University Press, 1989), 24.
51. Alice O'Connor and Mary L. Henzel, *The Root of Republican Government: Terms of Office in the Legislative Branch* (Washington, D.C.: Jefferson Foundation, 1984), 85.
52. See the speech by Melancton Smith contained in Ketcham, ed., *Anti-Federalist Papers*, 350. See also Wood, *Creation of the American Republic*, 521, and Fish, *Civil Service and Patronage*, 80.
53. See Herbert J. Storing, ed., *The Anti-Federalist* (Chicago, Ill.: University of Chicago Press, 1981). The Antifederalists were not alone in their praise for rotation, nor in their desire to see rotation applied to senators and the president. Thomas Jefferson complained of its absence in a letter written to James Madison in December of 1787: "I dislike, and greatly dislike [in the Constitution] the abandonment in every instance of the principle of rotation in office, and most particularly in the case of the President." The following year Jefferson went so far as to suggest the need for a new amendment to the Constitution which would restore the principle of necessary rotation. See Foley, ed., *The Jeffersonian Cyclopedia*, 786. Benjamin Franklin also spoke out in favor of rotation for the president and members of the Senate. See Elliot, ed., *Debates on the Adoption of the Federal Constitution*, 369.
54. Quoted in Paul Leicester Ford, ed., *Pamphlet on the Constitution of the*

United States [1888] (New York: Da Capo Press, 1968), 9.

55. Ketcham, ed., *The Anti-Federalist Papers,* 350.

56. Storing, ed., *The Anti-Federalist,* 190.

57. Monroe is quoted in W. B. Allen and Gordon Lloyd, eds., *The Essential Antifederalist* (Lanham, Md.: University Press of America, 1985), 149. Lee's observation appears in Walter H. Bennett, ed., *Letters From the Federal Farmer to the Republican* (University: University of Alabama Press, 1978), 73. Lansing is quoted in Cecil L. Eubanks, "New York: Federalism and the Political Economy of Union," in *Ratifying the Constitution,* ed. Michael Allen Gillespie and Michael Lienesch (Lawrence: University Press of Kansas, 1989), 321. The quotation from Gerry appears in Ford, ed., *Pamphlets on the Constitution,* 9.

58. Jonathan Elliot, ed., *Debates on the Adoption of the Federal Constitution,* vol. 2 (New York: Burt Franklin, 1988), 292-293.

59. Paul Leicester Ford, *Essays on the Constitution of the United States* [1892] (New York: Burt Franklin, 1970), 234.

60. Elliot, *Debates on the Adoption of the Federal Constitution,* vol. 2, 320-321.

61. Bennett, ed., *Letters From the Federal Farmer to the Republican,* 74-75.

62. Ibid., 74.

63. Quoted in Wood, *Creation of the American Republic,* 522.

64. Cecelia Kenyon, "Men of Little Faith: The Anti-Federalists on the Nature of Representative Government," *William and Mary Quarterly* 12 (January 1955): 3-43. On the differences between actual and virtual representation, see Russell L. Hanson, *The Democratic Imagination in America* (Princeton, N.J.: Princeton University Press, 1985). On the connection between representative and constituents in Federalist and Antifederalist thought, see Cass R. Sunstein, "Interest Groups in American Public Law," *Stanford Law Review* 38 (November 1985): 29-87. Rotation was conducive to a great many other advantages, including a check on factions, the diffusion of a more general spirit of emulation, a device to bring forward the genius and abilities of the continent, and a way to increase knowledge and information about the country. See the speeches of Melancton Smith in Elliot, ed., *Debates on the Adoption of the Federal Constitution,* vol. 2, 310.

65. From a letter dated May 20, 1792; quoted in Frederick W. Whitridge, "Rotation in Office," *Political Science Quarterly* 4 (June 1889): 283.

66. See Raymond G. Gettel, *History of American Political Thought* (New York: D. Appleton-Century Co., 1928), 254.

67. Leonard D. White, *The Jeffersonians* (New York: Macmillan, 1951), 397.

68. Quoted in Gettell, *American Political Thought,* 254.

69. This summation is from Fish, *Civil Service and Patronage,* 66.

70. James Sterling Young, *The Washington Community, 1800-1828* (New York: Harcourt, Brace and World, 1966), 51, 61.

71. Stuart Rice, *Quantitative Methods in Politics* (New York: Alfred A. Knopf, 1928), 296-297; Robert Struble, Jr., "House Turnover and the

Principle of Rotation," *Political Science Quarterly* 94 (Winter 1979/80): 649-667.

72. See Jackson's inaugural address in Walter E. Volkomer, ed., *The Liberal Tradition in American Thought* (New York: Capricorn Books, 1969), 151.
73. Ibid.
74. Kohl, *The Politics of Individualism,* 124.
75. Volkomer, ed., *The Liberal Tradition in American Thought,* 151.
76. Leonard D. White, *The Jacksonians* [1854] (New York: Macmillan, 1963), 300-301.
77. White, *The Jacksonians,* 320-324. The application of rotation to elected officials occasioned far less objection.
78. Arthur M. Schlesinger, Jr., *The Age of Jackson* (New York: Book Find Club, 1945), 46.
79. Ibid., 47. Schlesinger also notes that in private correspondence with President Jackson, the English philosopher Jeremy Bentham confided his support for the doctrine of rotation.
80. Quotation in Kohl, *The Politics of Individualism,* 124.
81. Max Farrand, *The Development of the United States* (Boston: Houghton Mifflin, 1918), 157. Weberian language seems appropriate as Farrand says of individuals appointed under the spoils system: "The men were not like the old ruling class whose members were in politics largely from a sense of duty and public service, or for the honor of it, or even for the sake of power; but they were in politics as a business, not for the irregular profits to be derived therefrom, but to make a living."
82. The association of rotation in office with democracy was so strong that there was a movement in many states to extend the principle to judicial officers. By the 1840s, for example, judges were being elected for limited terms in New York, Louisiana, Missouri, Texas, Illinois, Iowa, and Wisconsin. See H. Von Holst, *The Constitutional and Political History of the United States,* vol. 3, trans. John J. Lalor and Paul Shorey (Chicago: Callaghan, 1881), 150-152. A few years after Jackson's presidency, Joseph Story, professor of law at Harvard University, strongly opposed short terms for legislators on grounds familiar to the Pennsylvania Republican Society:

> A very short term of service would bring together a great many new members, with little or no experience in the national business; the very frequency of the elections would render the office of less importance to able men; and some of the duties to be performed would require more time, and more mature inquiries, than could be gathered, in the brief space of a single session, from the distant parts of so extensive a territory.

Joseph Story, *A Familiar Exposition of the Constitution of the United States* [1840] (New York: Harper and Brothers, 1893), 52.
83. Frederick Grimke, *The Nature and Tendency of Free Institutions* [1848] (Cambridge, Mass.: Belknap Press of Harvard University, 1968), 187. A timely response to Grimke can be found in a pamphlet produced by

Frances Bowen in 1853. Bowen denied that rotation was essential to democratic government. See White, *The Jacksonians,* 559.

84. For Senator Allen's speech, see Holst, *The Constitutional and Political History of the United States,* 149. Lincoln followed the principle of rotation as a representative from Illinois when he stepped down from office to rotate his seat with another Whig. See Sula P. Richardson, *Congressional Terms: A Review of Efforts to Limit House and Senate Service* (Washington, D.C.: Congressional Research Service, 1989), 8. Fish, *Civil Service and Patronage,* 166. It is also worth reviewing the evidence compiled by Fish on the mechanisms used to circumvent rotation in office.

85. Theodore D. Woolsey, *Political Science or The State* (New York: Charles Scribner's Sons, 1889), 299.

86. A. Lawrence Lowell, *Public Opinion and Popular Government* (New York: Longmans, Green and Co., 1913), 244.

87. Bryce explained the virtue of rotation: "It is supposed to stimulate men to execution, to foster a laudable ambition to serve the country or the neighborhood, to prevent the growth of an official caste, with its habits of routine, its stiffness, its arrogance." Bryce, *The American Commonwealth,* 138.

88. R. L. Ashley, "Terms of Public Office," in *Cyclopedia of American Government,* ed. Andrew C. McLaughlin and Albert Busnell Hart (New York: D. Appleton and Co., 1914), 517; and Lawrence B. Evans, "Tenure of Office," in *Cyclopedia of American Government,* ed. McLaughlin and Hart, 517.

89. James Albert Woodburn, *The American Republic and Its Government* (New York: George Putnam's Sons, 1903), 254.

90. Beard, "Rotation in Office," 235. Other prominent historians sharing Beard's view are Frank J. Goodnow, H. Von Holst, and Carl Russell Fish. See, for example, Frank J. Goodnow, *Comparative Administrative Law* (New York: G. P. Putnam's Sons, 1903).

91. Nelson W. Polsby, "The Institutionalization of the U.S. House of Representatives," *American Political Science Review* 62 (March 1968): 144-168. For slightly different perspectives on the development of legislative careerism, see H. Douglas Price, "Congress and the Evolution of Legislative 'Professionalism,'" in *Congress in Change,* ed. Norman J. Ornstein (New York: Praeger, 1975); Peter Swenson, "The Influence of Recruitment on the Structure of Power in the U.S. House, 1870-1940," *Legislative Studies Quarterly* 7 (1982): 7-36; and Nelson C. Dometrius and Lee Sigelman, "Costs, Benefits and Careers in the U.S. House of Representatives: A Developmental Approach," *Congress and the Presidency* 18 (Spring 1991): 55-75. On the growth in the length of the average House term, see Rice, *Quantitative Methods in Politics,* 297. Data for the second half of the twentieth century can be found in Norman J. Ornstein, Thomas E. Mann, and Michael J. Malbin, *Vital Statistics on Congress, 1991-1992* (Washington, D.C.: American Enterprise Institute, 1992), 19-20.

92. See Burton J. Bledstein, *The Culture of Professionalism* (New York: Norton, 1978); and Wilbert E. Moore, *The Professions: Roles and Rules* (New York: Russell Sage, 1979). See Robert J. Struble, Jr., "House Turnover and the Principle of Rotation," *Political Science Quarterly* 94 (Winter 1979/80): 643-667. Members of the House changed in a number of important ways during the end of the 19th century. See Allan G. Bogue, Jerome M. Clubb, Carroll R. McKibbin, and Santa A. Traugott, "Members of the House of Representatives and the Processes of Modernization, 1789-1960," *Journal of American History* 63 (1976): 275-302. Charles S. Hyneman, "Tenure and Turnover of Legislative Personnel," *The Annals of the American Academy of Political and Social Science* 195 (January 1938), 21-22. Political scientists continued to champion the professionalization of state legislatures right through the early 1970s. For additional references to this sizable literature, see Alan Rosenthal, "The Legislative Institution: Transformed and at Risk," in *The State of the States*, ed. Carl E. Van Horn (Washington, D.C.: CQ Press, 1989).

93. Interest in rotation has not been entirely limited to post-seventeenth century Anglo-American political theory. In various works, Condorcet, Tocqueville, and Michels all endorsed, to varying degrees, the principle of rotation in office. See Walsh, *The Political Science of John Adams,* 16; James Wilford Garner, *Political Science and Government* (New York: American Book Co., 1928), 701; and Robert Michels, *Political Parties* [1915], trans. Eden and Cedar Paul (New York: Free Press, 1962), 120-122 and 36.

94. Daniel J. Boorstin, *Hidden History* (New York: Vintage Books, 1989), 221-225.

95. No major report on constitutional reform during the past decade has included a discussion of rotation in office or term limits. One has to go back to deliberations on the Twenty-second Amendment to find a serious reference to America's experience with rotation in office.

3. FEDERALISTS V. ANTIFEDERALISTS: THE TERM-LIMITATION DEBATE AT THE FOUNDING

Michael J. Malbin

Mark Petracca's essay makes it clear that rotation in office is not a new idea. "New"—in the broad sweep of history—is a label that more properly belongs to the ideas of the Federalists, ideas that underlie the most complete theoretical argument against mandatory rotation. In *Federalist* Number 9, Alexander Hamilton presented the Constitution as being based on a new science of politics. What made that science new were its ideas about representation and the large republic that representation made possible. This chapter reviews the connection between term limits and representation in the debates between Federalists and Antifederalists. Following that review are extended excerpts from one of those debates.

Term Limits and Representation

The Antifederalist critique of the Constitution was based upon a classic view of democracy in which democracy is assumed literally to mean government by the people, directly.[1] In this view representation is at best a necessary evil, a device to be used when direct democracy is impossible, but not something that *adds* to the public good. A good representative body, under this conception, is one that closely reflects or mirrors the instincts and wishes of the people. The Antifederalists were opposed to a large republic because they believed representatives would perform properly only if the people kept careful watch over them. The need for an active and watchful citizenry required small legislative districts, short terms of office (one year at most), and mandatory rotation.

The Federalists, in contrast, believed that in a small republic the public would inevitably divide into a relatively small number of factions, a situation in which the majority faction could too easily tyrannize the minority. The Federalist solution, expressed most clearly by James Madison in *Federalist* Number 10, was to enlarge the sphere of the republic to incorporate a multiplicity of factions. This, in turn, would prevent the formation of a permanent majority by requiring factions to compromise and form shifting coalitions. The large-republic solution was not possible without a system of representation. For that reason, instead of seeing representation as an evil, the Federalists viewed it as the precondition for a great good: a large, diverse, democratic republic.

The Federalists knew that representatives can never simply reflect the wishes of their constituents. Instead, they act as filters, as Madison wrote in *Federalist* Number 10; they "refine and enlarge" the public views. However, refining and enlarging does not necessarily mean improving. Representation can be a great benefit; it can also bring about serious problems. The one thing it cannot be is a neutral conduit, because the representative's personal ambitions and perspectives inevitably interact with his or her duties.

The Constitution, therefore, attempts to harness the ambition of office holders to serve the public good.[2] It gives powers to office holders, lengthens terms, and provides rewards for public service, so that capable and ambitious people will seek to serve what they perceive to be the long-term best interests of their constituents and country and not merely to realize the public's immediate, short-term desires. The Constitution does this by offering the office holder a personal stake in maintaining a longer time horizon than the span between elections. With such a perspective, the Federalists believed that a representative democracy could subject the public's desires to a process of deliberation that, in the long run, would result in policies more likely to serve the public interest.

The key to the Federalist view of representation was the idea of using rewards to channel personal ambition to serve the public good. If the system failed to reward those willing to take political risks in the name of the public's long-term interests, the power of those who pandered to momentary passions would grow unchecked. In that case, "refining and enlarging" would mean "purifying and inflaming."

Contemporary supporters of term limits, like the Antifederalists, believe that the longer time horizons of career politicians turn out to serve the long-term interests of the politicians and not those of the public. With the wisdom of hindsight, some Federalists might agree with a part of this criticism of the contemporary legislature. But the two perspectives would diverge over solutions. Many term-limit advocates believe that the ills caused by ambition should be prevented by doing away with the political career. A Federalist, in contrast, would consider this approach to be worse than futile. Ambition will assert itself in any case, they would say; the aim should be to redirect it usefully.

These statements about how Federalists and Antifederalists would view term limits are not deductive guesses. As Mark Petracca has noted, the issue was debated during the campaign to ratify the U.S. Constitution. The most interesting of these debates, involving some of the country's leading Federalist and Antifederalist thinkers, took place in the state of New York. (Selections from the debates follow this introduction.) On June 24, 1788, Gilbert Livingston proposed that the U.S. Constitution be amended so that U.S. senators would be limited to six years of service in any twelve-year period. The amendment also would have permitted state legislatures to recall senators at any time. Although the New York convention recommended adoption of the amendment, the first Congress did not include it in the Bill of Rights sent back to the states for ratification.

Unlike most of the participants in the late-twentieth-century debate, the main speakers on both sides in 1788 took pains to connect their views about the proposal at issue with their larger views about the principles of representation. Consider Gilbert Livingston's fear that without mandatory rotation, the nation's capital would become an "Eden," a kind of "hallowed ground." His complaint sounds contemporary—straight from a radio talk show. But unlike the talk shows, it was linked very clearly to a view of what the job of the representative ought to be. That view is expressed most clearly in the selections by Melancton Smith, one of the most thoughtful Antifederalists.

On the opposite side, Robert R. Livingston and Alexander Hamilton made it abundantly clear that their reasons for opposing rotation flowed directly from their views about ambition. Livingston worried that the amendment would take away "the strongest stimulus to public virtue—the hope of honors and rewards." Hamilton worried what truly ambitious people might do if deprived of attaining such rewards inside the system. The effect would be to encourage such people either to line their own pockets or to build public support for overriding the Constitution to perpetuate themselves in office.

Hamilton's specific objections to rotation do not seem overly persuasive today. Because serving in a legislature is not the peak of ambition today, it seems far-fetched to think of legislators, frustrated by term limits, turning into modern-day Caesars. (The argument is more pertinent to presidential term limits.) As for Hamilton's concern that term limits would encourage corruption, one could counter by citing abundant evidence of legislative nest feathering without term limits.

Hamilton's underlying concerns, however, remain relevant. Consider the sentences with which we close the selections from the New York debate:

> Men will pursue their interests. It is as easy to divert human nature as to oppose the strong currents of selfish passions. A wise legislator

will gently divert the channel, and direct it, if possible, to the public good.

It is hard to imagine a clearer statement of the premises that underlie Federalist notions of representation. Similarly, it would be hard to imagine a clearer statement on the other side than Melancton Smith's preference for relying not on the ambitions of the legislator but on the virtue of "a numerous body of enlightened citizens, ready for the call of their country."

The differences between Hamilton and Smith—between Federalists and Antifederalists—are reproduced almost exactly in the contemporary debate over term limits. Even more importantly, the same difference in perspective is reflected in virtually every debate that has ever occurred in American history over how to improve our governing institutions. It is a living debate that addresses enduring questions of principle. An awareness of these principles can only improve the deliberations of today.

Debate on Mandatory Term Limits

The excerpts that follow are from a debate that occurred on June 24 and 25, 1788, before the New York State convention to ratify the U.S. Constitution. The debate covered two subjects: mandatory rotation and recall (the power to remove U.S. senators in mid-term). In these excerpts, ellipses generally indicate that the speaker was talking about recall or a subject other than rotation. The numbers in square brackets refer to pages in Jonathan Elliot, ed., *The Debates in the Several State Conventions on the Adoption of the Federal Constitution,* vol. 2 (New York: Burt Franklin, 1966), a reprint of the edition of 1888.

> *Gilbert Livingston [287]:* What are the checks provided to balance this great mass of power? Our present Congress [under the Articles of Confederation] cannot serve longer than three years in six: they are at any time subject to recall. These and other checks were considered necessary at a period which I choose to honor with the name of virtuous. . . . True it is, sir, there are some powers wanted to make this glorious compact complete. But, sir, let us be cautious that we do not err more on the other hand, by giving power too profusely, when, perhaps it will be too late to recall it. Consider, sir, the great influence which this body, armed at all points, will have. What will be the effect of this? Probably a security of their reelection as long as they please. Indeed, in my view, it will amount nearly to an appointment for life. What will be their situation in a federal town? Hallowed ground! Nothing so unclean as state laws to enter there, surrounded, as they will be, by an impenetrable wall of adamant and gold, the wealth of the whole country flowing into it. . . .

Their attention to their various business will probably require their constant attendance. In this Eden they will reside with their families, [288] distant from the observation of the people. In such a situation, men are apt to forget their dependence, lose their sympathy, and contract selfish habits. Factions are apt to be formed, if the body becomes permanent. The senators will associate only with men of their own class, and thus become strangers to the condition of the common people. They should not only return, and be obliged to live with the people, but return to their former rank of citizenship, both to revive their sense of dependence, and to gain knowledge of the country. This will afford opportunity to bring forward the genius and information of the states, and will be a stimulus to acquire political abilities. It will be the means of diffusing a more general knowledge of the measures and spirit of the administration. These things will confirm the people's confidence in government. When they see those who have been high in office residing among them as private citizens, they will feel more forcibly that the government is of their own choice. The members of this branch having the idea impressed in their minds, that they are soon to return to the level whence the suffrages of the people raised them, this good effect will follow: they will consider their interests as the same with those of their constituents, and that they legislate for themselves as well as others. They will not conceive themselves made to receive, enjoy, and rule, nor the people solely to earn, pay, and submit. . . . [289] I therefore move that the committee adopt the following resolution, as an amendment to this clause:

> Resolved, That no person shall be eligible as a senator for more than six years in any term of twelve years, and that it shall be in the power of the legislatures of the several states to recall their senators, or either of them, and to elect others in their stead, to serve for the remainder of the time for which such senator or senators, so recalled, were appointed.

Robert R. Livingston [291]: The amendment appears to have in view two objects—that a rotation shall be established in the Senate, and that its members shall be subject to recall by the state legislatures. . . .

[292] The people are the best judges who ought to represent them. To dictate and control them, to tell [293] them who they shall not elect, is to abridge their natural rights. This rotation is an absurd species of ostracism—a mode of prescribing eminent merit, and banishing from stations of trust those who have filled them with the greatest faithfulness. Besides, it takes away the strongest stimulus to public virtue—the hope of honors and rewards. The acquisition of abilities is hardly worth the trouble, unless one is to

enjoy the satisfaction of employing them for the good of one's country. We all know that experience is indispensably necessary to good government. Shall we, then, drive experience into obscurity? I repeat that this is an absolute abridgement of the people's rights.

John Lansing [293]: The objects of this amendment are, first, to place the senators in such a situation of dependence on their several state legislatures, as will induce them to pay a constant regard to the good of their constituents; secondly, to oblige them to return, at certain periods, to their fellow-citizens, that, by mingling with the people, they may recover that knowledge of their interests, and revive that sympathy with their feelings, which power and an exalted station are too apt to efface from the minds of rulers.

It has been urged that the senators should be acquainted with the interests of the states in relation to each other, and to foreign powers, and that they should remain in office, in order to acquire extensive political information. If these were the only objects, the argument would extend to the rendering [of] their dignity perpetual—an idea which probably none of the gentlemen will consent to; but, if one third of the senators go out every two years, cannot those who succeed them acquire information from the remaining members, with respect to the relative interests of the states? It is to be presumed that the Senate will be composed of the best informed men, and that no such men will be incapable of comprehending the interests of the states either singly or collectively. If it be the design of representation that the sense [294] and spirit of the people's interests and feelings should be carried into the government, it is obvious that this design can be accomplished in no way so perfectly as by obliging our rulers, at certain periods, to relinquish their offices and rank. The people cannot be represented by men who are perpetually separated from them. . . .

[295] It is further objected to this amendment, that it will restrain the people from choosing those who are most deserving of their suffrages, and will thus be an abridgement of their rights. I cannot suppose this last inference naturally follows. The rights of the people will be best supported by checking, at a certain point, the current of popular favor, and preventing the establishment of an influence which may leave to elections little more than the form of freedom. The Constitution of this state says, that no man shall hold the office of sheriff or coroner beyond a certain period. Does any one imagine that the rights of the people are infringed by this provision?

Richard Harrison [298]: The gentlemen carry their amendment further than the power of recall; they say that a rotation in office ought to be established; that the senators may return to the private walks of life, in order to recover their sense of dependence. I cannot agree with them in this. If the senator is conscious that his reelection depends only on the will of the people, and is not fettered by any law, he will feel an ambition to deserve well of the public. On the contrary, if he knows that no meritorious exertions of his own can procure a reappointment, he will become more unambitious, and regardless of the public opinion. The love of power, in a republican government, is ever attended by a proportionable sense of dependence.

Alexander Hamilton [301]: In the commencement of a revolution which received its birth from the usurpations of tyranny, nothing was more natural than that the public mind should be influenced by an extreme spirit of jealousy. To resist these encroachments, and to nourish this spirit, was the great object of all our public and private institutions. The zeal for liberty became predominant and excessive. In forming our Confederation, this passion alone seemed to actuate us, and we appear to have had no other view than to secure ourselves from despotism. The object was certainly a valuable one, and deserved our utmost attention; but, sir, there is another object, equally important, and which our enthusiasm rendered us little capable of regarding: I mean a principle of strength and stability in the organization of our government, and vigor in its operations. This purpose could never be accomplished but by the establishment of some select body, formed particularly upon this principle. There are few positions more demonstrable than that there should be, in every republic, some permanent body to correct the prejudices, check the intemperate passions, and regulate the fluctuations, of a popular assembly. It is evident that a body instituted [302] for these purposes must be so formed as to exclude, as much as possible, from its own character, those infirmities, and that mutability, which it is designed to remedy. It is therefore necessary that it should be small, that it should hold its authority during a considerable period, and that it should have such an independence in the exercise of its powers, as will divest it, as much as possible, of local prejudices. It should be so formed as to be the centre of political knowledge, to pursue always a steady line of conduct and to reduce every irregular propensity to system. Without this establishment, we may make experiments without end, but shall never have an efficient government. . . .

From these principles it follows that there ought to be two distinct bodies in our government—one which shall be immediately constituted by and peculiarly represent the people and possess all the popular features; another formed upon the principle and for the purposes before explained. . . .

Now, sir, what is the tendency of the proposed [recall] amendment? [303] To take away the stability of government by depriving the Senate of its permanency. . . . In whatever body the power of recall is vested, the senator will perpetually feel himself in such a state of vassalage and dependence, that he never can possess that firmness which is necessary to the discharge of his great duty to the Union.

Melancton Smith [309]: The amendment embraces two objects—first, that the senators shall be eligible for only six years in any term of twelve years; second, that they shall be subject to the recall of the legislatures of their several states. It is proper that we take up these points separately. I concur with the honorable gentleman that there is a necessity for giving this branch a greater stability than the House of Representatives. I think his reasons are conclusive on this point. But, sir, it does not follow, from this position, that the senators ought to hold their places during life. Declaring them ineligible during a certain term after six years, is far from rendering them less stable than necessary. We think the amendments will place the Senate in a proper medium between a fluctuating and perpetual body. As the clause now stands, there is no doubt that senators will hold their office perpetually; and in this [310] situation they must of necessity lose their dependence, and attachments to the people. It is certainly inconsistent with the established principles of republicanism that the Senate should be a fixed and unchangeable body of men. There should be, then, some constitutional provision against this evil. A rotation I consider as the best possible mode of effecting a remedy....

It is a circumstance strongly in favor of rotation, that it will have a tendency to diffuse a more general spirit of emulation, and to bring forward into office the genius and abilities of the continent: the ambition of gaining the qualifications necessary to govern will be in some proportion to the chance of success. If the office is to be confined to a few, other men, of equal talents and virtue, but not possessed of so extensive an influence, may be discouraged from aspiring to it. The more perfectly we are versed in the political science, the more firmly will the happy principles of republicanism be supported. The true policy of constitutions will be to increase the information of the country, and disseminate the knowledge of government as universally as possible. If this be done, we shall have, in any dangerous emergency, a numerous body of enlightened citizens, ready for the call of their country. As the Constitution now is, you only give an opportunity to two men to be acquainted with public affairs. It is a maxim to me that every man employed in a high office by the people, should, from time to time, [311] return to them, that he may be in a situation to satisfy them with respect to his conduct and the measures of administration.

If I recollect right, it was observed by an honorable member from New York, that this amendment would be an infringement on the natural rights of the people. I humbly conceive, if the gentleman reflects maturely on the nature of his argument, he will acknowledge its weakness. What is government itself but a restraint upon the natural rights of the people? What constitution was ever devised that did not operate as a restraint on their original liberties? What is the whole system of qualifications, which take place in all free governments, but a restraint? Why is a certain age made necessary? Why a certain term of citizenship? This Constitution itself, sir, has restraints innumerable. The amendment, it is true, may exclude two of the best men; but it can rarely happen that the state will sustain any material loss by this. I hope and believe that we shall always have more than two men who are capable of discharging the duty of a senator. But, if it should so happen that the state possessed only two capable men, it would be necessary they should return home, from time to time, to inspect and regulate our domestic affairs. I do not conceive the state can suffer any inconvenience. The argument, indeed, might have some weight, were the representation very large; but as the power is to be exercised upon only two men, the apprehensions of the gentleman are entirely without foundation.

Alexander Hamilton [320]: Sir, in contending for a rotation, the gentlemen carry their zeal beyond all reasonable bounds. I am convinced that no government, founded on this feeble principle, can operate well: I believe also that we shall be singular in this proposal. We have not felt the embarrassments resulting from rotation that other states have; and we hardly know the strength of their objection to it. There is no probability that we shall ever persuade a majority of the states to agree to this amendment. The gentlemen deceive themselves; the amendment would defeat their own design. When a man knows he must quit his station, let his merit be what it may, he will turn his attention chiefly to his emolument: nay, he will feel temptations, which few other situations furnish, to perpetuate his power by constitutional usurpations. Men will pursue their interests. It is as easy to change human nature as to oppose the strong current of the selfish passions. A wise legislator will gently divert the channel, and direct it, if possible, to the public good.

Notes

1. For the best explanation of the Antifederalists' views about representation, see Herbert J. Storing, *What the Anti-Federalists Were For,* published separately under that title (Chicago: University of Chicago Press, 1981),

Part II

THE POLITICAL CAMPAIGN ANALYZED

4. TERM LIMITS FAIL IN WASHINGTON: THE 1991 BATTLEGROUND

David J. Olson

After term limits were adopted in Oklahoma, Colorado, and California in 1990, Washington State became the national battleground for the issue in 1991. Following an intensely fought campaign, voters shocked most observers by turning down the initiated measure by a 54 to 46 percent margin in an election attracting a record off-year turnout of 67.9 percent of registered voters.

This chapter analyzes the political battle over term-limit legislation by initiative in Washington in 1991. The study is both descriptive and analytic. It tells the story of the rise and fall of the term-limit idea, identifying key players in the drama and the roles they played. And it examines how the initiative process was structured by interest groups, campaign strategy, the media, public opinion, and political parties.[1]

The Setting

The Context

Washington provides a conducive setting for citizen-initiated change movements. Its medium size and population concentration make such movements more feasible than in very large states or those in which the population is widely dispersed. With five million people, Washington ranks eighteenth in the nation and is the second largest of the thirteen Western states. Securing certified petitions for referenda or initiated ballot measures in this mid-sized state requires a manageable 150,001 signatures.[2] Additionally, over half the state's population is clustered in the three-county Puget Sound region, providing a close concentration of voters for signature drives or election campaigns.

Washington exhibits a wide-open and freewheeling style in its politics. The inherited legacy is a "lusty, gutsy politics" with pronounced strains of populism and radicalism.[3] The state's radicalism includes ideologies of both the left and the right, with the former more sustained in the first third of this century and the latter peaking during the McCarthy period at mid-century. Whether of the left or right, radicalism is deeply embedded in the state's populist practices. Tendencies toward radical and populist politics are reified in the use of the initiative and the referendum.

Washington's independent style of politics is both due to and a cause of the weakness of political parties. Absent strong parties, issues and candidates assume a central electoral importance, creating politics in which media and interest groups occupy important roles. In addition to being weak in the state, the Republican and Democratic parties were remarkably evenly matched in electoral outcomes throughout the seventies and in the period from 1982 to 1986, more so than in any of the other dozen mountain or Pacific states of the West.[4]

Perhaps most reflective of party weakness in Washington is the use of the blanket primary, adopted by initiative in 1936. In the blanket primary, parties lose control of the process of selecting candidates for office, because voters have the option of crossing party lines from office to office in the primary contests. Some scholars argue that parties in Washington are even less powerful than their weakening counterparts elsewhere in the country. Certainly, citizens of the state profess antiparty attitudes; a majority of voters identify with neither party, calling themselves independents.[5] The tenuous and fluid attachments voters have for parties, the weakness of the parties themselves, and their competitive nature all make Washington a state conducive to setting public policy through citizen-initiated measures.

Term-limitation initiatives base their appeal partly on the increasing cost of election campaigns and partly on the widening disparity between incumbents' campaign war chests and those of challengers. Washington legislative elections have witnessed sizable growth in campaign contributions and expenditures, and incumbents consistently spend more than their challengers in contested elections. The margin of financial advantage in Washington, however, may not be as large as in other states. In the 1990 Washington state elections, incumbents held an expenditure advantage over challengers, but in the senate races that advantage was just slightly under 1.5 to 1, while in house races it was less than 2 to 1.[6] This can be contrasted to the 1990 California state elections, where incumbents outspent challengers by an 8 to 1 margin.[7]

The central argument used to justify term limitations is the minimal level of turnover among elected officials. Washington presents a mixed picture of turnover across the two branches of the state legislature. Over the decade from 1979 to 1989 the legislature experienced an 81 percent turnover in its general membership, with 90 percent turnover for house members and 63 percent turnover in the state senate.[8] The house figure placed Washington in a tie with West Virginia for highest turnover, while the senate rate was among the lowest turnovers. The comparatively low turnover of state senate seats would appear to encourage term-limit initiatives in Washington, while the house's highest-in-the-nation turnover might have the opposite effect.

Turnover among Washington's national office holders is much lower than for state legislators. Here Washington has a long history of incumbent reelection, highlighted by the careers of Senators Warren G. Magnuson and Henry M. Jackson, who together compiled sixty-five years service in the U.S. Senate. Through seniority each assumed powerful positions; at home they became known as "the gold dust twins" for their legendary ability to deliver federal largess to the state until the early 1980s. Representative Tom Foley from the fifth congressional district compiled twenty-five years service on his way to becoming Speaker of the House in 1989. His long tenure and powerful position became a central issue in the 1991 term-limit campaign.

Political clout in the other Washington has always had a high priority in the state's politics. Traditional political wisdom in Washington viewed seniority and incumbent reelection favorably because of the power they gained for the state's congressional delegation. This was partly due to the state's regional isolation and its medium size, but it also derived from the sizable number of military installations in Washington, from Boeing's dependence upon military contracts, and from the state's economic dependence on federally owned natural resources (timber, water, fisheries, and hydroelectric power). For all of these reasons, the Washington delegation is known for its unified behavior across party lines on issues having a regional impact.

These traditional beliefs in the value of seniority were challenged directly in 1991 by the term-limit initiative.

The Initiative in Washington

As a device to give voters the direct power to enact legislation, the initiative is highly compatible with Washington's independent, open style of politics, its weak parties, its independent voters, and its radical and populist past. Products of Washington's robust progressivism at the turn of the last century, the initiative, the referendum, and recall were enacted in 1912.

Initiatives in Washington may be either direct or indirect. Under the direct option, a number of residents equal to 8 percent of the number of votes cast in the preceding gubernatorial election must sign a petition for a measure to be certified and placed on the ballot at the next general election. An indirect initiative also requires that 8 percent of voters sign a petition, but the proposal goes directly to the legislature. If enacted unchanged, it becomes law. If the legislature rejects the initiative or amends it, both the original proposal and the legislative alternative are placed before voters at the next election. Washington does not allow use of the initiative to amend the state constitution.

Over the seventy-six-year history of the initiative in Washington, nearly half of all direct initiatives and exactly half of indirect initiatives have been enacted into law. Hugh Bone points out that even these adoption rates do not convey the full importance of the initiative in Washington state politics:

> In addition to Initiative 276 (mandating comprehensive "open" government), the voters brought about two reapportionments, permanent registration, the blanket primary, civil service, and repeal of the poll tax through the initiative process. It has also been used to liberalize liquor policies, to bring about programs sought by pensioners, sportsmen, "good government" groups, chiropractors and consumers, among others.[9]

The referendum device allows 4 percent of the voters to petition to have a law passed by the legislature submitted to the voters before it becomes effective. Washington voters nearly always override legislative enactments subjected to referendum. They also tend to participate actively in such "people's" measures: initiatives and referenda routinely out-poll statewide races for positions such as treasurer and auditor.

Although designed to be the "people's voice" by turn-of-the-century progressive and populist reformers, initiatives can and have become tools for private interests. Interest groups take an active role in initiatives, providing organizational, personnel, and financial support for passage or defeat of particular measures. Still, of the twelve initiated measures enacted over the past decade and a half, five passed even though advocates were outspent by opponents. This pattern in Washington can be contrasted to Shockley's findings for Colorado, where all initiated measures drawing strong corporate opposition were defeated.[10]

In summary, Washington appears to provide a setting conducive to initiative politics. The state is of manageable size and its population is regionally concentrated. The legacy of radical and populist politics legitimates popular mobilization of voters to direct legislative action. The parties are decidedly weak in their organization and in their command over voter loyalties. Washington also proved ripe for term-limit advocates because of increasing campaign costs and incumbents' electoral advantages, especially for congressional and state senate races. Finally, the ease of access to the initiative process, the robust use of this device in the past, and the frequency of its successful use all invited term-limit advocates to embrace it.

The Rise and Fall of Term Limits

A group calling itself LIMIT (Legislative Initiative Mandating Incumbent Terms) drafted the language of I-553 in late December 1990 and early January 1991. The most restrictive term-limitation proposal to go before voters in the 1990s, it limited legislators to no more than ten consecutive years in the state legislature, with state senators restricted to two four-year terms and state representatives to three two-year terms. Twelve consecutive years in the U.S. Congress were to be the limit, with two six-year terms for senators and three two-year terms for representatives specified. The governor and lieutenant governor might serve for eight years. Limits would take effect immediately and would be retroactive. Incumbent officials, except the governor, who had reached their term limit would be allowed one more election for the office. Finally, officials could run again for the same seat only after a six-year break.

Passage of I-553 would have barred incumbent Governor Booth Gardner from running for a third term in 1992. House Speaker Tom Foley and all 7 of his House colleagues, and 109 of the 147 state legislators, could seek and serve just one additional term before leaving office in 1994. The lieutenant governor would be blocked from reelection in 1996, and the state's two U.S. senators would be disqualified from reelection in 1998 and 2000.

Several false starts preceded LIMIT's successful initiative drive. The provisions of these unsuccessful precursors were much less restrictive than those of I-553. I-522 would have limited state legislators to eight years and members of Congress to twelve years, without retroactivity, and would have placed restrictions on campaign contributions and on gifts and other perks for elected officials. The chairs of both state party organizations immediately announced their opposition to the I-522 measure. Two months later backers of I-522 withdrew their effort and joined forces with LIMIT.

Initially legislators competed for control of the term-limitation terrain by submitting bills in the 1991 legislative session. These included a bill limiting legislative service to twelve years in the U.S. House or Senate, a bill limiting all statewide elected officers to twelve-year terms, and a resolution requesting that Congress initiate a constitutional amendment to limit service of its members to twelve years. Sponsors of these measures also joined forces behind I-553.

Due partly to the intensity of their anger over what they saw as abuses of office by elected officials and incumbent advantages in reelection campaigns, partisan advocates of term limitations embraced the most restrictive alternative. This may have served them well in launching their campaign, building an organization, attracting committed volunteers, and perhaps even in obtaining signatures during the petition drive. But in the battle to win the final election it undermined their cause.

LIMIT and the Origin of Mobilization

In the 1990 congressional elections, a group of self-described left-wing Democrats—including community organizers, SANE/FREEZE supporters, gay and lesbian rights proponents, and peace activists—backed Mike Collier in a primary challenge against six-term incumbent Norm Dicks from Washington's sixth congressional district. First elected in 1976, Dicks's seniority had gained him power in the House Appropriations Committee. A conservative Democrat, he specialized in defense issues and in guarding the Boeing company's military contracts.

After initially ignoring Collier's challenge, Dicks blitzed the district at the end of the primary campaign, outspending his opponent by a 16 to 1 margin. He got 72 percent of the vote.

Sherry Bockwinkel, later to become state chair of the I-553 campaign, dates her initial embrace of term limits to the failed Collier challenge. Gene Morain, later treasurer of LIMIT, was on the steering committee of the Collier campaign. Dicks had refused to debate Collier, they said, and good government groups like the League of Women Voters had even refused to provide a forum for a debate. Moreover, district newspapers had failed to cover the primary closely because, Bockwinkel thought, they coveted the incumbent's sizable media spending account.

The disappointment of the primary defeat refocused the challengers' energies on finding systematic ways of countering incumbent advantages. From the experience, Bockwinkel concluded: "There's only two parties left: the incumbents and the rest of us." [11] The day of Collier's defeat was the day Oklahoma passed a term-limit initiative. Bockwinkel and Morain obtained copies of the initiative from the Oklahoma secretary of state's office and placed their names on the mailing lists of term-limit groups in Oklahoma, California, and Colorado.

Bockwinkel moved on from the failed Collier challenge to join the general-election campaign of Helen Myrich, who ran for an open house seat in Washington's thirtieth legislative district. Myrich lost the election by just 439 votes, after being outspent $52,824 to $35,065 by her opponent. The house Democratic caucus gave only $650 to the Myrich campaign.[12] The reluctance of the caucus to fund the candidate sufficiently for an open seat, while it gave generously to incumbents, only confirmed for Bockwinkel that the election funding process was fundamentally flawed. "That's what said to me that incumbents are too important." [13]

The 1990 campaign experience convinced LIMIT organizers that incumbent advantages in fund-raising, franking privileges, media access, and paid staff made them invulnerable to successful challenge. Passage of term-limit initiatives in Oklahoma, Colorado, and California persuaded them that major structural change in the form of term limits would provide relief. A dozen partisans met weekly in living rooms to discuss term limits, to plan strategies, to review texts of initiatives elsewhere, and to begin drafting their own initiative language. [14]

The smoldering anti-incumbent group received a critical stimulus to action and valuable lessons on organizing initiatives at a conference on term limits sponsored by two national term-limit groups, Citizens for Congressional Reform (CCR) and Americans to Limit Congressional Terms (ALCT). The San Jose conference of December 13, 1990, which featured national and state proponents of term limits, is coming to be known as "the Port Huron of the 1990s." Bockwinkel and Morain attended at the invitation of the sponsoring groups, who had learned about them from their requests for information. At the conference they received literature on term limits elsewhere, viewed draft initiative language, talked with term-limit leaders from Oklahoma, Colorado, and California, and established ties with groups like Americans Back in Charge (ABIC), which had led the Colorado initiative drive. They met term limit "stars" like Lloyd Noble II, a key supporter of Oklahoma's initiative, and John H. Fund, who had written op-ed pieces for *The Wall Street Journal* promoting term limits. [15]

The conference attracted mainly very conservative Republicans and libertarians. Because Bockwinkel and her supporters from Washington came from the left wing of the Democratic party, Bockwinkel felt "out of place" and "stuck out like a sore thumb" among the wealthy, white, male Republicans at the conference. [16]

Following the San Jose conference, Bockwinkel and Morain returned to Tacoma and drafted I-553. On January 9, 1991, LIMIT filed its term-limit initiative with the secretary of state's office. It was given its number and ballot wording: "Shall there be limitations on terms of office for Governor, Lieutenant Governor, State Legislators, and Washington State members of Congress?"

The I-553 Signature Campaign

Between filing the initiative on January 9 and the July 5 deadline for turning in signed petitions, LIMIT secured 254,263 signatures in support of I-553. Of these, 211,257 were deemed valid by the secretary of state. This was far more than the 150,001 required for ballot certification and represented the fourth-highest total in 79 years of initiated measures in Washington.[17]

At first, in the purely local phase of the signature campaign, LIMIT remained a small, grass-roots organization of several dozen highly committed volunteers. Bockwinkel was the only paid staff member. Volunteers were drawn largely from Tacoma and surrounding Pearce County. LIMIT held monthly meetings at a Tacoma church; a potluck dinner was served, business was conducted, and petitions were distributed. Though small, the feisty group received important media publicity by tweaking the establishment at every opportunity. LIMIT took its signature drive to shopping malls, fairs, grocery stores, post offices, state ferries, gun shows, the Kingdome, and Tacoma Dome. Additionally, LIMIT obtained mailing lists from Citizens Against Government Waste and other groups whose members might be sympathetic to term limits. It circulated information by postcard mailings and distributed leaflets in public spaces. Still, by the end of February it had collected only about twelve thousand signatures.[18]

Fund-raising, too, went slowly during the purely local phase. LIMIT raised $1,248 from seventeen individuals between November and January 3, by which time it was $400 in the red. It secured two loans for $15,000, one from LIMIT treasurer Gene Morain, the other from a local doctor. At the end of March, as the local phase came to a close, I-553 had received only limited media notice and LIMIT was running a hefty $10,000 deficit. Signatures were coming in too slowly and elected officials at the state and national levels were largely oblivious to LIMIT and I-553. It was at that point that national term-limit organizers came to Washington and formed a national-local partnership.

Cleta Mitchell, a former Oklahoma house Democrat who led the term-limit effort in her state, came representing Americans Back in Charge and spent the last week of March promoting the initiative. She was joined by Shari Williams, director of the successful Colorado campaign and now executive director of Americans Back in Charge, and by LaDonna Lee from Americans to Limit Congressional Terms in Washington, D.C. The national term-limit leaders consulted with LIMIT on strategy, held press conferences, met with editorial boards, and gave public speeches on behalf of I-553. They energized the volunteers and gave visibility to the initiative.

The most important visiting delegation came from CCR. From the San Jose conference forward, CCR had known of LIMIT's activities and maintained contact with its leadership. In late February, CCR

TABLE 4-1   Citizens for Congressional Reform
Contributions to LIMIT—
(April 1991 through July 8, 1991)

Month	Monthly subtotal	Cumulative subtotal
April	$27,655.00	$27,655.00
May	44,315.89	71,970.89
June	95,000.00	166,970.89
July 8	10,000.00	
Total		$176,970.89

Source: Public Disclosure Commission, Olympia, Washington.

commissioned a poll of four hundred state residents by the Charlton Research Company. A month later, when the results showed 68 percent support for term limits in the state,[19] CCR made the decision to commit major funding to LIMIT's campaign. This infusion of money gave new life to LIMIT.

CCR describes itself as a nonpartisan, grass-roots group whose aim is to make Congress more accountable. Headquartered in Washington, D.C., it claims a national membership of two hundred thousand. CCR began in 1990 as an outgrowth of Citizens for a Sound Economy (CSE), which advocates free market principles, attacks government regulation in all its forms, and urges the privatization of government entities such as the Postal Service and Amtrak. Board members of CSE range from conservative Republicans to libertarians.

CCR reflected the political ideology of its origins. Its executive director was thirty-two-year-old Ron St. John, formerly head of an industry group that fought insurance reform in Arizona. Michael Hinds, who had worked in the Reagan administration and on the Bush campaign, served as CCR's director of field operations. Besides term limits, CCR's goals include ending the franking privilege, reducing committee staff, and instituting a pay-for-performance system for members of Congress.

On its own LIMIT had raised only $4,790.65 by the beginning of April 1991; by mid-month it showed a debt of $10,000. Beginning with a $100 contribution on April 8, CCR made substantial, periodic transfers of money to the LIMIT ballot access account, as reported in Table 4-1. CCR contributed a total of $27,655 in the first month of its partnership with LIMIT. The financially strapped LIMIT suddenly found itself awash in cash and able to produce campaign literature, reproduce petitions, pay hired staff, rent office space and equipment, and substantially expand its activities.

In addition to bankrolling LIMIT, CCR took unilateral steps to ensure a successful signature gathering campaign. It separately contracted in early April with the California-based company, National Voter Outreach (NVO), headed by Barry Smith. Smith coordinated professional signature agents from out-of-state and in-state volunteers, paying agents sixty cents for each signature obtained, plus bonuses. He provided training, supplies, and supervision for the agents, arranged for their rental housing at different locales, and reimbursed their expenses. NVO utilized sophisticated advertising techniques to prepare areas targeted by the signature gatherers.

The strategy proved enormously successful. LIMIT watched the NVO activities with amazement. The opposition, too, recognized the professionalism of the effort. Mark Brown, who later masterminded the opposition, commented in mid-June: "The organizers know what they're doing. I see them everywhere. At teachers rallies, fairs, malls. And my gut tells me this would be very difficult to beat at the polls." [20] By the certification deadline NVO had brought in 121,561 signatures, for which it was paid $82,348.70 from CCR funds.[21] Without the paid NVO signature gatherers, LIMIT would have generated only 89,696 signatures, 60,305 short of certification requirements.

Although critical to the successful petition drive, the use of paid signature gatherers proved to be highly controversial in at least three respects. First, though the practice is legal in Montana, Wyoming, and some other western states, and has become a cottage industry in California, Washington State law prohibits the hiring of solicitors to circulate petitions.[22] In the 1980s, California-based firms exported the industry by contracting to gather signatures in Arizona, Montana, and Oregon. Before I-553 in 1991, however, Washington had had few visible paid signature drives. The appearance of NVO enraged Republicans and Democrats alike. Republican secretary of state Ralph Munro blasted the tactic: "I'm violently opposed to buying signatures. It sets a very bad precedent." [23] (Despite its illegality, the practice was never legally challenged because similar challenges in other states had been dismissed by the courts.)

Second, as self-anointed guardians of the purity of the initiative, the press reacted uniformly with furious indignation at what it considered a prostitution of the process through paid signature gathering. "Democracy for sale, 40 cents a head," blazed the headline of one influential columnist in the state's largest newspaper. Describing signature agents as "bounty hunters," Herb Robinson argued: "The tactic is out of whack with our populist doctrine, which honors the initiative and referendum as grassroots democracy at its best." [24] Beginning with the practice of using hired signature gatherers, term-limit proponents lost favor with the print media, which eventually nearly uniformly condemned I-553.

Third, and most significantly, LIMIT was not a party to the signature-gathering contract between CCR and NVO. When LIMIT leaders asked to see the contract, they were denied. Thus, the autonomy of the local group declined in direct proportion to its acceptance of money from the national group.

Frictions developed between LIMIT and CCR in other areas as well. Early in April, CCR insisted that LIMIT open a separate bank account into which it wired funds directly, denying LIMIT's treasurer access to the account. Similarly, CCR sent field representatives from Washington, D.C., to Washington State. Instead of merging their efforts with those of LIMIT, the CCR field representatives conducted their own parallel campaign. The high salaries, lavish expense accounts, and different lifestyles of the CCR operatives shocked the leadership of LIMIT and caused some of its volunteers to resign from the cause. Early on, LIMIT asked CCR for assistance in raising local funds to be controlled by LIMIT. CCR denied the request, leading LIMIT to conclude that CCR desired to keep it financially dependent upon the national group.

Compounding the frictions between LIMIT and CCR were the divergent ideologies of the two groups. LIMIT's leaders were left-wing Democrats; CCR relied heavily upon right-wing alliances to advance its conservative agenda. The coalition between populist activists of the Left and Right appeared inherently unstable. Yet the campaign frictions and ideological differences were overcome in order to sustain the signature-gathering campaign. The liberal Bockwinkel offered this rationale for accepting conservative money: "Wring 'em dry. Let 'em spend it on this one instead of spending it on taking peoples' civil liberties away. . . . Then we'll save the left's money to fight the war machine." [25]

In fact, Bockwinkel and LIMIT had nowhere else to go for money. And CCR had nowhere else to go to advance its agenda in 1991. For LIMIT partisans, the price paid for ballot certification was controversy and friction, considerable loss of control over campaign strategy, and alliance with their ideological opposites. Given the alternative, it seemed a small price to pay.

By the July 5 petition-filing deadline, LIMIT had secured over a quarter of a million signatures; by July 10 it reported contributions of $240,092.16 and a membership of 7,600 volunteers. Entering the campaign for passage of I-553, it represented a formidable and well-financed organization. Meanwhile, the opposition to I-553 had remained unorganized, unfunded, and silent.

Opposition to Term Limits

Until just days before the petition-filing deadline, LIMIT continued to be dismissed as yet another disgruntled group pushing a single-issue cause. However, when LIMIT filed its quarter of a million signatures, the opposition quickly formed a formal organization. Calling itself "No on 553," its leader was Mark Brown, deputy director of the state employees' union and a seasoned campaign strategist whose reputation for skilled leadership would grow through the term-limit campaign. Vito Chiechi, a veteran Republican legislative staffer and party tactician, joined Brown as co-treasurer of the group, thus securing the appearance of bipartisanship for the opposition. No on 553 received initial financial contributions from state labor unions and the state trial lawyers association, enabling it to begin operations.

An otherwise unlikely set of allies from four distinct groups came together to form No on 553. A first set consisted of "good government" and environmental groups: the Washington State League of Women Voters, the Washington State Grange, Common Cause of Washington, and the Washington Environmental Council. This set of interests headlined most public activities of No on 553. Second, an early and substantial contributor to the opposition was organized labor: the Washington Federation of Employees, Washington State Labor Council, Washington Teamsters, and the Aerospace Machinists Union. A third set drew from influential business groups: US West, Washington Natural Gas, and the Sabey Corporation, among others. Lastly, an assortment of interest groups ranging from the Washington State Trial Lawyers Association to Democratic party committees and caucuses completed the No on 553 roster. This coalition, better known for their political differences and bitter battles, formed the opposition to term limits.

Reacting to the formation and composition of No on 553, LIMIT claimed for itself the grass-roots designation. Chair Bockwinkel equated the No on 553 forces to the establishment: "The opposition in every term limit campaign has always been the establishment. They're not concerned about government reform. They're concerned about keeping the people in power who they've worked on for 30 years." [26]

The No on 553 group turned for support and advice on strategy to its counterpart organizations in Oklahoma, Colorado, and California. Unlike limit proponents, it received no support from these states; the only advice it received came from California, where forceful opposition had narrowed the favorable margin of Proposition 140's passage. No on

553 then turned to "Let the People Decide," the only national organization specifically established to oppose term limits. Let the People Decide provided a one-thousand-dollar contribution and various pamphlets and fliers but little else, as the group was suffering from financial and organizational problems of its own.

During the first half of the term-limit campaign, No on 553 adopted three parallel strategies: it polled state residents on term limits, instituted legal action to remove I-553 from the ballot, and sought the financial and personal involvement of the state's congressional delegation in defeating I-553. Each strategy proved to be highly counterproductive.

The poll conducted on its behalf by The Analysis Group cost No on 553 half the money it had raised and yielded results that were "grim" and "frightening." Seventy-two percent of the respondents said they favored I-553, although the loss of political clout worried some, as did the potential loss of their own member of Congress.

Lacking apparent public support, and with limited financial and organizational resources, No on 553 filed a lawsuit. Upon the recommendation of the congressional delegation, No on 553 asked the state supreme court to remove the initiative from the ballot. The lawsuit argued that terms of elected officials were governed by the state and U.S. constitutions, which prescribed the qualifications and requirements for public office, and that the initiative was not a valid means of changing those documents. The state attorney general's office defended I-553's place on the ballot, arguing that the initiative should first be voted upon. If it was enacted, then legal action could be entertained. By an 8-1 vote the supreme court agreed with the defendants and dismissed the legal challenge to I-553.[27]

Besides the loss itself and the expenses incurred, the legal challenge proved counterproductive by creating opportunities for initiative proponents. LIMIT issued numerous press releases condemning the plaintiffs as incumbents and special-interest groups attempting to deny the people a vote. Bockwinkel asked: "Are they so afraid of losing? I say, let the people decide," borrowing a phrase from the national organization that opposed term limits.[28] Throughout the two weeks between filing of the lawsuit and the court's decision, LIMIT enjoyed access to and coverage by the press it previously had been denied. Editorial page commentary also shifted from harsh denunciation of the term-limit initiative to condemnation of the preemptive lawsuit. Prior to the legal challenge not a single editorial had favored I-553; after the filing not a single editorial on the suit favored removing I-553 from the ballot.[29]

Confronted by discouraging poll results and the failed lawsuit, representatives of No on 553 journeyed to the nation's capital in the second week of September, seeking campaign support and funds from national organizations and the state's congressional delegation. They found Let the People Decide in the midst of closing its shop due to funding problems. Some national interest groups balked at the funding request, having lost on term limits in the three prior states where they attempted to block its passage. Other organizations, particularly labor, said they would contribute but only if the state's congressional delegation gave priority to defeating the initiative.

The aims of No on 553 were dashed when the congressional delegation reaffirmed that it would stay out of the term-limit battle. The delegation's calculus appeared to be three-fold. First, to campaign personally against I-553, delegation members reasoned, would appear terribly self-interested and self-serving. Second, they did not want to enter a race if they did not have to, particularly when doing so would expose them unnecessarily to a potential loss. Third, they strongly believed the initiative's provisions were unconstitutional as applied to members of Congress.

The trip thus proved unsuccessful. A $1.1- to $1.5-million budget for a statewide media and direct-mail campaign was rejected by the delegation. Without this support, No on 553 lacked the ability to pry contributions out of the national lobbying organizations. As a former aide to the governor explained: "Before people committed themselves, they were looking for the signal from elected officials that this was clearly important to them. The signal never came." [30]

The Campaign at Mid-Point

By mid-September, the contrast between proponents and opponents of the initiative was so dramatic that passage of I-553 by a wide margin appeared all but inevitable. Surveys revealed overwhelming popular support for the measure. The two polls, one by proponents taken in February and the other by opponents in August, showed respectively 68 percent and 72 percent support for term limits.

No on 553 had raised $48,070.17 by mid-September, primarily from organized labor; professional, business, and good government groups; and Democratic office holders and campaign committees at the state level. Having spent most of its account on the survey and the failed lawsuit, No on 553 had a balance of just $832.34 in mid-campaign and its prospects for major national funding appeared bleak. By contrast, LIMIT enjoyed a 7.5 to 1 financial advantage over the opposition, having raised $364,077.28, 92 percent of which originated from CCR. It had a balance of $6,144.53 and a seemingly unending source of additional funds from CCR.

No on 553 came into existence just four months prior to the election and, until two months prior to the vote, had no paid staff, no campaign office, and no field representatives. Instead it relied upon volunteers from its loosely knit coalition. LIMIT had evolved from a handful of deeply committed grass-roots activists to a substantial organization claiming 7,600 volunteers from across the state. Its regional field directors were coordinated by a twelve-person paid staff housed in a large suite of offices at its state headquarters. Additionally, LIMIT personnel had over a quarter of a million names and addresses of people who had signed the original petition, in addition to lists of people and groups known to be supportive.

Entering the campaign's home stretch, LIMIT enjoyed substantial advantages in popular support for I-553, a hefty financial advantage, and a robust organization. On the other side, No on 553 knew from its survey which soft spots to exploit to undermine I-553's popular support. It had the endorsement of major economic and public interest groups and the editorial support of nearly all of the state's newspapers. The odds still seemed overwhelmingly arrayed against No on 553, and at the campaign's mid-point, no observer predicted defeat for I-553.

The Home Stretch

On September 25, six weeks before the election, the Washington State congressional delegation reversed its position of no involvement and agreed to help raise funds for No on 553. Its earlier decision had generated substantial home-state anger. Led by labor, economic interest groups accused the delegation of ducking the issue, which in part was a fight to save the members' positions. A month after the switch, more than $300,000 poured into the No on 553 campaign coffers.[31]

Encouraging news also came to No on 553 from a poll Republican representative Sid Morrison conducted to sample state opinion on a contemplated run for the governorship. The poll revealed a 10 percent reduction, to 62 percent, in support for the initiative.

Three and a half weeks prior to the election, No on 553 launched an aggressive campaign against I-553. It had identified likely voters, and voters likely to be swayed by one argument or another, and used finely tuned direct-mail techniques to reach them. Its theme was "There's Too Much to Lose." The argument was that Washington State would be jeopardized by I-553's passage through the loss of seniority and leadership positions in Congress. A second direct mailing to a half-million "perfect voters" argued that placing limits on the congressional delegation was "unilateral disarmament" when it came to protecting state water from diversion to California; retaining inexpensive energy from the Bonneville Power Administration; keeping large oil tankers out of Puget Sound; and barring offshore drilling for oil along the state's pristine coastline.

The opposition to term limits spent no money on television or newspaper ads, although it continued to receive considerable free media, particularly in newspaper editorials. Instead, it budgeted two-thirds of its resources for a saturated radio campaign, beginning the first of three waves of ads three and a half weeks before the election. LIMIT, too, relied primarily on saturated radio ads, largely repeating the anti-incumbent and abuse-of-office themes that had worked so well earlier.

A series of events that began to unfold in early October substantially aided term-limit opponents. The Tacoma *Morning News Tribune* ran a major investigative story on October 13 entitled: "Push For Limits: Is It the People or the Powerful?" [32] It identified CCR as the offspring of Citizens for a Sound Economy, which it characterized as a "right wing think-tank," and pointed out that brothers David and Charles Koch of Wichita, Kansas, who *Fortune* magazine ranked as the eighteenth richest men in the world (with a fortune estimated at $4.7 billion), were the major bankrollers of I-553 and the LIMIT organization. It also reported that Koch Industries, with holdings in energy, real estate, manufacturing and cattle, ranked as the second-largest privately held company in the United States and noted that David Koch had run for vice president on the Libertarian Party ticket in 1980. The story jolted LIMIT into a defensive posture from which it failed to recover, in part because it had little knowledge of the source of the CCR monies pouring into its treasury.[33]

Attempting to counter the article's effect, LIMIT searched for a national political luminary of liberal persuasion to reinforce the bipartisan image of term-limit supporters. After considering Ralph Nader, LIMIT settled on former California governor Jerry Brown. Brown accepted and appeared in the state three weeks before the election, campaigning for term limits as "a natural reaction to the utter breakdown of the political process." [34] The media gravitated to Brown, but his arguments for term limits elated No on 553 strategists, who had placed at the center of their "clout" argument the suggestion that California stood to benefit most by Washington's "unilateral disarmament." Brown's presence in the state allowed No on 553 to link California interests to I-553 proponents.

Eighteen days before the election a survey of state voters showed that support for I-553 had slipped to 57 percent, down 15 percent from early August.[35] Three days later, Booth Gardner, one of the state's most popular governors, announced that he would not stand for reelection for a third term in 1992. The withdrawal fueled speculation about whether his decision had been prompted by the term-limit initiative.

With ten days left, Congressman Al Swift, a seven-term Democrat, returned to the state and, in what became known as "the Al Swift sacrifice," made an "irrevocable pledge" to seek just one additional term. In doing so, he acknowledged the problem incumbents had in campaigning against term limits: "The frustration I have felt in speaking out against this very popular response to the intense frustration people are feeling these days is that you have no credibility as a member of Congress who would be affected by it." He concluded: "This announcement changes that." [36]

Swift rented a plane and flew around the state barnstorming against I-553. The dramatic gesture captured media attention as Swift warned against the loss of clout: "So what is at stake? Just for starters: our power, our electricity rates, our water, a fair portion of Pacific Rim trade, and, at its very core, our ability to have control of our own fate when our giant neighbor to the south decides otherwise." [37] By returning to the state, Swift altered the low profile the congressional delegation had taken, gave needed visibility to the issue, redirected attention away from Congress as an institution toward individual members of Congress, and emphasized the stakes voters had in retaining their individual members. Republican representative Morrison reinforced the new theme: "I would hope the sacrifice of a fine member of our team will wake up the voters." [38]

Nine days out, Representative Jim McDermott delivered a stinging attack against the bankrollers of LIMIT in a House floor speech which gained wide publicity in the state. McDermott charged that "a few of the world's richest men are trying to hoodwink the citizens of my state. . . . I will not stand by and watch a few right-wing billionaires try to perpetrate a legal and political fraud on the people I represent." [39] By now the issue of where LIMIT's money came from had become central to the campaign. No on 553 emphasized the issue in its final wave of radio advertisements.

Governor Jerry Brown returned to Washington State the day after McDermott's speech to campaign for term limits, again at the invitation of LIMIT. This visit proved as disastrous as his first to the cause of the initiative proponents. Members of the congressional delegation seized upon Brown's role in pushing for term limits, suggesting that a hidden California agenda lay behind his alliance with LIMIT. Now House Speaker Tom Foley took up the issue: "In January of 1993, one out of eight members of Congress will be a Californian." He then linked the governor's support for term limits to the advancement of California interests: "It's wonderfully ironic that a former governor of California would favor term limits for Washington's members of Congress. Jerry Brown has supported diversions of water from the Northwest to California. It's not surprising he favors tilting the balance." [40]

The role of Tom Foley in opposing term limits proved crucial to its defeat. Reluctant from the beginning to enter the battle, he had preferred that I-553 not become a referendum on Tom Foley. Throughout the campaign he insisted that the initiative was unconstitutional as applied to members of Congress, but he had not actively campaigned for its defeat and gave only lukewarm support to No on 553 as late as six weeks before the vote. He also knew, however, from the several polls taken late in the campaign, that support for the initiative had eroded. [41]

Despite his efforts to make it otherwise, the Speaker was very much an issue in the initiative campaign. News accounts and media editorials consistently pointed out the costs to the state of barring Foley from running again after 1992. Proponents and opponents focused on the Speaker in their advertising campaigns over I-553. One repeatedly aired radio ad by term-limit supporters included a mean-spirited and personal attack on the Speaker. [42]

With four days remaining until the election, Speaker Foley held a press conference in Washington, D.C., to denounce the initiative. He then flew back to the state to campaign against it. Newspapers headlined, "Foley Heads Home to Stump against Term-Limit Initiative" and "Foley Calls Term Initiative 'Anti-People.' " He labeled the initiative an attempt by extreme right-wing activists "to hijack the initiative process in the state." "This is a very big muscular out-of-state finance machine," Foley argued, "that has brought enormous amounts of money into the state, most of it from a single organization." [43] He crisscrossed the state over the weekend in a major media blitz from Seattle to Spokane. The usually cautious and understated Speaker now addressed the issue with fervor, conviction, even passion. With his position as Speaker on the line, he explained in concrete terms how the loss of clout would affect the state. He was joined by bipartisan representatives of the delegation in the final days of campaigning against I-553. On November 6, 1991, I-553 failed passage by a 54 to 46 percent margin with a record turnout of 67.9 percent of registered voters.

Explaining the Outcome

The 1991 defeat of term limits in Washington after three successful efforts in 1990 shocked national and local observers. Term-limit proponents from across the nation gathered at LIMIT headquarters on election eve confident of victory. Their disappointment the following day quickly turned to anger and internal bickering. Term-limit opponents celebrated the upset; most pointed to the Speaker as the key to the turnaround. Tom Foley no doubt played a crucial role, but a host of equally important factors help explain the defeat of I-553.

Public Opinion Polls

At least six surveys probed voter sentiments over the ten months of the initiative campaign. They provide insight into the basis of support for and the vulnerabilities of term limits. A late February CCR poll revealed 68 percent support for term limits, but when respondents were told that passage would force out Speaker Foley, only 40 percent said they would be more likely to vote for I-553, while 44 percent said they would be less likely to do so. Similarly, an August poll commissioned by No on 553 revealed 72 percent support for I-553 but also identified supporters who could be moved to "undecided" by the "loss of clout" argument and others who feared the loss of their own member of Congress. These two soft spots became a target for the No on 553 campaign strategy.

Representative Morrison's October 8 survey showed that support for I-553 had dropped to 62 percent; the ten percent defection from early August had moved into the undecided, not the negative, category. A fourth poll, taken on October 19, showed a decline of support to 57 percent.[44] Finally, a tracking poll on November 4 and 5 showed term limits failing passage. Thus, rather than a sudden, precipitous reversal on the weekend before the election in response to the Speaker's blitz, or a free fall toward the end of the campaign, surveys show a consistent loss of support for I-553 between August and mid-October as limit opponents geared up their campaign against the measure.

The week following the election, No on 553 and the Democratic Congressional Campaign Committee jointly commissioned The Analysis Group to survey 500 Washington voters on why they voted as they did. The survey reported that two thirds of I-553 voters knew that Speaker Foley opposed the measure, whereas less than a third knew that their member of Congress was opposed. Term-limit supporters said the need for new blood among elected officials was the single most important reason for their support (Table 4-2). Respondents who voted against term limits felt that "voters should be able to vote for whomever they want" (24 percent) and they feared the loss of clout in the Washington congressional delegation (21 percent) (Table 4-3). Only 8 percent of term-limit opponents said the potential loss of Speaker Foley was the prime reason for their opposition. Nineteen percent responded that it was Washington acting alone among the states that made the prime difference to them. Foley's role thus appears

TABLE 4-2 Reasons Given by Voters Favoring I-553 for Their
Support of Term Limits

*Question: Let me read you a list of reasons that other people have given and
tell me which you think was the most important to you personally in deciding
to vote in favor of Initiative 553. Remember to give the reason that influenced
you most at the time of your vote.*

We need new faces and new ideas	42%
Elected officials vote themselves pay raises and are mainly interested in themselves	11
Things are logjammed and nothing gets done	10
Special interests and political action committees have too much influence	10
Politicians don't listen to the people	8
Corruption and lack of ethics	6
Opposition to term limits came from out of state money and special interests	4
Perks and privileges like bounced checks at taxpayers' expense	4
Politicians vote policies like the S&L bailout to help special interests rather than the people	3
(none)	2
(don't know)	2

Source: The Analysis Group, Washington, D.C., November 1991.

Note: Percentages do not add up to 100 because of rounding.

to have been important, but not nearly as crucial as the other reasons
for opposing I-553.

For all its financial advantages in the campaign, LIMIT had access
to only the first poll taken in February, while No on 553 had access to all
four polls taken during the latter stages of the campaign. The surveys,
moreover, provided important guidance for the opponents' campaign
strategy, allowing them to identify vulnerabilities in LIMIT's support
and to tailor their campaign accordingly. Without doubt, the findings of
the postelection survey will be valuable in future term-limit campaigns.

Campaign Finance

Though LIMIT enjoyed a 2 to 1 margin over No on 553 in
financial contributions, this apparent advantage was no advantage at all

TABLE 4-3 Reasons Given by Voters Opposing I-553 for Their Opposition to Term Limits

Question: Let me read you a list of reasons that people have given and tell me which you think was the most important to you personally in deciding to vote against Initiative 553. Remember to give the reason that influenced you most at the time of your vote.

Voters should be able to vote for whomever they want	24%
The loss of the clout of the Washington congressional delegation	21
It does not make sense to be the only state to have term limits	19
The loss of Speaker Foley	8
The law was unconstitutional	8
The change is too radical and would wreck Washington State's leadership	7
The loss of your own member of Congress	4
The loss of influence on environmental issues like supertankers	2
The initiative was financed by out-of-state money from the far right	2
The loss of jobs that rely on federal dollars and programs	1
Losing control of Columbia River water to California	1
Keeping low electrical rates	0
(none)	3

Source: The Analysis Group, Washington, D.C., November 1991.

in the end. First, as the advocate of change in the status quo, LIMIT had to spend $240,092.16, or one-third of its eventual total, just to obtain access to the ballot for the initiative. From mid-September, when the home stretch of the campaign began, until Election Day, LIMIT and No on 553 raised roughly comparable amounts: $366,935.71 for LIMIT and $316,250.95 for No on 553. Thus, for the actual conduct of the campaign, the opposing sides had roughly comparable funding. In the last three weeks of the campaign, No on 553 spent $200,000 on saturated radio advertising; LIMIT could afford only $177,000 on radio ads because the rest of its funds had been committed elsewhere. Second, LIMIT ran a very expensive operation, with its large suite of rented offices, field representatives across the state, and a paid staff of thirteen. By contrast, No on 553 had one paid staffer over just the last two months of the campaign situated in a modest office with no field representatives.

Several features are striking about the financing of the LIMIT campaign. Table 4-4 shows, first, that fully 70 percent of all contributions toward passage of I-553 originated with CCR. Second, the combined contributions from CCR, Americans Back in Charge, National Committee to Limit Terms, and Americans to Limit Congressional Terms—all national term-limit organizations from outside Washington State—represented 82 percent of total contributions.

No on 553 used the fact that four-fifths of the opposition's money came from four national conservative and libertarian groups as a centerpiece of its campaign strategy. It argued that out-of-state interests were attempting to buy an initiative. LIMIT experienced considerable difficulty in countering the argument, particularly after the press had picked it up.

A third striking feature of LIMIT financing was the absence of national or local economic interest groups as contributors. Only one organized interest group appears, the National Federation of Independent Business from San Mateo, California, which made a $6,141.56 in-kind contribution in the form of a bulk mailing to its members.

LIMIT received about 1,800 modest individual contributions, most between ten and fifty dollars. In contrast, No on 553 secured very few individual contributions, relying instead on organized economic and labor interest groups and incumbent office holders, who together accounted for 84 percent of its money. State and national economic organizations gave almost $200,000, three-fourths of which came from national economic interest groups (Table 4-5). Nearly all of the national contributions came in during the final thirty days of the campaign, following the decision by the House delegation to commit itself to the term-limit battle. The infusion of money from national interest groups provided LIMIT a limited opportunity to neutralize the charge that it was funded by out-of- state money. LIMIT tried to argue that funding for its opponents originated with the "incumbent protection society," but because more than 90 percent of LIMIT's funds came from out-of-state, compared to just 52 percent of No on 553's, the argument was difficult to make.

Organized labor provided just over $70,000, or one-fifth of No on 553's total. Just under $40,000, or a tenth of the total, came from party campaign committees or incumbent office holders, all from the Democratic party, except for $5,000 from Republican representative Sid Morrison.

Unlikely Coalitions

Finance patterns associated with I-553 reflect the unusual coalitions that formed around the term-limit initiative. LIMIT

TABLE 4-4   Major Contributors to LIMIT

Contributor	City and state	Amount
Citizens for Congressional Reform	Washington, D.C.	$491,148.52
Americans Back in Charge	Denver, Colo.	50,000.00
National Committee to Limit Terms	Sacramento, Calif.	34,478.00
Washington State Citizens for Congressional Reform	Tacoma, Wash.	11,000.00
Americans to Limit Congressional Terms	Washington, D.C.	9,173.00
National Federation of Independent Business	San Mateo, Calif.	6,141.56
Leslie Graves	Spring Green, Wis.	5,000.00
Harold Kean	Seattle, Wash.	5,000.00
Eric O'Keefe	Spring Green, Wis.	5,000.00
Howard Rich	New York, N.Y.	5,000.00
Barry Seid	Chicago, Ill.	5,000.00
Valhi Inc.	Dallas, Texas	5,000.00
Sherry Bockwinkel	Tacoma, Wash.	3,428.96
Boyd Lundstrom	Tacoma, Wash.	3,150.00
Joseph Curiel	Tacoma, Wash.	640.00
Gene J. Morain	Tacoma, Wash.	550.00
Edgar Cochran	Royal City, Wash.	500.00
Costco Leasing	Tacoma, Wash.	500.00
Paul Farago	Key West, Fla.	500.00
Citizens for Roy Ferguson	Bellevue, Wash.	500.00
Lucas Petroleum Group	Houston, Texas	500.00
Committee to Re-elect John Moyer	Spokane, Wash.	500.00
George Paris	Bothell, Wash.	500.00
Citizens for Congressional Reform	Wichita, Kan.	453.00

Source: Public Disclosure Commission, Olympia, Washington, "1991 Campaign Finance Reports," January 9, 1992.

combined local left-wing Democratic challengers with national libertarian tax-revolt partisans. The outsiders cared little about obtaining endorsements and failed to receive support from in-state business, labor, professional, party, and good-government groups. The alliance, inherently unstable, was sustained over the duration of the initiative by real mutual dependence (one faction provided the financial resources, the other the organizational muscle and volunteers) and by remaining focused on the term-limit objective as the two factions' single purpose.

The coalition of term-limit opponents was also inherently unstable and had difficulty during the initiative campaign in taking unified,

TABLE 4-5   Major Contributors to No on 553

Contributor	City and state	Amount
Philip Morris USA	New York, N.Y.	$25,000.00
Washington State Labor Council	Seattle, Wash.	24,500.00
Kaiser Aluminum	Spokane, Wash.	16,694.63
Washington Federation of State Employees	Olympia, Wash.	12,534.80
Aerospace Machinists	Seattle, Wash.	10,000.00
Association of Trial Lawyers of America	Washington, D.C.	10,000.00
The Boeing Company	Seattle, Wash.	10,000.00
Burlington Northern	Fort Worth, Texas	10,000.00
National Rifle Association	Washington, D.C.	10,000.00
PULSE—Washington Education Association	Federal Way, Wash.	9,000.00
United Sign Associates	Spokane, Wash.	7,586.87
Pacific Public Affairs	Seattle, Wash.	6,757.90
US West Communications	Olympia, Wash.	5,500.00
Akin Gump Hauer & Feld	Washington, D.C.	5,000.00
Aluminum Co. of America	Wenatchee, Wash.	5,000.00
Anheuser-Busch Companies	St. Louis, Mo.	5,000.00
Central States Management Corp.	Washington, D.C.	5,000.00
Consolidated Rail Corp.	Washington, D.C.	5,000.00
Cox Cable	Atlanta, Ga.	5,000.00
CSX Corp.	Richmond, Va.	5,000.00
Foley Congressional Campaign Committee	Spokane, Wash.	5,000.00
House Leadership Fund	Potomac, Md.	5,000.00
Macandrews & Forbes Holdings Inc.	New York, N.Y.	5,000.00
Citizens for Sid Morrison	Yakima, Wash.	5,000.00

(Continued on next page)

coherent, and sustained action. Mark Brown characterized No on 553 as the "broadest and oddest" coalition in recent state politics. It was composed of unlikely partnerships of business and labor, environmentalists and developers, Common Cause and party partisans, the National Rifle Association and the League of Women Voters, and the Washington Environmental Council and the Dow Chemical Corporation. In the end, the coalition achieved unity by focusing on the single goal of defeating term limits.

Media and Term Limits

The visual, print, and audio media played markedly different roles in the term-limit campaign. Television remained largely oblivious to the issue until the last stages of the campaign and even then gave it only fleeting coverage. Neither LIMIT nor No on 553 spent money on

TABLE 4-5   *(Continued)*

Contributor	City and state	Amount
National Cable Network	Washington, D.C.	5,000.00
Norfolk Southern	Washington, D.C.	5,000.00
Olin Ordnance	St. Petersburg, Fla.	5,000.00
Raytheon Co.	Lexington, Mass.	5,000.00
RJR Nabisco	Washington, D.C.	5,000.00
Steven Ross	New York, N.Y.	5,000.00
Southern Pacific Transportation	San Francisco, Calif.	5,000.00
Textron Inc.	Providence, R.I.	5,000.00
TRW Space & Defense	Redondo Beach, Fla.	5,000.00
Union Pacific Railroad	Washington, D.C.	5,000.00
Charles Walker & Associates	Washington, D.C.	5,000.00
Washington Teamsters	Seattle, Wash.	5,000.00
Democratic Congressional Campaign Committee	Washington, D.C.	3,000.00
INC Services Corp.	Washington, D.C.	3,000.00
McCaw Communications	Kirkland, Wash.	3,000.00
PTSGE	Seattle, Wash.	3,000.00
Simpson Investment Co.	Seattle, Wash.	3,000.00
Washington State Trial Lawyers Association	Seattle, Wash.	2,750.00
Snohomish County Democrats	Everett, Wash.	2,510.00
AFSCME Council 2	Lynnwood, Wash.	2,500.00
Centel Corp.	Chicago, Ill.	2,500.00
Public Employees Action Committee	Pacific, Wash.	2,500.00
Weyerhaeuser Co.	Tacoma, Wash.	2,500.00
Ed Younglove	Olympia, Wash.	2,500.00

Source: Public Disclosure Commission, Olympia, Washington, "1991 Campaign Finance Reports," January 9, 1992.

television ads. A limited number of news commentaries, mostly opposing the initiative, did air toward the end of the campaign.

By contrast, the print media focused on the term-limit initiative early and gave it close coverage throughout the campaign. Neither LIMIT nor No on 553 purchased more than an occasional newspaper ad, but leaders from both groups visited major newspaper editorial boards. The opposition to term limits received enormous amounts of free newspaper space in the form of editorials and commentaries. Eighteen of twenty major newspapers surveyed in Washington condemned term limits as unwise, counterproductive, or even foolish. Appalled by LIMIT's use of paid signature gatherers and by the size of its external funding from CCR, newspapers ran several in-depth investigative stories on the Koch brothers, their funding of CCR, their right-wing ties, and their libertarian political agenda.

Perhaps more important than the print and visual media combined, radio played a central role in the term-limit initiative. LIMIT enjoyed an easily available and highly sympathetic forum in the radio media, particularly on call-in talk shows. As the campaign entered the home stretch, LIMIT budgeted $175,000 for saturated radio advertising. No on 553 allotted $200,000, or well over half its total budget, for the same purpose. LIMIT experienced difficulty controlling the content and timing of its ads as out-of-state term-limit organizations brought in their own ads and ran them as and when they chose. No on 553 had greater autonomy in organizing its radio ads, tailoring them to specific media markets across the state, and altering their content as the last three weeks of the campaign unfolded.

Political Parties and Term Limits

The term-limit initiative originated outside political party structures and focused its attack on entrenched interests within the parties. Thus, it is not surprising that neither the Democratic nor Republican party organizations at the state level supported I-553. Still, the two parties approached the term-limit issue in different ways.

The Republican party is of several minds over term limits. Former high-level Reagan and Bush administration officials lead several national term-limit organizations. This has led some to suggest that term limits are a Republican plot to wrestle control of the U.S. House away from Democrats. Both President Bush and Vice President Quayle have spoken in support of term limits. Moreover, the national Republican party platform calls for a constitutional amendment to place "some restrictions on the number of terms elected officials can serve." [45]

At the state level in Washington, however, the Republican party was paralyzed by the term-limit issue. There was no plank on term limits in the 1990 Washington State Republican party platform, nor did the issue even surface for debate at the 1990 state party convention. This silence was due not to ignorance but to internal division on the issue. When I-553 became one of the state's most controversial issues in 1991, neither the Republican State Central Committee nor any Republican county or district committees took stands on the issue, which split and immobilized the party. Individual Republican elected officials did become active, on both sides.

In contrast, the Democratic party united strongly against the term-limit initiative. Democrats had much to lose if I-553 passed. The incumbent governor would not have been able to run for reelection in 1992. All five Democratic House members, including Speaker Foley, would have had to end their service in 1994. A similar term deadline faced 19 of the 24 Democratic state senators and 14 of the 58 Democratic state house members. Democratic U.S. senator Brock Adams would be limited to one more reelection in 1992. A seasoned Democrat managed the campaign for No on 553. Democratic elected officials contributed money to the opposition, as did county and district party committees and party legislative caucuses. Of the forty thousand dollars raised by No on 553 from party sources, all but five thousand dollars came from Democrats.

At the national level, the Democratic Congressional Campaign Committee (DCCC) gave strategic assistance to No on 553. It contributed money, sent a staff person to the state for three days to help raise local money, urged national economic organizations to contribute, researched the background of CCR and the Koch brothers for Congressman McDermott's House floor speech, jointly sponsored with No on 553 the postelection poll, and convinced poll takers for another initiative to include a question on I-553. In this sampling of opinion on I-553, the DCCC was seeking to determine whether by mid-October the level of public opposition to term limits had reached the point where individual members of the House delegation, particularly Speaker Foley, could campaign actively against term limits in the state. When DCCC learned that support for I-553 had slipped to 57 percent, its staff began urging members of the delegation to confront the initiative at home and in person.

Defining and Redefining Term Limits

The battle over I-553 involved a struggle over the meaning of term limitations. At one level the meaning of term limits is very simple—they would limit the length of service of elected officials. The apparent simplicity of the issue explains its popular appeal. In a protracted campaign over adopting term limits, however, the simplistic definition yields to more complex formulations as attention shifts to secondary and derivative effects of term limits.

For well over half of the I-553 campaign LIMIT enjoyed a virtual monopoly in defining term limits, with no organized opposition to provide alternative interpretations. LIMIT presented the initiative as an opportunity to strike out at Congress and to send a message about the practices of career politicians. To LIMIT, Congress as an institution remained governed by nineteenth century rules rewarding longevity in office through the seniority system. Term limits would serve to modernize the Congress, which had failed miserably in balancing the national budget, solving the savings and loan crisis, and addressing the balance-of-trade problem. LIMIT also attacked an assortment of abuses by career politicians: unearned salary hikes, automatic reelection due to PAC funding advantages, check kiting schemes, luncheon privileges, perpetual reelection machines, fixing parking tickets, and special parking privileges. The abuse of state power by incumbents who became preoccupied with and permanently successful at reelection rather than performing their proper legislative role were identified by LIMIT as the flaws in the system for which term limits promised relief.

As initially defined by LIMIT, term limits reflected mass disenchantment and alienation over the institutions of power and the agents of rule. This definition appealed powerfully to populist sentiments of both the left and right. It resonated equally powerfully with disaffected citizens who felt like spectators in elections. Uncertainties about the more complex effects of term limits and even about their constitutionality allowed disenchanted voters an opportunity to send a message about their discontent with politics as usual without having to defend or justify their full consequences. As long as LIMIT held a monopoly over the definition of the issue, from 68 to 72 percent of Washingtonians supported the initiative.

Opponents of I-553 initially argued that the initiative, particularly as it applied to national elected officials, was unconstitutional, but the arcane claim to unconstitutionality failed to counter LIMIT's original definition of the issue or to redefine it.

As the campaign entered the home stretch, No on 553 adopted a four-pronged strategy for redefining the term-limit initiative. The first addressed the benefits for the state of seniority within the Washington congressional delegation. There were reminders of the federal largess delivered to the state by former senators Magnuson and Jackson. Prospectively, No on 553 identified areas where term limits could jeopardize Washington State's interests, using the theme, "There's Too Much to Lose." The potential diversion of Columbia River water to California frightened agricultural interests dependent upon irrigation, fishing interests, barge shipping operations, and environmental groups, all of whom had petitioned the delegation in the past to prevent such diversions. The specter of higher energy charges if the Bonneville Power Administration honored calls by recent administrations to raise electric rates threatened consumers and energy-dependent industries. Finally, the prospect of offshore drilling for oil and gas on the state's coastline and of lifting the ban on transshipment of oil in lower Puget Sound triggered strong environmental concerns. By this reasoning, term limits threatened the proven power of seniority to protect Washington State from disadvantageous federal policy.

Fairness was a second issue in redefining term limits. Opponents of I-553 argued that if the initiative passed Washington's congressional delegation would be alone in playing by the new rules. Calling the measure "unilateral disarmament," No on 553 pointedly noted that its nemesis to the south, California, had not included national elected officials in its term-limit proposition. LIMIT attempted, ineffectively, to counter the argument by claiming that term limits would pass in other states in the future.

A third strategy branded term limits as basically undemocratic. No on 553 argued that voters should be able to vote for whomever they chose and that term limits would restrict that choice.

Redefining term limits as being about political clout, fairness, and democratic choice helped to change the debate over I-553, but a final strategy proved most critical to defeating the initiative. LIMIT had previously defined term limits as an opportunity for striking out at the institution of Congress, which voters disliked, without attacking their own representatives, whom they did like. At first members of the delegation hid from the term-limit issue, at the most labeling it unconstitutional. By the home stretch of the campaign they had reversed their position and confronted the issue directly and personally, turning the campaign into a judgment about individual members of Congress, not about Congress as a whole.

By the end of the campaign, No on 553 had redefined term limits as a personal attack on members of the delegation. The National Committee to Limit Terms aided this redefinition immeasurably by running personal and mean-spirited ads that accused the Speaker of abusing his office. Congressman Swift's announcement that he would end his political career personalized the issue and raised the stakes for voters in the election. When Governor Gardner announced that he would not seek a third term the perception was enhanced that term limits discouraged popular officials from seeking reelection. And the Speaker's media blitz across the state exposed him to voters, who believed him more than the caricatures of him provided by LIMIT. Members of the delegation returned to the state emphasizing the importance of political clout, fairness, and democratic choice. But in the end it was their personal appearance that made the largest difference.

Notes

1. The approach used in this research was to interview partisans favoring and opposing the term-limit initiative, gather publicly available data on campaign organization and finance, analyze public opinion surveys made available to the author, interview key actors involved in the process, collect

campaign literature and position papers from those involved, and assemble media accounts of the initiative campaign.

2. The figure is derived from the requirement for signatures amounting to 8 percent of the prior gubernatorial vote.

3. Hugh A. Bone, "The Political Setting," in *Political Life in Washington,* ed. Thor Swanson, William F. Mullen, John C. Pierce, and Charles H. Sheldon (Pullman: Washington State University Press, 1985), 7.

4. Ronald J. Hrebenar and Robert C. Benedict, "Political Parties, Elections and Campaigns, II: Evaluation And Trends," in *Politics and Public Policy in the Contemporary American West,* ed. Clive S. Thomas (Albuquerque: University of New Mexico Press, 1991), 142.

5. William F. Mullen and John C. Pierce, "Political Parties," in *Political Life in Washington,* 57-67.

6. Public Disclosure Commission, *1990 Election Financing Fact Book* (Olympia: Washington State Department of Printing, 1991), 36.

7. Reported in *The Wall Street Journal,* June 19, 1991, A8.

8. National Conference of State Legislatures, "State Legislative Turnover, 1979-1989" (n.p., August 28, 1991).

9. Hugh A. Bone, "The Political Setting," in *Political Life in Washington.*

10. John S. Shockley, *The Initiative Process in Colorado Politics: An Assessment* (Boulder: Bureau of Government Research and Service, University of Colorado, 1980).

11. *Seattle Post Intelligencer,* July 18, 1991, A8.

12. Public Disclosure Commission, *1990 Election Financing Fact Book* (Olympia: Washington State Department of Printing, 1991), 94.

13. *Seattle Post Intelligencer,* July 18, 1991, A8.

14. In drafting I-553, Bockwinkel said: "Our biggest debate was on the number of terms." *The Olympian,* June 21, 1991, A1.

15. John H. Fund, "Term Limitation: An Idea Whose Time Has Come," *Policy Analysis,* October 30, 1990.

16. *Seattle Post Intelligencer,* July 18, 1991, A8.

17. The record for signatures on initiatives is held by a 1973 measure controlling salaries of elected officials (699,098), followed by a 1988 minimum-wage initiative (300,900), and a 1991 property tax valuation rollback (275,000).

18. *The Morning News Tribune* (Tacoma), February 27, 1991, D9.

19. When respondents were told that passage would force the ouster of Speaker Foley, 40 percent said they would be more likely to vote for I-553, while 44 percent said they would be less likely to do so.

20. *Seattle Times,* June 12, 1991, A1.

21. Public Disclosure Commission files, Olympia, 1991.

22. The statute reads: "Every person shall be guilty of a misdemeanor who: For any consideration or gratuity or promise thereof solicits or procures signatures upon an initiative or referendum petition." *Revised Code of Washington,* 29.79.490.

23. *The Seattle Times,* June 12, 1991, B1. LIMIT chair Bockwinkel

responded that people were not buying signatures but being paid to circulate petitions.

24. Herb Robinson, *The Seattle Times,* June 21, 1991, A10.
25. *Seattle Post Intelligencer,* July 18, 1991, A1.
26. *The Seattle Times,* July 20, 1991, A8.
27. In doing so, the court acknowledged that "the underlying constitutional issues are complex, as well as of great public significance" but deferred a substantive ruling by saying that the court lacked sufficient time for "adequate briefing, argument and deliberation."
28. *Seattle Post Intelligencer,* August 15, 1991, A1.
29. Some sense of the favorable press proponents of I-553 received can be gained from editorial headlines: "Let initiative go to the voters" (*Seattle Post Intelligencer*), "Let People vote on Initiative 553" (*Morning News Tribune* of Tacoma), "Term Limits lawsuit should wait for voters" (*Valley Daily News*), "Right or 'wrong,' the people have a right to be heard" (*Aberdeen Daily World*), "Court shot at term limits could prove bad gamble," (*Vancouver Columbian*), "Court should refuse initiative challenge" (*Centralia Daily Chronicle*), and "Leave 553 on the ballot" (*Eatonville Dispatch*). What had been harsh editorial opinion against I-553 now turned against the preemptive lawsuit: "Stupid, stupid, stupid. That's the only way to describe the last-ditch lawsuit aimed at knocking Washington's term limit initiative off the November ballot." *Morning News Tribune* (Tacoma), August 15, 1991, A10.
30. *The Seattle Times,* September 25, 1991, G1.
31. Campaign officials attribute two-thirds of this amount directly to the intervention of the delegation, which pried contributions from national economic organizations.
32. *Morning News Tribune* (Tacoma), October 13, 1991, A1.
33. LIMIT leaders report having pressed CCR for information on the source of its contributions, but CCR remained elusive. LIMIT's treasurer became suspicious about the funding source after making an urgent call to CCR for money to cover an overdue payroll and receiving $15,000 the next day from Wichita.
34. *The Seattle Times,* October 17, 1991, B10.
35. The proponents of a "death with dignity" initiative conducted the poll and included a question on term limits at the request of the Democratic Congressional Campaign Committee. The results of this poll were not shared with No on 553 strategists until just days before the election.
36. *The Seattle Times,* October 25, 1991, A1.
37. *Seattle Post Intelligencer,* October 26, 1991, A1.
38. Ibid.
39. *Seattle Post Intelligencer,* October 29, 1991, A3. McDermott's speech drew on the investigative reporting of the Tacoma *Morning News Tribune* (October 13, 1991, A1), and on research provided by the Democratic Congressional Campaign Committee.
40. *San Diego Union,* November 3, 1991, A1.

41. As crucial as Foley's role was, campaign insiders still give as much or more credit to Al Swift, who stepped out at a critical time in the process, campaigned actively, and sacrificed his political future.
42. The ad, produced in Sacramento by the National Committee to Limit Terms (NCLT), aired without LIMIT's concurrence. It contained the tag line, "Ready to take back our government? Prop. 553." In Washington, initiatives are not referred to as "propositions," as they are in California. Although the spot generated highly negative media reactions, NCLT continued running it until the end of the campaign, ignoring pleas by LIMIT to cancel it.
43. *The Seattle Times,* November 3, 1991, B1.
44. Again, the movement away from support for I-553 was into the undecided category. The Democratic Congressional Campaign Committee did not share these results with local No on 553 leaders until the weekend before the election, prompting the latter to speculate that the poll's purpose was to test the waters for Foley's entry into the battle.
45. Republican Party National Platform, 1988, p. 39.

5. TRANSPLANTING TERM LIMITS: POLITICAL MOBILIZATION AND GRASS-ROOTS POLITICS

Stuart Rothenberg

The term-limitation movement, which began in three western states, has spread from California to Massachusetts and from Colorado to Florida. The movement is so striking not only because it has developed nationally, but also because of the speed at which it has spread and the diverse state political cultures in which it has taken root. The grass-roots appeal of term limits supersedes ideology and political party, and the movement is active in states which allow voters to impose the limits through the initiative process, as well as in those states (such as Texas and New Jersey) where any term-limit proposal would have to be approved by the very legislators whose terms would be limited.

Although term limits met relatively little resistance in their earliest battles, they have their critics, and the defeat of the 1991 Washington term-limit ballot measure—Initiative 553—demonstrates that such initiatives can be defeated.

The term-limit movement is only the latest example of an important but understudied phenomenon: nationwide explosions of populist ideas that breed supportive and opposing organizations in their wake. In the past, new ideas seemed to spread first within a region and then to adjacent states before becoming national phenomena. Modern communications, reinforced by the increasing professionalization of political campaigns, clearly have bred new methods of dissemination, as ideas and organizations leapfrog to fertile political environments.

This chapter will examine the "nationalization" of the term-limitation movement by exploring the role of national elites and groups as well as the activities of the opposition. It will also compare the term-limit movement with other grass-roots movements to look for clues to how and why such movements succeed and why they may ultimately disappear.

National Groups and the Spread of Term Limits

Any successful grass-roots movement needs organization and money, both of which require the support of activists and, ultimately, trained professionals. As with previous populist efforts, the congressional term-limitation drive has both local and national components. Local leaders plot strategy and oversee daily operations in individual states but they are aided, in varying degrees, by national organizations that offer guidance, expertise, and logistical support.

Over the past few years, five national groups—four based in Washington, D.C., and one in Denver, Colorado—have been the major players in the term-limitation movement. Americans to Limit Congressional Terms (ALCT), Citizens for Congressional Reform (CCR), and Americans Back in Charge (ABIC) have supported the cause, whereas Let the People Decide (LTPD) and the American Federation of State, County, and Municipal Employees (AFSCME) have opposed limits. Each of these groups has adopted a particular style and approach to the series of state skirmishes that together constitute the term-limitation movement.

Americans to Limit Congressional Terms

Republican political consultants Eddie Mahe and LaDonna Lee of the Eddie Mahe Company began to look at term limits early in 1989. That summer, Mahe and Lee established ALCT, bringing Democrats into the group's hierarchy and incorporating it as a 501(c)(3) tax-exempt, bipartisan organization.[1] ALCT was the first national group established for the sole purpose of promoting term limits for members of Congress.

ALCT is a prototypical Washington-based organization that caters to the national media and a number of Washington constituents. Early on, the group's leaders decided against creating local chapters, preferring instead to work with state groups that had no formal connection with ALCT. "Our premise was that this would be a national movement and that we could help by networking with the movement," said LaDonna Lee, a member of ALCT's board and president of the Eddie Mahe Company.[2]

ALCT has done little grass-roots political work and virtually no on-site work. Instead, it has acted as a spokesman for the national term-limit movement (members of the group are frequently quoted in national news stories) and as a general advisor and conduit for information.

ALCT kicked off its advocacy campaign with a mid-winter press briefing in 1990 and sponsored a Washington, D.C., term-limit conference in December of 1990, one of two major early conferences held by advocates of limits. The group also completed a mailing to local radio talk shows across the country. "We got more responses—more requests for interviews—than we could handle. We referred them to local people when we could. Otherwise, someone from ALCT would do the interview," said Lee.

But time was not kind to ALCT. During the second half of 1991, it began to experience organizational problems, and its president, Cleta Mitchell, resigned to join Americans Back in Charge, a different term-limit organization. From that point, ALCT restricted itself primarily to raising money through direct mail and to monitoring state developments.

Citizens for Congressional Reform

Citizens for Congressional Reform was begun in November of 1990 as a project of Citizens for a Sound Economy, a nonpartisan membership organization promoting free-market alternatives to government programs. In February of 1991, CCR was spun off from its parent and incorporated as two separate organizations—a tax-exempt, nonprofit 501(c)(3) group, and a 501(c)(4) lobbying organization. CCR itself was replaced by U.S. Term Limits in 1992, but during its existence it billed itself as a grass-roots membership group with over 200,000 members nationwide, and its agenda called for ending a number of incumbent advantages, including the frank, in addition to term limits. CCR was active on term limits in a number of ways:

Research and information. CCR supplied local term-limitation groups with information about the issue, including draft language for an initiative. "We actually provide the language to make certain that it is constitutional and can be defended," said Ron St. John, who served as executive director of CCR for four months early in 1991. CCR also frequently provided state limitation efforts with lists of its local members who were both potential contributors and workers.

Ballot access services. CCR was well known for providing advice on how initiatives could make it to a state's ballot. The organization contracted with professional signature-gathering companies to ensure that initiative efforts gathered enough valid signatures to qualify for the ballot.

Monitoring and coordination. CCR monitored developments in the states and maintained a national clipping service to show local groups what was happening nationally. It also worked to ensure that multiple groups working for limits in the same state coordinated and combined their efforts rather than proceeding independently. In Arizona, for example, CCR encouraged Arizona Citizens for Congressional Reform and Citizens for Limited Terms to agree on a single term-limitation proposal. In noninitiative states, CCR monitored state activity and provided information to local organizations.

Money and fund-raising. CCR had the greatest financial resources of any of the national term-limit organizations. St. John readily admitted that the issue was "a phenomenal one on which to raise money," and CCR gave substantial direct and in-kind contributions to a number of state term-limit efforts, including those in California, Wyoming, and Massachusetts. CCR spent nearly $500,000 in Washington State. (Approximately one-third of the total went to a California-based professional signature company to assure ballot status.)

CCR divided states into categories depending on the extent of opposition it expected and it did not rule out such activities as telephone banks, television commercials, or independent expenditure campaigns in those states where it expected term limits to meet stiff opposition.

Americans Back in Charge

ABIC evolved from Coloradoans Back in Charge (CBIC), a state campaign committee established during the winter of 1989-1990 to build and tap popular support for a state initiative limiting the terms of state legislators, state constitutional officers, and Colorado's congressional delegation. CBIC spent $300,000 on signature gathering and a small radio advertising campaign, and the group's success drew requests for information from term-limit groups in more than two dozen states.

Campaign consultant Paul Ogle, who played a key role in CBIC and is president of ABIC, said that in late November 1990 he "felt that if we didn't establish an organization to help other states [pass term-limit initiatives], a lot of what we learned would be lost." Shari Williams, who managed the Colorado initiative campaign and served as executive director of CBIC, was recruited to be the executive director of ABIC. The group identifies three major areas of activity:

Legal.   ABIC hired attorney Cleta Mitchell, a former Oklahoma Democratic state legislator to become director and general counsel of the Term Limits Legal Institute. Mitchell was hired to provide legal research and advice to state limitation groups and to academic legal scholars who wanted to write on the subject. She also submitted a written brief and made oral arguments before the Florida supreme court when that court was reviewing the Florida term-limit ballot measure.

Ballot access.   ABIC provides advice to state groups on collecting signatures for ballot status (especially on how to use volunteers) and on the wording of term-limit proposals.

Campaign strategy and tactics.   More than any of the other national groups, ABIC provides campaign advice (campaign plans and issue positioning) to state groups. Ogle and Williams "audit" initiative campaigns and detail its strengths and weaknesses. They show campaigns how to get media attention, how to put together a volunteer organization, and how to raise money. The two ABIC strategists are political "nuts and bolts" experts who made trips to Washington State, Arizona, Texas, Ohio, Florida, New Mexico, Nebraska, Massachusetts, and California during 1991. Doug Watts, an experienced political consultant, has also worked with state groups to sharpen their message and with state spokesmen to improve their public speaking skills.

Because campaign planning and execution are among ABIC's greatest strengths, the organization works heavily in initiative states, but it also gives advice to groups operating in other states. For example, Ogle spoke at a February 1991 press conference sponsored by Texans for Term Limitations to kick off the state group's efforts to pressure the state legislature into passing a term-limit bill.

Let the People Decide

Let the People Decide was established as a 501(c)(4) lobbying organization during the spring of 1991. Although the group has had limited resources and no obvious successes, it is the one visible national organization devoted to opposing term limits. In a move that surprised many, LTPD scaled back its already token efforts on October 1, 1991, exchanging its Washington offices for quarters in Virginia and virtually closing down operations.

LTPD has one full-time employee (an executive director) and two advisory panels, one composed of political scientists and historians and the other of lawyers. Its board of advisors includes many well-known former public officials, such as former House Speaker Carl Albert (D-Okla.), former representative and defense secretary Melvin Laird (R-Wis.), and former senators Charles Percy (R-Ill.) and William Proxmire (D-Wis.). As part of its October 1991 downsizing, LTPD let go its public information director.

LTPD, which originally operated out of the offices of a Washington law firm, will not disclose its financing. It receives most of its money from organized labor but operates on a shoestring budget. The group has been involved in activities such as:

Monitoring and coordination. LTPD tracks term-limit developments across the country, frequently supplying information to other national groups interested in the issue, including Common Cause and Americans for Democratic Action, as well as to groups not yet concerned about the issue but that might become involved in the future. "We work to get the issue on other national groups' radar screens," said Rachel Dale, who served as the group's public information director. "Once a national group, like the American Association of University Women, takes a position, [LTPD] distributes materials to its members across the country."

Research and information. LTPD offers a basic information packet about term limits to anyone who requests information. The group answers questions from elected officials about term limits and about how the movement is proceeding nationally.

Advocacy. LTPD recommends speakers (frequently from its advisory panels) to talk about term limits and generally looks for opportunities to make the anti-term limit case.

Legal. LTPD provides legal guidance through Arnold & Porter, a high-powered Washington law firm that acts as the group's pro bono counsel. Dale said that the law firm was "actively involved in providing legal advice" to term-limit opponents and will "litigate if and when it becomes appropriate." LTPD was involved in the Florida supreme court's review of the Florida term-limit ballot measure.

Let the People Decide does no field work; though it has never ruled out such activity, the group's overall approach and capabilities all but preclude it. LTPD has been so inactive that it did not hold a press conference or send out a press release following the surprising defeat of the Washington State term-limit measure. Apparently, LTPD has not been able to convince potential financial supporters that a national organization is a necessary element in stopping term limits.

American Federation of State, County, and Municipal Employees

In 1990 and again in 1991, the AFL-CIO executive council, reflecting the views of most union leaders, adopted a resolution opposing congressional and state legislative term limits. But organized labor has been surprisingly hesitant to participate in mobilizing or orchestrating opposition to term limits. The most active union has been AFSCME, which has a unique relationship to elected officials given its position as bargaining agent for public employees.

Like the other national term-limit groups, AFSCME gathers information about term-limit campaigns in the states and passes it along to other interested parties. It offers advice and some financial support to state groups that oppose limits. AFSCME has also encouraged its state affiliates to become involved in efforts to defeat term-limit initiatives. Mark Brown, of the Washington Federation of State Employees, has been a vocal opponent of limits and mobilized opposition among Washington State AFSCME members.

But AFSCME's role in assisting opponents of term limits is limited. "We don't have the time or resources to get heavily involved," said AFSCME political director Rick Scott. "I have the same amount of money and the same staff that I had before [term limits became an issue]."

The Creation and Growth
of the Term-Limit Movement

National term-limit groups have played a critical role in placing their issue before the American public and are largely responsible for the speed with which the movement has spread from coast to coast. However, those groups did not create the movement, nor are they primarily responsible for its successes and failures. The term-limit movement became a national phenomenon as voters became frustrated with the nation's political institutions and as the term-limitation issue gained visibility in the national media, particularly because of the 1990 initiative campaigns in Oklahoma, Colorado, and California.

The leaders of national organizations acknowledge that, for the most part, they have responded to requests for information and advice from existing state groups. They have not created local groups to spread the cause from state to state. Badgers Back in Charge, the Wisconsin term-limit group, is one of the few state organizations that owes its existence directly to a national group. Badgers was born from a conversation between Paul Ogle of Americans Back in Charge and Terry Kohler, a Wisconsin conservative activist and financial supporter.

State term-limit leaders say almost unanimously that they took their cue from the three 1990 term-limit states. "The fact that other states succeeded gave us the impetus to get going," said the leader of one Midwest term-limit group. That is also how the Washington State limitation movement began. Frank Eisenzimmer of Let Incumbents Mosey into the Sunset (LIMIT), Oregon's major term-limit group, said that he was "generally aware of what was going on in other states," and when a tax-limitation group he was involved with looked around for another project, term limits seemed like "the obvious next step." Other state leaders acknowledge their debt to Oklahoma, Colorado, and California but spread the credit around. Phil Handy, for example, who has been the most visible figure in Florida's Citizens for Limited Political Terms, remembered that a *Wall Street Journal* op-ed article by editorial writer John Fund provided the spark that got him interested and involved in term limits.

Most state groups were established by a few activists who had heard of term limits and were looking for a way to shake up the system. Many of them have had some campaign experience but are not high-level party insiders or members of their state's political establishment. A few could be described as political cranks who latch onto populist proposals, but most are politically interested activists who understand how the system works and what changes are realistic.

Wisconsin's Kevin Hermeling of Badgers Back in Charge, a hostage during the Iran crisis, has run for Congress and the state legislature; state representative John Timmer and consultant Jeff Hayzlett of South Dakotans for Limited Terms have managed ballot measures before; Oregon's Eisenzimmer worked during 1989 and 1990 for the passage of Measure 5, a successful tax-limitation ballot measure that cut property taxes over a five-year period; and Washington's Sherry Bockwinkel was a photojournalist who had managed a couple of candidate and ballot campaigns before helping launch her state's term-limit initiative. Very few state leaders are insiders like Florida's Handy, a former state finance director for Republican governor Bob Martinez, or Texas's Rob Mosbacher, a former GOP candidate for lieutenant governor and the son of the former secretary of commerce.

If it is clear that state term-limit groups have sprung from home soil, it is equally true that national groups deserve some of the credit for the spread of the term-limitation movement. Aside from their considerable cheerleading and media efforts (including press conferences and press releases), national groups helped local activists with limited campaign experience understand how to proceed.

The single most significant national event may well have been the December 1990 term-limit conference in San Jose, California, cosponsored by CCR and ABIC. That conference, attended by about 150 limitation activists from more than a dozen states, encouraged local leaders by showing them how limitation efforts had succeeded in three states and provided them with advice that they have used successfully in their states.

"We just had the limitation concept but we didn't know what to do with it until Rob Mosbacher attended the San Jose conference," said Mark Sanders, a spokesman for Texans for Term Limitations. "In particular," he noted, "it taught us the importance of a bipartisan movement." Washington State's Bockwinkel agreed, adding, "If the San Jose conference hadn't occurred, we might not have gotten this far [in Washington State]."

National groups have provided only limited financial backing to state term-limit efforts except in Washington, where CCR made a major financial investment. But they have offered expert advice on tactics, strategy, and the mechanics of the initiative process in dozens of states. Indeed, one area where national groups have tried to play a significant role and have succeeded to a large extent has been ballot access. CCR and ABIC, in particular, have advised state groups on how to draft their initiatives and get them on the ballot. At the very least, every state group has examined the California, Colorado, and Oklahoma measures before deciding how to construct its own proposal.

Not surprisingly, given the diversity in the limitation movement, there are several distinct perspectives on the importance of the national groups. South Dakota's limitation group has been in frequent contact with CCR and ABIC, but the state leadership has extensive experience in both candidate and ballot campaigns and has developed an elaborate volunteer organization and a grass-roots campaign with little national input and no outside financial support. In Washington State, on the other hand, CCR played a major role through its heavy financial involvement. "We would have been lucky to make the ballot [in 1991] and probably would have waited until 1992 if CCR had not come in and helped us get signatures [by financial support that allowed for paid signature gatherers]," acknowledged Washington term-limit spokesman John Burick shortly before the unsuccessful 1991 vote.

Florida's Phil Handy works with one national group, ABIC, but had virtually nothing to do with CCR. "CCR made their financial involvement subject to a six-year term limit for the U.S. House of Representatives," said Handy, adding that he prefers an eight-year limit and refused to change the length of service in order to get help from CCR. "They don't have a nickel in the race," he said proudly in November of 1991.

National term-limit groups agree that the movement would still be alive and kicking if they did not exist. But they also note that the limitation movement almost certainly could not have spread as far or as fast without groups like CCR and ABIC. "Term-limit supporters are out there," says Shari Williams of ABIC, "and while they benefit from our experience, they'd still be out there if we weren't around." "The American people are dictating the direction of term limits, we aren't," agreed Mary Ann Best, who took over as executive director of CCR in the summer of 1991 and served in that capacity until the end of the year, when CCR went out of business.

In addition to national groups promoting the term-limit cause, there has been considerable cross-pollination from other state efforts. Washington's Bockwinkel appeared at an Oregon term-limit press event, and her group was in frequent contact with term-limit forces in Michigan and Florida. Texas's term-limit organization brought California limitation leader Pete Schabarum to the state for a fund-raiser.

The National Opposition

The success of grass-roots groups depends, in part, on resources and skill in applying them. Equally important, however, is "the behavior of status quo interests that oppose mobilizing masses." [3] Although grass-roots movements may have a variety of resources at their disposal, they are seeking to *change* policy and therefore must overcome all of the advantages possessed by those who oppose change.

The term-limitation movement's early successes and growth during 1990 and 1991 was due in no small part to the virtual invisibility of the opposition. Although every state has its share of term-limit opponents, only in California and Washington State have they coalesced into effective opposition.

Nationally, much of the opposition to limits has come from elected officials. As the epitome of the status quo, elected officials constitute one of the groups least likely to sway public opinion against the term-limit idea. Other groups, including organized labor, the League of Women Voters, the American Association of University Professors, and certain state chapters of national organizations (such as the Grange) have also opposed term limits, but there is little indication that these groups reflect rank-and-file views, and only in Washington did opponents take the sort of dramatic steps that could turn around public opinion on the issue (see Chapter 4).

As noted above, LTPD has never become a major player in the term-limitation debate and its attempts to coordinate opposition have paled in comparison with those of CCR or ABIC. AFSCME has encouraged its state chapters to weigh in against limits and has supported term-limit opponents financially, but organized labor as a whole has never treated the issue as if it were critical. "The opposition to term limits from the union movement has collapsed," lamented one term-limit opponent before Washington's Initiative 553 was defeated, complaining that organized labor had not become fully involved in the battle because its congressional allies had not taken the term-limit threat seriously enough.

Organized opposition to the Washington term-limit initiative finally emerged a few months prior to the November vote. First, a number of state groups coalesced to form the "No on 553." In mid-September, Linda Marson joined No on 553 as campaign manager. Marson and AFSCME field staffer Mark Brown were active throughout October trying to drum up opposition. Among the large, national organizations that joined were the National Rifle Association, the League of Women Voters, the Sierra Club, the Teamsters, Common Cause, the National Organization for Women, and the Rainbow Coalition. Corporate participants included Boeing, Kaiser Aluminum, US West, Philip Morris, and Anheuser-Busch.[4] Late in the campaign, the Democratic Congressional Campaign Committee (DCCC) sent out a press release from committee chairman Vic Fazio (D-Calif.) seeking to discredit the term-limit movement by raising questions about David and Charles Koch, two wealthy supporters of

CCR, the most visible national term-limit group that operated in Washington State.

Ultimately, the most effective opposition came from House Speaker Tom Foley, whose last-minute statewide blitz against the ballot measure, combined with the questions raised by opponents about the effect of limits on the state's political clout in Congress, generated enough opposition to defeat Initiative 553. Foley's role should not be underestimated. The term-limit proposal was defeated, in part, because of strong opposition from Foley's own district. The fact that the initiative threatened the Speaker's position elevated the clout issue and activated groups that otherwise might have stayed out of the fight. For example, the National Rifle Association, which has not taken a position on term limits, contributed ten thousand dollars to No on 553. "Tom Foley is a friend of gun owners, and we wanted to see him back in Congress," explained Jim Baker, the NRA's chief lobbyist.

Although opponents lacked an active national organization that would devote itself completely to defeating the initiative, powerful, nationally known organizations from the business and labor communities did join other interest groups and national Democratic political strategists in their efforts to defeat term limits.

Grass-Roots Lessons

The vote against I-553 was important on several levels. First, and most immediately, it rejected a proposal that would have had a dramatic impact on Washington's congressional delegation. Second, and even more importantly, it raised questions about the national vulnerability of the term-limit movement, which only weeks earlier had been regarded as unbeatable. Finally, it forced supporters and opponents to reevaluate their assumptions and strategies.

Defining and Redefining Issues

The lack of an effective opposition to term limits before Washington was remarkable because term limits passed only narrowly in California, the one state where opponents had put together an organized campaign. Until No on 553 and House Speaker Foley began their final efforts against the Washington State measure, opponents never tried to redefine the issue, as nuclear freeze opponents did during the early 1980s.

The nuclear freeze movement, much like the term-limit movement, spread quickly across the country and permeated every demographic and social group. Nine of the ten states that held freeze referenda during 1982 passed them, and public opinion polls during that period showed that about seven out of ten Americans supported a bilateral, verifiable nuclear freeze. Politicians jumped aboard the freeze bandwagon, and the issue picked up a momentum. Yet within a couple of years, the national drive for a nuclear freeze had disappeared as a political issue. The freeze movement died not because supporters suddenly became disinterested, but because freeze opponents succeeded in redefining the issue to make many Americans feel ambivalent about it. While grass-roots supporters of the freeze portrayed the issue as a simple choice between a spiraling and costly arms race and sanity, freeze opponents reframed the debate along national-security lines and the general state of Soviet-American relations. Opponents tapped public concern about Soviet intentions, played on President Ronald Reagan's popularity and persuasiveness, and argued that the freeze would make the United States less secure.[5]

Term-limit opponents did not successfully cross-pressure voters until the Washington contest, when they redefined the issue into one of clout. Before Washington, limit opponents sounded either self-serving, when defending the institution of Congress, or irrelevant, when presenting legal arguments against limits. That changed when Speaker Foley made the November 1991 vote a referendum on whether the state should or should not place itself at the mercy of other states, particularly California. Suddenly, the issue no longer was whether politicians were responsive to their constituents or whether congressional turnover was a good idea. Instead, I-553 became a question of water rights, potential environmental threats to Washington's coastline, electric rates, and pocketbook issues in general.

In short, until the Washington State vote the choice between limits and no limits was no choice at all. The costs associated with limits seemed low, so the status quo did not appear to be any safer than a change in policy. Foley and No on 553 changed all that.

The Importance of Bipartisanship

The term-limitation movement has generally succeeded in avoiding the partisan trap that ultimately helped undermine other populist proposals, including the nuclear freeze.

While many freeze leaders sought to make their cause a broad-based, middle-class movement, it became a partisan and ideological effort when conservative groups (such as the Coalition for Peace through Strength) and the White House mobilized against it and Democratic candidates sought to seize it as their party's issue in 1982 and 1984. "Whatever its original intentions," wrote Adam Garfinkle, "the freeze movement has sharpened the expression of national disagreements over strategic issues and helped make them hostage to narrow partisan goals." [6]

Although term-limit forces have had to try to explain away the Bush administration's support for limits, the involvement of GOP consultants in term-limit campaigns, and the position of the 1988 Republican party platform, they have generally succeeded in recruiting Democrats to their cause and stressing the bipartisan nature of the issue.

Opponents in Washington State had particular problems trying to paint the term-limit movement as a Republican or conservative plot, because its state leader, Sherry Bockwinkel, was a liberal Democrat who had worked for many liberal causes in the past. She made no secret of the fact that the state movement was born of people with her beliefs.

National Democratic party campaign professionals did, ultimately, interject themselves into the Washington vote, and they may have succeeded in swinging a few voters against I-553. The DCCC's three-page press release of November 1, 1991, called term limits an attempt "by very narrow special interests designed to reduce the influence of ordinary citizens." It then linked term limits to CCR contributor David Koch, who had run for vice president on the 1980 Libertarian ticket, and portrayed the Koch brothers as the driving force behind I-553, obviously hoping to raise questions about the grass-roots nature of the entire term-limit movement. The release even listed more than a dozen of the Libertarian party's more controversial positions.

Populist Politics

Term-limit forces had a substantial advantage over freeze advocates because of the differences in the nature of the subjects. "The term-limit issue is different than most because it is so easily understood and so easily explained," argued ABIC's Ogle. "You need only three words: limit politicians' terms." The same sort of straightforward, easily appreciated message was used by tax cut advocates during the late 1970s and early 1980s.

Freeze advocates, on the other hand, were dealing with a complicated foreign-policy matter that involved weapons systems, arms negotiations, and national security—relatively complicated subjects that voters frequently leave to politicians. While the freeze solution was easy to characterize, the nature of the subject matter inevitably raised questions about any populist solution.

Like opponents of the clean-air movement of the 1970s, who relied on traditional forms of lobbying to sway important legislators rather than on a national campaign to change public opinion, term-limit opponents mounted court challenges in California, Washington, and Florida to overturn the results of initiatives or keep them off the ballot entirely. Although such challenges can slow the momentum of the term-limit movement, they do not address the public's feelings of anger about politicians, and they give the decidedly unpopular message that opponents do not want to let the people decide for themselves.

Term Limits After Washington State

National and state term-limit leaders stress that the defeat of I-553 will not derail their movement, and they note that more than a dozen states plan to have term limits on the ballot in 1992. But both sides acknowledge that they learned something from the outcome in Washington State, and the lessons they have drawn could have an important effect on the future of the term-limit movement.

Term-Limit Supporters

Supporters of limits say they learned three main lessons. First, they believe that the retroactivity of the Washington measure cost them the election. "I'd advise people against including retroactivity in term-limit proposals," said ABIC's Paul Ogle unhesitatingly. "Politically, retroactivity isn't pragmatic," agreed Jeff Hayzlett, a strategist for South Dakotans for Limited Government.[7]

Second, term-limit advocates believe the clout issue was magnified by the fact that Washington was the only state with a term-limit measure in 1991. "With Oregon, Idaho, and other states likely to have term-limit measures on the ballot in 1992, there will be much more of a national movement," predicted John Burick, a leader of the Washington State effort. Strategists are already suggesting that eliminating retroactivity will undermine the clout issue. "Without retroactivity, states will have six or eight years to look at the issue. They will be able to repeal limits before they go into effect if other states don't also adopt them," said Ogle.[8]

Third, even before the Washington vote state term-limit organizations stressed the importance of locally based campaigns and the dangers associated with outside help. As one state operative said back in October of 1991, "I can't imagine anything worse than dropping term-limit direct mail in this state with a Washington, D.C., postmark." Some term-limit advocates believe that CCR's heavy involvement in Washington gave the opposition an issue; they are not eager to be seen as captives of national organizations. "We want to make outside money an issue *we* can use," said one term-limit advocate.

But few state organizations are likely to turn down help from ABIC or any other national group if it is their only chance to win. "We'd love to get as much done in the state as possible," commented

Oregon term-limit leader Frank Eisenzimmer, "but if it takes outside help, we'll ask for it." The Washington result had an almost immediate organizational impact on the term-limit movement. CCR, which had been an important actor in the movement but which had also generated a great deal of controversy, went out of business at the end of 1991. On January 1, 1992, a new group, U.S. Term Limits, opened its doors to take the place of CCR. The new organization, which promotes term limits at the congressional, state, and local levels, purchased CCR's mailing list and received some of the CCR's research files. In addition, one former CCR staffer went to work for U.S. Term Limits, as did a former staffer of ALCT.

Interestingly, the Term Limits Legal Institute, which remains a project of ABIC and continues to be run by Cleta Mitchell, relocated to Washington, D.C., early in 1992. "We don't want to run a national campaign from D.C., but I hope to establish a network of lawyers and legal scholars in support of term limits, and many of them are in D.C.," says Mitchell. She also argues that a Washington base gives the Institute immediate credibility.[9]

Term-Limit Opponents

Term-limit opponents believe that the defeat of I-553 will encourage opposition in other states. "Washington told the folks that this is a winnable fight. Nobody likes to suit up for a fight they think they are going to lose," argued AFSCME's Scott. Members of Congress, in particular, may be more willing to become actively involved in fighting term limits now that they have seen what Speaker Foley accomplished.

Ironically, the defeat of I-553 could reinvigorate Let the People Decide. Term-limit opponents believe that they need a mechanism for passing along the lessons of Washington State, and Let the People Decide is already in place. Still, LTPD executive director Linda Kingsbury-Rogers expects her organization to have a limited role that will most likely include acting as a clearinghouse for information about term limits.

Opponents have concluded that they need to focus on specific tactics to defeat term limits. They point to Houston, Texas, where opponents of limits actually *added* term-limit proposals to the ballot to confuse the electorate, hoping that one of their own less restrictive measures would pass, rather than the more onerous one proposed by Citizens for Term Limits.

Both sides agree that the main lesson of Washington is the importance of agenda setting. "The key is who gets to the voters first with their description of the issue," said Rick Scott. "People in the states now know they are going to have a fight," agreed Mary Ann Best of CCR.

Conclusion

National term-limit organizations played an important role in stimulating the public's interest in term limitations, in motivating key state leaders, and in supporting state limitation efforts. They have sped up the process by providing the resources and skills to allow dozens of states to have term-limit measures ready for the ballot—or to be considered by legislators in noninitiative states—by the end of 1992. But CCR, ABIC, and ALCT did not create the mood of voter anger and frustration that became so obvious in 1990, and most state term-limit battles have not seen the intense conflict witnessed in Washington State. The term-limitation movement remains a grass-roots effort that depends heavily on the commitment and energy of state organizers and dedicated volunteers.

The future of the term-limit movement is still very much in doubt. Opponents now understand that term limits are not inevitable, but they must not assume that the defeat of I-553 is the beginning of the end of term limits. The elements which came together to defeat I-553 in Washington may not exist in many other states, and term-limit opponents may find in the future that the lack of a strong organization to advise opponents in dozens of states is a serious problem.

Finally, the Washington experience suggests that it is a mistake to look only at groups like CCR and ABIC, both of which have devoted many of their resources to the term-limit effort, when examining the role of "national" organizations. To do so ignores the activities of other significant actors—the political parties, unions, corporations, and interest groups—with national reach and powerful resources.

Notes

1. The Internal Revenue Code recognizes many types of organizations. A 501(c)(3) organization is exempt from federal taxes and contributions to it are tax deductible. A 501(c)(4) organization—which, unlike a (c)(3), is allowed to lobby—is tax-exempt but contributions to it are not tax deductible.
2. Unless otherwise noted, quotations not attributed to a published source are based on personal communications and interviews with the author conducted between August and October 1991.
3. L. Marvin Overby and Sarah J. Ritchie, "Mobilized Masses and Strategic Opponents: A Resource Mobilization Analysis of the Clean Air and

Nuclear Freeze Movements," *Western Political Quarterly* (June 1991): 329-351.

4. Many print and television reporters picked up on the Koch connection to CCR and term limits. For example, see Timothy Egan, "Campaign on Term Limits Breeds Unusual Alliances," *The New York Times,* October 31, A1 and B9; Lou Cannon, "Washington State Activists See Approval of Sweeping Initiative on Term Limits," *The Washington Post,* November 3, 1991, A4.

5. For the figures on public support for the freeze, see Overby and Ritchie, "Mobilized Masses," 332. Also see Patrick B. McGuigan, *The Politics of Direct Democracy* (Washington, D.C.: The Free Congress Research and Education Foundation, 1985), 67-85. James Ring Adams notes a similar development during the tax revolt: "The vote for Proposition 13 was to the Tax Revolt what Bastille Day was to the French Revolution. The successful assault on authority completely changed the rules. Governor Brown, a close observer of the public mood, moderated his harsh attacks on the measure and began making publicized preparations to implement it." James R. Adams, *Secrets of the Tax* Revolt (San Diego: Harcourt Brace Jovanovich, 1984), 166. Oregon term-limit organizer Frank Eisenzimmer notes that his state's 1990 property-tax-limitation measure met much more opposition than has the current term-limit drive. He cites the Oregon Education Association and the Oregon Public Employees Union as two groups that were heavily involved in trying to defeat the tax measure. On the successful redefinition of the nuclear-freeze issue, see Overby and Ritchie, "Mobilized Masses," 338-342.

6. Adam M. Garfinkle, *The Politics of the Nuclear Freeze* (Philadelphia: Foreign Policy Research Institute, 1984), 184-221. Also see David S. Meyer, *A Winter of Discontent: The Nuclear Freeze and American Politics* (New York: Praeger, 1990).

7. Personal interview with the author, November 1991.

8. The quotations in this section were obtained by the author in personal interviews conducted in December 1991 and January 1992.

9. Personal communication with Cleta Mitchell, April 1992.

Part III

THE LIKELY EFFECTS ON POLITICAL CAREERS

6. THE GUILLOTINE COMES TO CALIFORNIA: TERM-LIMIT POLITICS IN THE GOLDEN STATE

Charles M. Price

Introduction

On Tuesday, November 6, 1990, California voters said, "Off with their heads!" In narrowly approving Proposition 140, one of the most controversial initiatives in state election history, the voters established term limits for a range of public offices. The margin was 52 percent to 48 percent. Ironically, because of the low turnout, the 3,744,447 who voted in favor of Proposition 140 were less than 20 percent of the 19,244,902 adult citizens of the state. Briefly, Proposition 140 limited members of the assembly to three terms (six years) and all other state elected officials except judges (but including senators and constitutional officers) to two terms (eight years). The measure also reduced the legislative budget by nearly 40 percent and eliminated the legislators' retirement program.

This chapter analyzes the impact of the adoption of Proposition 140 on California's government, particularly the legislature. Will term limits alter patterns of recruitment to the legislature? Will legislators elected in the years ahead be any less capable or responsive because of term limits? Will the imposition of legislative term limits affect the power relationships between the governor and the legislature and between the legislature and special interests in the state?

Studying the effects of term limits in California should help us understand how such a reform might affect government at the federal level. As Bruce Cain notes, "California's experience with term limits has the potential of more external validity for students of national politics (and Congress in particular) than the experiences of other states. This is because there are a number of parallels between the situations in Sacramento and Congress." Among the similarities Cain mentions are (1) split government with a Republican executive and Democratic-controlled legislature, (2) comparably high reelection rates for Congress and the California legislature, and (3) high professionalization of both Congress and the California legislature.[1]

The Attack on the Professional Legislature:
Prelude to Term Limits

Until 1965, the California legislature was like nearly all other state legislatures—poorly paid, part-time, rural-dominated, and understaffed. State legislatures were "horse and buggy" operations—a sad national joke. However, a series of U.S. Supreme Court decisions that culminated in *Reynolds v. Sims* in 1964 (377 U.S. 533) required that both upper and lower houses of state legislatures be apportioned on the basis of population. These decisions, combined with professionalizing reforms promoted by Jess Unruh, speaker of the California assembly, transformed the California legislature in the late 1960s into what the Citizens Conference on State Legislatures ranked as the premier state legislature in the nation.[2] Under Unruh's prodding the legislature became full time. It set its members' salaries; determined its own calendar; hired expert staff; refurbished its offices, committee hearing rooms, and chambers; and offered an array of perquisites to its members.

Typical of the lofty praise the California legislature received was William Muir's observation:

> Scholars, legislators and lobbyists alike have declared California's state legislature the best.... What, then, was the California legislature? In a nutshell, it was a gathering of political representatives, most of whom were energetic, attentive, and informed individuals, learning from the best of its membership within a fair and versatile system the skill of coalition-building and the competence to govern a free people under law.[3]

A reaction to these professionalizing reforms developed in the 1970s and 1980s. Critics complained that professional legislators were greedy, pampered, partisan, wasteful, and arrogant, and that their offices were grossly overstaffed. Partisan wrangling and political paralysis were leading to lawmaking by initiative rather than by the legislature. In addition, two FBI investigations of the California legislature in the 1980s culminated in the indictment and conviction of several legislators, staffers, and a prominent businessman on charges of extortion and racketeering.

The situation was exacerbated when, in the spring of 1990, state legislative leaders decided that it would be better to remove the issue of legislative salaries from the legislature to an independent Citizens' Compensation Commission because of the bitterness engendered when legislators voted themselves pay raises. To sugarcoat the proposition advancing this new back-channel pay-raise procedure, legislative leaders included in their amendment several ethics reforms (such as banning honoraria) that they knew the public strongly supported.

Not surprisingly, the public approved Proposition 112, with its ethics measures. However, many who voted for it were unaware of the Citizens' Compensation Commission feature. Within a short time the commission raised legislators' salaries from $41,000 to $52,500 yearly; the salaries of other elected state officials were raised as well.

The California legislature of the 1980s seemed constantly engulfed in negative publicity, leading Democratic leaders to complain that the media focused only on the legislature's negative features and not on its positive accomplishments. The nation's preeminent state legislature had fallen upon hard times.

The image problems of the California legislature are not unique. State legislatures across the country have been hit by FBI stings and messy political scandals in recent years. At the August 1991 meeting of the National Conference of State Legislatures, political scientist Alan Rosenthal warned state legislators: "You people are in trouble, and you may as well appreciate it. . . . I don't think you do. . . . State lawmakers are unknown, unloved, unliked. . . . You get no respect." [4]

In an August 1991 speech announcing her resignation from the Democratic party to become an independent, Senator Lucy Killea eloquently summarized some of the problems the contemporary legislature faces:

> This institution, the Senate, the Assembly, the Legislature as a whole, is in serious trouble. . . . No matter how noble our innermost motivations are, no matter how solid our records individually, the fact is that time after time we give the public very good reason to think that our first priority is to make sure that we get our full per diem—that our first priority is to carve out districts favorable to our own ambition—that our first priority is to maintain a hefty balance in our campaign treasury to discourage a challenger. [5]

Background: Propositions 131 and 140

There were two separate term-limit propositions on the ballot in California in 1990—Propositions 131 and 140. Proposition 131— authored by the incumbent attorney general, Democrat John Van de Kamp—combined campaign finance reform with term limits. Van de Kamp had also drafted two other initiatives: Proposition 128, an antipesticide, environmental measure ("Big Green"), and Proposition 132, a drug enforcement proposal.

Since 1980, many candidates for state office in California have sponsored initiatives, in part for the publicity value and in part because the stalemate between the governor and the legislature has meant that new measures have a better chance of being enacted by the electorate than by the legislature.[6] Currently, Governor Pete Wilson is championing a welfare-reform initiative which, if it qualifies, will be on the November 1992 ballot.

Assuming that he would capture the Democratic nomination for governor, Van de Kamp designed his three initiatives as the cornerstones of his campaign against Pete Wilson, then the favorite to be the Republican candidate. Van de Kamp expended a considerable amount of time, money, and energy in the months preceding the June primary to qualify his initiatives for the November 1990 general-election ballot. Unfortunately for Van de Kamp, however, while he succeeded in qualifying his initiatives for the ballot, he lost the Democratic gubernatorial primary to Dianne Feinstein, former mayor of San Francisco. In November, all three Van de Kamp initiatives were rejected by California voters, and Dianne Feinstein lost a close race to Pete Wilson.

Proposition 131's main thrust was campaign-finance reform: contributor limits, expenditure caps, and an option for state candidates to receive partial public funding for campaigns. According to Ruth Holton, chief lobbyist for California Common Cause, the largest interest group supporting Proposition 131, Van de Kamp added a term-limit section to his initiative to make it more palatable to the many California voters unenthusiastic about using taxpayer funds for political campaigns. As senate Republican minority leader Ken Maddy caustically put it, "Proposition 131 was simply a political gimmick for candidate Van de Kamp." [7] Because it seemed likely in spring 1990 that a very harsh term-limit initiative would be on the November ballot, Van de Kamp hoped that if voters were given a more reasonable alternative they would support it.

Under Proposition 131, holders of offices identified in the state constitution would have been limited to two consecutive four-year terms. State legislators and members of the Board of Equalization could serve for twelve consecutive years (assembly members six consecutive two-year terms and senators and board members three consecutive four-year terms). Under the Van de Kamp initiative, elected officials who had "maxed out" could sit out a term and then run for the same office again. If elected, they would be eligible to serve again for the full period specified in the initiative.

Proposition 140 was authored by Pete Schabarum, a conservative Republican, former assemblyman, and retired Los Angeles County supervisor. Although Proposition 140 was aimed at "career" politicians, its author had held elective office since 1966—some 24 years. Schabarum's coauthors were former leaders in Howard Jarvis's 1978 property-tax-relief campaign (Proposition 13): J. G. Ford, president of the Marin County United Taxpayers Association, and Lewis K. Uhler, president of the National Tax-Limitation Committee and a leading advocate of the balanced budget constitutional amendment.

Eight years after the adoption of Proposition 13, a number of antitax activists had become increasingly angered by what they believed were violations by office holders of the "Spirit of 13." However, because the incumbents had a lock on their offices (due to their name identification, gerrymandered districts, and superior financial resources), the tax protesters looked to term limits as a way of ousting the incumbents. Thus, Operation Broomsweep was launched.[8]

Proposition 140, besides establishing strict term limits, reduced the California legislature's budget by nearly 40 percent and eliminated the legislators' pension system.

Schabarum, the lead spokesman for the cause, contributed more than six hundred and fifty thousand dollars from his own campaign funds (he was retiring from public office) to hire a professional petition firm to help collect the 615,957 signatures needed to qualify the constitutional-amendment initiative for the ballot.

Proposition 140's term-limit features were far stricter than those of Proposition 131. Members of the state assembly were limited to three two-year terms. Holders of all other state offices—senators, governor, lieutenant governor, attorney general, secretary of state, controller, treasurer, superintendent of instruction, and members of the Board of Equalization—were limited to two four-year terms in any one office. The limit was a lifetime ban.[9]

Although Proposition 140 was not retroactive, the term limits of all state elected officials began with the 1990 election. Thus under California's staggered-term system, incumbent state senators reelected in 1992 will have to retire from the senate in 1996.

The Campaigns for and against
Propositions 131 and 140

The campaigns for and against the term-limit initiatives were bitter and vitriolic—typical of most controversial proposition campaigns in California. Much of the battle was waged on television in thirty-second campaign spots. In all, opponents of term limits spent about $6 million. The proponents of Proposition 140 spent about $1.3 million in their winning campaign. They directed most of their attack against corruption, waste, and "career politicians" at the capitol (in particular, assembly speaker Willie Brown and senate president pro tem David Roberti). While term-limit advocates could be found in both major parties, those leading the fight for the strict limitations of Proposition 140 tended to come from the militant right—

taxpayer groups and the so-called caveman faction of the Republican legislative caucus. Senate Republican leader Ken Maddy noted, "Some Republicans who were mistreated in the redistricting process over the last two decades supported Proposition 140 because they believed an overhaul of the system would give the Republican party greater opportunities."

The chief Democratic opponents of term limits in the state, Speaker Willie Brown and senate president pro tem David Roberti, spent as much time attacking the moderate Proposition 131 as battling Proposition 140. Also opposing Proposition 140 were liberal interest groups representing teachers, women, and state employees. In addition, some special interests currying favor with Democratic legislative leaders contributed to the effort to resist term limits. For example, Phillip Morris contributed several thousand dollars to the campaign.

Virtually all incumbent Democratic legislators and most Republican moderates were opposed to term limits, although more favored Proposition 131 than Proposition 140.

Republican state senator Bill Craven articulately expressed why so many California legislators opposed Proposition 140:

> I thought it was a vindicative act on the part of its inceptors—Supervisor Schabarum and Lew Uhler. In a year in which we must provide services to more Californians than ever in our history, we have had our budget reduced by 40 percent, lost our retirement benefits, and have had term limits imposed on us. This places legislators in the same category as felons. In their case, they have a prohibition from running, and we are prohibited for life for running for the same office.

Democratic state senator Mike Thompson of Napa argued that Proposition 140 was not needed because there have always been term limits for state legislators—elections. Republican Stan Statham, a fifteen-year veteran of the assembly, contended that, with term limits in place, "you'll have two kinds of legislators: those who are learning and those who are leaving. You won't have the longevity and expertise needed." Democratic state senator Robert Presley compared the post-Proposition 140 legislature to an airport: "Some will be going and some will be coming. Some will want to do some work but they won't be able to find the counter."

Critics of Proposition 140 argued that legislators serving their last term would not worry about reelection and, consequently, would be less responsive to the public. Democratic assemblyman Robert Campbell contended, "I believe that this proposition does even more harm to the legislative process than many of the other propositions that have limited

TABLE 6-1   Voter Awareness and Attitude on Propositions 140 and 131

	Have seen/ heard of proposition	Plan to vote yes	Plan to vote no	Undecided	Have not seen/ heard of proposition
Proposition 140					
August	20%	12%	5%	3%	80%
early October	50	35	11	4	50
late October	67	39	17	11	33
Proposition 131					
August	22	15	5	2	78
early October	48	35	9	4	52
late October	65	37	19	9	35
After being read summary in late October					
Proposition 140		61	26	12	
Proposition 131		45	36	19	

Source: Poll 1569, October 1990, Field Institute, San Francisco.

government's ability to deal with solving the many problems that society has."

In contrast, conservative Republican Chris Chandler, who announced his retirement from the legislature in 1992, argued that "after having been in this place since 1986, I've become convinced that the only way we have of moving away from a full-time, life-term legislature is by the artificial means of term limitation." Another legislator commented, "I understand the voters' frustration. They saw no other way to clean house."

Throughout the campaign, surveys conducted by California pollster Mervin Field indicated that Propositions 131 and 140 had roughly the same margin of support among those who knew something about them (Table 6-1). However, as Table 6-1 shows, when respondents who did not know about the subject matter of either proposition were read brief summaries, substantially more favored 140. On Election Day, voters narrowly approved Proposition 140 and decisively rejected Proposition 131. It seems likely that many late-deciding voters voted against Proposition 131 because they did not want taxpayer funds going to fund politicians' campaigns. They voted for Proposition 140 because it offered term limits at no cost; indeed, the legislative budget reduction promised savings.

Perhaps most critical to Proposition 140's electoral success was the strong endorsement the measure received from the Republican gubernatorial candidate, moderate Pete Wilson. President George Bush also provided momentum for the cause when he announced that he favored term limits for California state legislators as well as members of Congress.

Proposition 140 and the Courts

Over the last several decades the California supreme court has had to rule on the constitutionality of highly partisan voter-approved initiatives. Until November 1986, moderates and liberals had for several decades comprised a distinct majority on the court. However, the defeat of three liberal justices in confirmation elections (including the controversial chief justice, Rose Bird, who was rejected by nearly two-thirds of the electorate in the 1986 election); the retirement of other liberal judges; and the conservative nomination of Republican governors George Deukmejian (1982-1990) and Pete Wilson dramatically shifted the court's ideological balance to the conservative side. Conservative judges, who dominate the seven-member court by a 6-1 margin, seem more inclined to affirm the constitutionality of initiatives.[10]

As is the case with many voter-approved initiatives, Proposition 140's constitutionality was challenged soon after enactment in a suit brought by the California legislature.[11] On September 12, 1991, Joseph Remcho, representing the legislature in the case, made the following arguments:

1. Proposition 140 did not amend but revised the constitution of the state. Major changes in California government, such as those introduced by Proposition 140, must be accomplished by the process of revision by a constitutional commission and not by amendment.
2. Proposition 140 deprived citizens of the right to vote for the candidate of their choice.
3. Proposition 140 violated the single-subject requirement for constitutional amendments because it had separate and unrelated subjects: term limits, reduction of the legislative budget, and elimination of the legislators' pension system.
4. Proposition 140 discouraged the legislature from meeting its constitutional responsibilities to serve as a coequal branch. To be effective the legislature must act collectively and must depend upon the collective wisdom and institutional memory of its members, goals compromised by Proposition 140. Moreover,

although the legislature's budget was reduced by nearly 40 percent, the executive's budget was untouched.

5. Finally, Proposition 140's ad campaign in the fall of 1990 targeted Willie Brown and David Roberti personally and thus constituted a bill of attainder.[12]

Republican attorney general Dan Lungren presented the state's defense of the proposition. He argued that Proposition 140 was constitutional because it did not in any way change the formal structure of California government, although he did concede that power might shift away from the legislature to the governor. The attorney general also disputed that Proposition 140 revised the constitution and that the right to run for office was a fundamental right. Additionally, he argued that Proposition 140 did not violate the single-subject rule because the sections of the initiative were "reasonably germane." Finally, Lungren noted that because all legislators and other state elected officials, not just the legislative leaders, were affected by 140's term limits, the measure did not constitute a bill of attainder.[13]

The court ruled (6-1) on October 11, 1991, that Proposition 140's term limits and legislative budget cutback were constitutional, but that the pension elimination section was not. In his opinion for the majority, Chief Justice Malcolm Lucas commented:

> Restriction upon the succession of incumbents serves a rational public policy. This may deny qualified men an opportunity to serve, [but] as a general rule the overall health of the body politic is enhanced by limitations on continuous tenure. . . .
>
> [The state has a legitimate interest in] protecting against entrenched dynastic legislative bureaucracy.

Legislative leaders appealed their case to the U.S. Supreme Court, but it refused to review the case, thereby upholding the California court's decision.

The Impact of Term Limits on the California Legislature: The Choice to Run

To better assess the impact term limits will have on the California legislature in the years ahead, the author surveyed members of both houses using oral interviews or mailed questionnaires. Thirty-four state legislators out of a total of 118 (two seats were vacant) responded— approximately 29 percent of the membership.

Although an overwhelming majority of legislators opposed Proposition 140, more than half of those surveyed said that even if it had been in effect when they first ran, they would have run for state office

TABLE 6-2 Survey—Impact of Term Limits on Decision to Run for State Legislature

---

Question: Think back to when you first ran for the state legislature. If Prop. 140's term limits had been in effect then, would you still have run for the legislature?

Respondents	Yes	No	Don't know
Democrats	9	7	3
Republicans	5	4	1
Independents	4	0	1
Total	18	11	5

Source: Author's survey of members of the California legislature, September 1991.

anyway (Table 6-2). Senator Barry Keene stated, "I might have run to 'do my part' within the limitations of the system or to use the office as a stepping stone." Democratic assemblyman Jim Costa said he would have run anyway because "it's a tremendous opportunity to have an impact on issues one cares about, and at the same time help people and improve our quality of life."

However, a significant minority, about a third of those surveyed, expressed reservations about whether they would have run if Proposition 140 had been in effect. Freshman Democratic assemblyman Xavier Becerra of Los Angeles was not sure: "It was hard for me to leave the security of the attorney general's office. I had to give up my personal life and sacrifice a lot of family time when I ran for office." Assemblywoman Delaine Eastin noted, "I was working for a large corporation. It would have been difficult to sacrifice the benefits and ladder-climbing opportunities for a dead-end job." Democratic assemblyman Sal Cannella was also ambivalent, citing the special problems of members who lacked a professional career outside public service:

> My background is different from almost any other member of this house. Most are attorneys, or are in the medical profession, or have businesses of their own—construction, real estate, or whatever. I'm blue collar. I worked in a factory for thirty years before I came here. I had to give up everything when I was elected. I don't go back and pick up the thirty years' seniority I had in that job. [After leaving the legislature] I'll have to start all over again. Those who favor Prop. 140 keep talking about bringing back a citizen

legislature. That's baloney. The citizen is the blue-collar person working in a factory, driving a bus, teaching school, and they just can't go back to their job again after serving in the legislature.

These responses promise few changes in the social backgrounds of members elected in the years ahead. After all, most contemporary legislators would have sought elective office with or without Proposition 140. However, it does appear that less affluent aspirants will have even more problems than they have at present in running for office.

Reapportionment after Proposition 140

The term-limitation portions of Proposition 140 will not take effect until 1996, when assembly members elected in 1990 and incumbent senators reelected in 1992 will have to step down. Nevertheless, the impact of the measure on California state officials is already being felt. The resignation in early 1991 of Democratic assemblyman Mike Roos, formerly speaker pro tem, was a harbinger. A larger than usual number of legislators have announced plans to retire in November 1992. Clearly, many incumbent California state legislators are beginning to ponder the question, "Is there life after the legislature?" An unusually high number will be filing for congressional seats in 1992.

Nearly all legislators surveyed agreed that the reapportionment process of 1991 was complicated by Proposition 140 because of the "short-timer" mentality now prevailing in the legislature. As *Sacramento Bee* political editor Martin Smith noted, there were "fears among House incumbents that the California legislature, in drawing redistricting plans, [would] ignore their interests in order to create seats for state lawmakers who hope to move on to the nation's capital." [14] By doing so, of course, they would escape the term limitations of Proposition 140. Stan Statham, a member of the assembly for nearly 15 years, told the author, "For the first time in California's history, assemblymen and senators are more interested in drawing congressional lines than state legislator lines. I've enjoyed working in the assembly, and I wanted to stay for a while longer, but now I'm limited. For the first time I'm actually considering running for a congressional seat."

In the past several reapportionments, Democratic state lawmakers had allowed former Democratic representative Phil Burton to devise congressional redistricting plans. However, in the 1991 reapportionment, the legislature did not delegate congressional redistricting to leaders of the congressional delegation.[15] But because the Democratically-led legislature and Republican governor Pete Wilson ultimately

were unable to resolve their partisan reapportioning differences, the
state supreme court (and its masters' panel) eventually had to draw the
districts.

The resultant opportunities for state legislators to move up the
political ladder were unparalleled. First, the districts were designed
without incumbent bias. Second, because of population growth, California was allotted seven new House seats. Because all state legislative
incumbents faced the limits of Proposition 140 relatively soon, the
gamble of running for a House seat in a new district seemed more
attractive. Senator Bill Craven commented:

> It would be naive to think that many legislators are not eyeing new
> congressional seats to be established and perhaps hoping for a
> restructuring of districts which may well serve their best interests
> where there is no term limitation. The pay (in Congress) is about
> $75,000 more and there are excellent retirement benefits.

Effects on the Legislature as an Institution

Most legislators and political experts expect that coming legislative sessions, particularly those after 1996, will be far more chaotic than
previous ones. In the words of freshman Democratic assemblyman Sal
Cannella:

> If we have nearly 80 new people showing up in the Assembly on
> the 6th of January 1996, nobody will know what they're supposed
> to do. There will be no continuation of government. There will be
> no understanding of policy or legislative tradition. What are the
> rules? Who is going to be the speaker of the house, or the
> committee chairs?

In the ten years prior to the adoption of Proposition 140, biannual
turnover in the California legislature averaged 15 percent. California's
senate ranked third lowest in turnover among upper houses, while the
assembly ranked seventeenth lowest among lower houses.

Part-time, poorly paid amateur state legislatures tend to have a
higher voluntary turnover rate than professional ones, which provide
more attractive inducements for members to stay. Thus Karl Kurtz of
the National Conference of State Legislatures contends that term
limitations will have a particularly dramatic effect on professional
legislatures like California's.[16] Kurtz's projections of the average
number of new members in the California assembly over the next
twenty years are presented in Table 6-3.

According to Kurtz's projections, the turnover rate in the lower
house will ebb and flow, with a tidal wave of new members every sixth
year. Two caveats should be noted. Kurtz projects that voluntary

TABLE 6-3 Projection of California Assembly Under Term Limitation

Election Year	Number of Members Starting Term 1	Number of Members Starting Term 2	Number of Members Starting Term 3
1996	61	10	9
1998	19	52	9
2000	19	16	44
2002	50	16	14
2004	24	42	14
2006	24	20	36
2008	42	20	17
2010	27	36	17

Source: Karl T. Kurtz, "Assessing the Potential Impacts of Term Limits," State Legislatures 18, January 1992.

turnover after 1996 will continue at about 15 percent, in addition to turnover from term limits. This seems unlikely. Currently, after serving ten to fifteen years some legislators decide to retire voluntarily because they are tired of the legislative grind and want to make more money. However, under Proposition 140, tenure in either house will be so short that members who have worked hard to get elected will likely stay until they reach their six-year limit.

Another factor shaping term length is the court-designed 1991 reapportionment plan. It seems likely that in the 1992 and following elections there will be far fewer safe districts and many more competitive ones. This too will affect the number of new members elected in the years ahead.

Additionally, it seems highly likely in the future that there will be more backroom discussions between incumbent politicians on swapping legislative seats as term limits loom. Currently, a state senator would almost never run for the assembly—it would be a step down. But it seems very probable that in the post-Proposition 140 legislature incumbents may switch positions with one another to avoid term limits.

Proponents of Proposition 140 agree that it will produce more rapid turnover in the California capitol, but they believe this will be good. Prior to Proposition 140, it was sometimes difficult to find opposition candidates willing to run in districts represented by a popular, seasoned incumbent. Primaries and general elections would sometimes go uncontested. This is less likely to happen in the Proposition 140 era. Proposition 140 proponents also believe that legislators will not be able to develop the close and cozy relationships with lobbyists that some senior members now maintain. And more people will have a chance to serve.

It seems likely that substantial turnover in membership could easily weaken legislative leadership. Because legislative leaders will be able to hold office for just a few years, they may not be able to extract campaign contributions from special interests as easily as they have in the past. The diminishing ability of legislative leaders to raise large campaign war chests to give to their party colleagues, will, in turn, weaken their hold over them. It is possible that state political party organizations will play an enhanced role in post-Proposition 140 California. Because of a host of Progressive reforms imposed on them early this century, political party organizations have not been significant forces in the state's political milieu. Filling this void, to an extent, in the 1970s and 1980s have been the Democratic majority and Republican minority legislative leaders in each house. These legislative leaders raised campaign money from special interests and dispensed it to loyal and vulnerable members of their party in the chamber. Now that legislative leaders will be able to serve only a few years under term limits, their ability to attract contributions will be reduced. This may open the way to political party organizations functioning as the major dispensers of campaign money to candidates. In addition, because of a series of court rulings, California political parties *can* endorse candidates in the primary elections.

Furthermore, it is possible that if newcomers form a majority they will band together to elect their own members as legislative leaders. However, since most of these newcomers will have had relatively little mutual contact prior to their election, and given their partisan differences, a coup by freshmen seems unlikely.

There is one example in California political history of newcomers outnumbering veterans in one of the houses of the legislature. After the U.S. Supreme Court ruled in *Reynolds v. Sims* (1964) that both houses of the state legislature would have to be apportioned on the basis of population, Los Angeles County instantly gained thirteen senators in the forty-member senate; simultaneously, rural northern California lost much of its upper-house representation. Therefore, twenty-two of the forty senators elected in 1966 were freshmen. Within a few months many of these freshmen had voted to overthrow long-time incumbent Hugh Burns as president pro tem and elect a new leader (who was another senior member).

Michael Malbin suggests that term limits may increase the number of coalition elections of legislative leaders (i.e., a bloc of Democrats and Republicans voting for the same legislative leader).[17] This has happened occasionally in the pre-Proposition 140 legislature and may occur more often in the years ahead if short terms of office and weakened leadership reduce members' ties to their party. Some surveyed legislators disagree, maintaining that the many new members will be forced to look to party leaders for cues in voting and for campaign funds.

Many legislators surveyed emphasized that it takes time to develop into an effective member, and Proposition 140's limits will produce a largely inexperienced legislature struggling to deal with complex issues. Republican senate minority leader Ken Maddy stated, "It takes four to five years in the senate before you become a truly effective senator." Third-term Democratic assemblywoman Delaine Eastin said, "It takes a while to become experienced in the legislature. I feel as if I'm just getting to a point where I can be effective and get things done." Assemblyman Rusty Areias agreed:

> This is a pretty complicated place—a $55 billion budget, 128 different departments and agencies. It takes a couple of years for [new legislators] to learn their way around the process. They may be able to get a few things done in their second term, and then in their third term they'll be looking around for another job. Rural areas will be particularly disenfranchised. If this were 1996, with many legislators reaching their term limits, Republican assemblyman Bill Jones (Fresno) and Republican senator Ken Maddy (Fresno) would never have been able to get elected as minority leaders.

Senator Barry Keene noted that "140 creates a legislative body of those who don't know (incoming) and those who don't care (outgoing)." Republican assemblyman Stan Statham, a senior member of the GOP caucus, contended, "Only legislators who have been here a while (and feel secure) can stand up to the special interests." Senator Lucy Killea stated that although she favored the term-limit concept, the limits of Proposition 140 were too extreme: "Term limits of ten to fifteen years would allow enough time for sufficient experience and would provide for more gradual changes in the members of the legislative body."

The "Schabarumized" legislature may lack legislative policy experts because it takes time to understand complex issues. Democratic assemblyman Ted Lempert of San Mateo said:

> One of the first things I did when I first came up here was look for members I could trust on certain issues—Byron Sher on environ-

mental issues; Bruce Bronzan, health issues; or Becky Morgan, high-tech issues. These are high-caliber, experienced legislators who have developed an expertise on particular subjects. Then I wonder, if I were coming here in 1996 as a new legislator, who could I turn to in the legislature? Would I have to go to someone in the administration for that kind of expertise?

In contrast, freshman Republican Jim Bruelte, a Proposition 140 supporter, stated that he thought the legislature in the years ahead would be more effective because it would contain few professional politicians. Republican assemblyman Chris Chandler also felt expertise was overrated, saying that the legislature has too many "experts" telling the public what's good for them. "I think if we had more legislators listening to what the people want we'd be a lot better off. Name one thing these 'expert' legislators have come up with over the last ten years."

Of course, the unresolved question is: Will short-term legislators be more responsive to the public than careerists?

Legislator Characteristics

Most legislators believe that the type of person elected to the legislature after Proposition 140 will change but they disagree as to how. Assemblyman Xavier Becerra felt that educational background would not be as important for those running for the assembly after 1994: "It will just be people who can raise the big bucks running." Assemblyman Cannella stated that "140 was designed for the person in upper-middle management who could get a leave from his company or might be encouraged by his company to run for office so he could introduce legislation that might benefit that company. After six years, he could be recycled back to his former job."

Some members thought that term limits would discourage lawyers and other professionals from running for the legislature, but others disagreed. Senator Barry Keene remarked that the post-Proposition 140 legislature might have fewer lawyer-legislators (they now comprise 20 percent of the senate) because "many will consider it too great a sacrifice of productive years with limited opportunity to effect change." Senator Bill Craven disagreed: "I don't necessarily feel that there will be fewer lawyer-legislators. It may provide a stepping stone for a young attorney to establish some degree of public recognition who can still possibly conduct legal business as an aside to legislative duties." Agreeing with Craven, Senator Maddy commented, "Private institutions (utilities, banks, etc.), labor unions, and possibly law firms will furlough people to run, thus having "their representative" in office.

Most contemporary legislators are former legislative staff members or full-time local politicians. Staffers and local politicians tend to be bright, articulate activists who have good contacts, understand campaigns and fund-raising, and are familiar with the issues. It has been a concern of some that having so many ex-staffers serving as members is a form of legislative in-breeding. These critics believe there should be more diversity in occupational backgrounds of legislators.

Proposition 140 may slow the trend of staffers becoming legislators. First, Proposition 140's cuts in the legislature's budget have reduced the number of staff. Second, as Senator Bill Craven noted, "the legislative staff person moving to become a legislator is less likely since in almost every case it would mean for them a reduction in pension benefits as well as salary."

A number of legislators argued that wealthy people would have the easiest time running and getting elected to office. According to Senator Mike Thompson, "There will be more wealthy running for office because they can afford it—or retired because they have the time." This view squares with the conclusions of Morris P. Fiorina:

> Candidates who hope to serve in amateur legislatures differ in systematic ways from those who seek to serve in professional legislatures. Because service is part time and poorly remunerated, candidates must have independent sources of income and/or the freedom to take away from primary occupations without major financial or career costs. Thus, amateur political settings advantage the independently wealthy, professionals with private practices, independent business people, and others with similar financial and career flexibility.[18]

Fiorina also contends that good legislative salaries and other professional accoutrements encourage Democrats to run for office, whereas amateur legislatures are more appealing to Republicans. It should be emphasized in this connection that in 1990-1991 professional and nonprofessional trends crisscrossed in the California legislature. Proposition 140 makes the legislature less professional, but Proposition 112 of June 1990, which established an independent Citizens' Compensation Commission, was a professionalizing step.

Finally, Republican senator Marian Bergeson of Orange County suggested that term limits "give more women a chance to get elected to office." It is also possible that other underrepresented groups in the legislature might reach office because of the sheer amount of turnover.

The Balance of Power under Proposition 140

Most legislators surveyed are convinced that the legislature will lose power to the executive in future years because of Proposition 140. To be truly coequal and politically effective the legislature must pull together its members' disparate voices. Proposition 140 will decimate the experienced legislative leadership needed to forge legislative compromises and negotiate with the governor. Assemblyman Rusty Areias noted that every once in a while you need a "crotchety senator with a lot of seniority and power" to be able to stand up to the governor.

However, a few legislators do not believe that the legislature must play second fiddle to the governor. Senator Quentin Kopp noted, "Both legislators and governor face term limits under Proposition 140. Power will not inevitably flow to the governor and his administration."

The overwhelming majority of legislators surveyed are also convinced that under Proposition 140 the legislature will become more dependent on lobbyists and powerful interest groups because the latter will be so much more experienced. As one legislator noted, "There are no term limits on lobbyists." The deep staff cuts imposed on the legislature by Proposition 140's 40 percent budget reduction exacerbate this situation, especially as these cuts were made in professional and not political staff. (Political staff are adept campaign organizers and fundraisers; professional staff tend to be less partisan, policy experts.) Legislators will be forced to look to the "third house" for expertise. Already some lobbyists are stepping into the breach, reassuring legislators who agree to "carry" their bill that the lobbyist will do all the mundane details—contacting members of the appropriate committees, furnishing expert witnesses at legislative hearings, and setting up meetings to resolve conflicts with other interests.

In the post-Proposition 140 setting, lobbyists will be forced to try to make friends with successive waves of new legislators. Yet, this disadvantage is far outweighed by the experience and continuity in the ranks of the lobbyists. Senator Bill Craven remarked:

> Absent competent, experienced staff the members of the legislature must depend more heavily upon third-house information to get a grasp on the matters at hand. We will have less opportunity, by virtue of a lessened staff, to give total analysis and research to the issues in an objective manner, and there is no question that it will inhibit required legislative activity ... and [mean] a reduction in constituent rapport.

Senator Barry Keene believes that "the existing paralysis [in the legislature] will intensify because there will be a lack of skill in group decision making, less accountability, and loss of institutional memory under Proposition 140."

Holding a different viewpoint, Assemblyman Chris Chandler contended, "It is poppycock to suggest that the legislature is going to be more dominated by the third house because of Proposition 140. This all fits into this terrible, pat, trite, knee-jerk, business-as-usual mentality that is unfortunate. If every legislator voted as if this were his last term, this would be a better and more responsive place."

Conclusion

The impact of Proposition 140 is already being felt in the California legislature. More members than usual have announced their retirements from the legislature at the end of the 1992 session. Experienced staff members have lost their positions because of the budget cuts. Many state legislators have announced that they will be running for Congress. However, if former supervisor Pete Schabarum has his way, they will not evade term limits, even in Congress. Currently, Schabarum is the author of two new initiative proposals that he hopes will qualify for the November 1992 ballot: one would limit the terms of California members of Congress; the other would limit the terms of all local politicians in the state.

The post-Proposition 140 legislature will be similar in composition to the current one, but it will contain more women, and more Hispanic and Asian legislators. Most legislators seem convinced that in coming years the legislature will be dominated by the very wealthy or by businesses who "loan" executives to serve in the legislature for a few years, and this could lead to potential conflict of interest problems. The overwhelming majority of legislators are convinced that the legislature will become more chaotic and unwieldy, will lack strong leaders, will be more beholden to lobbyists and more subservient to the governor and administration.

Senator Bill Craven summed up many legislators' views of Proposition 140's impact on state government this way:

> My feeling is that when you limit a term, you also limit the interest and the feeling of responsibility in the elected official. I believe the public is best served when they hang the proverbial sword of Damocles immediately above the legislators' temple. Legislators, in turn, then very obviously recognize that if they do not perform appropriately, the electorate will cut the cord and eliminate them.

Notes

The author would like to thank Helen Neves, a graduate student in public administration at the University of Southern California, for her research assistance.

1. Bruce E. Cain, "Term Limits: Predictions about the Impact upon California" (Paper presented at the Conference on Legislative Term Limits sponsored by the Focused Research Program in Public Choice, University of California, Irvine, May 31-June 1, 1991), 1.
2. Citizens Conference on State Legislatures, *The Sometimes Governments,* ed. John Burns (New York: Bantam, 1971).
3. William K. Muir, Jr., *Legislature: California's School for Politics* (Chicago: University of Chicago Press, 1982), 191.
4. William Endicott, "Legislators Told They're In Trouble," *Sacramento Bee,* August 10, 1991, 3.
5. Speech by Lucy Killea to California senate, August 19, 1991.
6. Charles G. Bell and Charles M. Price, "Are Ballot Measures the Magic Ride to Success?" *California Journal* 19 (September 1988): 380-384.
7. Unless otherwise noted, all quotations not attributed to a published source are based on oral interviews with, or questionnaires completed by, members of the California legislature. The interviews were conducted and the questionnaires completed between August 19 and September 13, 1991.
8. Tom Waldman, "Pete Schabarum's Parting Shot," *California Journal* 22 (December 1991): 553-555.
9. There are two exceptions to the term-limit regulations on state office holders. Judges—supreme, appellate, superior, and municipal—have no term limits. The new elective position of insurance commissioner (established in 1990) was not included in the text of Proposition 140 because the proposition was drafted before the office became elective.
10. Upon completion of twelve-year terms, supreme court judges who wish to stay on the court must be reconfirmed by voters. For example: "Shall Chief Justice Rose Bird be reconfirmed to the state supreme court?" All three of the liberal judges mentioned in this passage faced reconfirmation at the first state election following their appointment.
11. *Legislature of the State of California et al. v. March Fong Eu, as Secretary of State, etc., et al.,* 54 Cal. 3d 492 (1991).
12. Petition for Writ of Mandate and/or Prohibition, *Legislature of the State of California et al. v. March Fong Eu, as Secretary of State, etc., et al.,* 54 Cal. 3d 492 (1991).
13. Response by Attorney General Daniel Lundgren to Petition for Writ of Mandate and/or Prohibition, *Legislature of the State of California et al. v. March Fong Eu, as Secretary of State, etc., et al.,* 54 Cal. 3d 492 (1991).
14. Martin Smith, "Congressional Fears," *Sacramento Bee,* August 6, 1991, D4.

15. In 1961, 1971, and 1981, the Democrat-controlled legislature, which had the power to reapportion California's congressional districts, allowed the leader of the state's congressional delegation (in 1971 and 1981, San Francisco representative Phil Burton) to draw the districts. The state legislature rubber stamped the boundaries drawn by Burton. After passing the legislature, reapportionment bills for the assembly, senate, and House of Representatives go to the governor, who may sign or veto them.
16. Karl T. Kurtz, "Assessing the Potential Impacts of Term Limitations," *State Legislatures* 18 (January 1992): 32-34.
17. Ibid. Malbin's comment was made at the Term Limits National Conference, Center for Legislative Studies, Nelson A. Rockefeller Institute of Government, State University of New York, Albany, October 11-12, 1991.
18. Morris P. Fiorina, "Divided Government in the States," in *The Politics of Divided Government,* ed. Gary W. Cox and Samuel Kernell (San Francisco: Westview Press, 1991), 192-193.

7. TERM LIMITATIONS AND POLITICAL CAREERS IN OKLAHOMA: IN, OUT, UP, OR DOWN

Gary W. Copeland

Limiting the number of terms a public official can serve is not a new idea. As we have seen, members of the Continental Congress were limited under the Articles of Confederation to a single three-year term and the matter was the subject of some debate between Federalists and Antifederalists during the Constitutional Convention and in the first Congress. It is common for terms of executives to be limited, and there are latter-day examples of legislative terms being limited in this country (San Mateo County, California) and in other nations (Costa Rica). However, 1990 marked a notable departure from common practice in this country as three states enacted term limitations for their state legislators and, in Colorado, for members of Congress as well. Oklahoma was the first of those states to act.

As part of the effort to understand the potential consequences of term limitations in Oklahoma, this chapter focuses on the legislative career and how it might be affected by those limits. It begins with a brief history of the term-limitation initiative in Oklahoma and describes the nature of the amendment. The chapter then examines how limitations will influence politicians' external and internal careers. The conclusion is that term limitations are certain to have a substantial impact on how politicians and potential politicians consider their political careers, on the decisions they make, and on the actions they take. Only time will permit firm conclusions, but some outcomes seem relatively certain.

Political scientists have little experience with the phenomenon of limitations on the number of terms an individual can serve in a legislature. Few political scientists had given the matter much serious thought until the events in Oklahoma unfolded and votes in Colorado and California loomed on the horizon. This chapter explores the new issue through various theories that political scientists have developed over the last several decades and through interviews with various political actors, primarily in Oklahoma.

Oklahoma's Term-Limitation Initiative
and Its Politics

The end of the decade of the 1980s saw the Oklahoma state legislature doing little to impress its electorate and much to distress it. Incident after incident brought embarrassment to the legislature and outrage from the citizens of the state. Examples include stopping the clock in the capitol just before constitutionally mandated adjournment and later arguing—successfully—in court that because the legislature never adjourned it remained in the same "legislative day," if not the same calendar day. In March 1989 voters severely limited the length of the legislative session both in terms of the total number of days and how long into the year the legislature could meet. Soon after, compensation to legislators skyrocketed based on a decision by an independent compensation board. Legislators were to be paid thirty-two thousand dollars a year for a maximum of ninety days in session. Then, in May of 1989, just days before the end of the legislative session, a coalition of disgruntled Democrats and minority Republicans joined to overthrow the sitting speaker of the house, leaving many wondering about the overall state of the legislature. The table—usually pretty full—was now fully set for an antiincumbent, antilegislature feast.

The feast that followed was served primarily by one man, Lloyd Noble II. Noble, once an unsuccessful legislative candidate, is a member of a distinguished Oklahoma family known for its civic contributions. His new political venture was destined to succeed from the start. Using his considerable resources, Noble commissioned a survey of Oklahoma voters to examine attitudes toward the legislature and term limitations. What he found was that 70 percent of those questioned supported the concept and fewer than 18 percent opposed it. Support, he further discovered, was consistent across the board; variables that normally produce differing political views, such as demographic characteristics or party identification, had no impact on support for term limitations.[1]

Noble spent the next several months preparing for the campaign. Three keys to the success of the initiative can be found during this period. First, Noble decided to seek a twelve-year limitation because his data indicated that support for limitations eroded as the length of the limit declined. (His poll showed that voters would likely approve a six- or even a four-year limitation, but Noble preferred to minimize his risks.)

Next, Noble moved to emphasize the initiative's bipartisan support. Former governor Raymond Gary, a popular Democrat, signed on as honorary chairman of Oklahomans for Legislative Reform, the group backing the initiative. Several other "good government" Democrats also joined the effort. One notable example was Cleta Deatherage Mitchell, a former Democratic power broker in the state house who became active nationally on the issue and now serves on the board of Americans to Limit Congressional Terms.[2] Finally, at least three of the four candidates in the 1990 gubernatorial run-off supported term limitations. The ultimate victor, Democrat David Walters, was a vocal supporter. Noble successfully convinced the voting public that his initiative had widespread support among a range of people with different views on most issues.

The final trick was to draft the wording of the proposed initiative very carefully. According to Patrick McGuigan, "State Senator Gary Gardenhire, a Norman Republican, joined attorney Wilson Wallace of Ardmore in taking the initiative through multiple drafts, to make it as politically realistic, and as legally sound, as possible." [3] The importance of this step was twofold. First, backers did not want support to erode over minor wording questions. Second, constitutional initiatives in Oklahoma can deal with only one topic and the courts have been strict in their interpretation of that requirement. An initiative such as California's Proposition 140 likely would be blocked before a vote in Oklahoma on the grounds that it dealt with more than one issue.

Based on this groundwork, Noble filed his petition and had ninety days to garner slightly more than 175,000 signatures.[4] The wording on the petition was straightforward and simple. In just a few lines it declares that no one may serve more than a total of twelve years in the state house, state senate, or the two combined. Those in office when the amendment was to take effect were covered by a "grandfather clause"; thus, previous service would not count. (It now appears, though, that those who had served twelve years but were not in office on the effective date are banned from any future service.) In just two months, proponents found 205,000 voters willing to attach their name to the proposed amendment. After certification of the petition, then Governor Bellmon, a supporter of the proposal, consulted with Noble regarding a date for the vote. Noble advocated its inclusion on the September 18 run-off ballot. His recommendation was driven by his desire to be the first in the nation to add limitations to a state constitution. He also wanted the proposal to attract attention both in- and out-of-state and not to be lost in the long and complicated ballot likely to be found in the general election. Bellmon acceded to the request and the stage was set for a vote on State Question 632.

Legislative term limitations will produce great changes in American elections and within its legislatures, but from the campaign waged in Oklahoma no one would guess that such a weighty issue was before the voters. What little campaigning there was on the issue was waged primarily by the proponents of term limitations.

The Noble organization was firmly in place and had solid financial backing when the date of the election was announced. It had already done its polling and had a plan for executing the campaign, having had to spend only about $240,000 on the whole effort. The organization's "Campaign Contributions and Expenditures Report" seems to indicate that over half of that total was spent during the petition phase to get the matter before the voters. The advertising budget appeared to be in the range of fifty to sixty thousand dollars. Advocates also received broad editorial support from newspapers throughout the state.[5]

Opposition nearly failed to materialize, but eventually an organization called "The Committee to Protect the Rights of Oklahoma Voters" (PROVE) emerged. Former state Democratic party chair Jim Frasier was its chairman and Glorine Henley, a former executive director of the state Democratic party, was treasurer. PROVE raised and spent just under $56,000. Most contributions came in large blocks from labor unions. In fact, all but $875 came from a total of seven labor unions—only one of which had an Oklahoma address (the state's AFL-CIO).[6] Some sitting legislators grumbled about the proposal, but few seriously sought to oppose it.[7] The most visible opposition finally emerged from retired U.S. House Speaker Carl Albert, but his contribution was too little, too late.

The result of having broad support going into a well-planned campaign and limited opposition to the end is predictable. By a two-to-one margin Oklahoma became the first state to enact term limitations for its state legislature on September 18, 1990.

Professionals or Amateurs: How Goes the Career?

Term-limitation proposals should catch the attention of those most directly affected by them—office holders. They certainly caught the attention of California house speaker Willie Brown and U.S. House Speaker Thomas Foley. But few legislators with whom I spoke in Oklahoma had given the matter much thought. One good reason accounts for the lack of anticipation and concern over term limits by Oklahoma's legislators. In Oklahoma, no one will be directly affected by term limitations until 2003, and most legislators do not expect to serve that long. As one state representative said, "We are struggling with reapportionment because we have only about three members who were here last time around." [8]

The analysis to be presented below will explore how term limitations will affect the careers of politicians and potential politicians. It will be years before we can speak definitively about the career consequences of term limitations, but the likely consequences are so wide-ranging that we need to begin the discussion now. Lacking experience with this phenomenon, our analysis is necessarily based upon theories in the professional literature and interviews with legislators, staff, lobbyists, and proponents and opponents of term limitations. Examination of the impact of term limitations on political careers will follow two routes before being synthesized. First, the "external career" will be examined. The external career refers to the making of a political career generally and how one makes judgments about which office to seek and when to move on to other activities or offices. The focus is outside of the legislature. The second career is the internal career, in the course of which one fulfills his or her role as a legislator. Member ambitions and goals within the legislature are the focus of the internal section. Finally, as we know, the two components are not independent, so we will conclude by drawing the external and the internal careers together and examining what it means for the legislature.

Ambition and the External Career

Running for political office is not easy. Those who seriously seek office expend considerable time and money in the endeavor. They subject themselves to personal and professional risks. Why do people, fully aware of the costs of seeking and holding political office, seek public positions? Ambition. It is nearly impossible to visualize an office holder who does not exhibit a considerable streak of ambition. Of primary relevance to this section is personal ambition—the drive to mold a successful career in public life.

In his treatment of ambition, Joseph Schlesinger argues that there are three fundamental types of ambition relevant to elected officials: discrete, static, and progressive. Schlesinger uses discrete ambition as a label for those who desire to serve for a discrete or limited period and then return to private life. Many elected officials in the United States in its early history had discrete ambition. Static ambition is characterized by the desire to gain an office and hold it for an indefinite period. Neither returning to private life nor seeking higher office drives the individual with static ambition. Progressive ambition is based on the assumption that some public offices are more desirable than others and that a shared hierarchy of desirability can be ascertained based on the prestige, power, remuneration, and other rewards provided by each office. Individuals who seek to move up that hierarchy are considered progressively ambitious. When one thinks about term limitations, then, what we have is an external device designed to force discrete ambition on a group of individuals who normally possess static or progressive ambition.[9]

Before examining how the attempt to restructure the forces of ambition will influence the thinking, decisions, and careers of state legislators in Oklahoma, we need to explore the opportunity structure that exists in that state. Oklahoma is a largely populist state and its state constitution very clearly reflects a progressive predisposition.[10] Hence, almost every office that can conceivably be filled by the ballot box (rather than by appointment or merit-based selection) is submitted to a vote. Among local offices, Oklahomans elect sheriffs, county assessors, county clerks, county treasurers, county commissioners, and the usual city officials. The state has six members of Congress and among the smallest populations found in congressional districts. It also elects a plethora of statewide officials (eleven, not counting U.S. senators or judges). Among those positions are lieutenant governor, auditor and inspector, state treasurer, and insurance commissioner. Politicians in Oklahoma, then, do have an unusually large range of opportunities to seek elected positions.

Why one runs or does not run for any particular office is beyond the scope of this paper, but it is possible to examine various ways state legislators may think about their political future under term limitations. We also consider how term limits might influence decisions made by individuals contemplating a run at the state legislature. Some proponents argue that those questions will become largely moot, as Oklahoma will have a "citizen legislature" composed of individuals whose ambition is sincerely discrete. Our interviews suggest that questions of ambition will remain very much relevant.

Will term limits influence personal decisions to seek political office? How will they affect decisions to remain in office or to seek higher or lower office? What kind of life might one envision after the calendar had turned the requisite number of pages to disqualify an individual from further service in office?

"Should I Run?" How and by whom that question is answered goes to the heart of the expectations of proponents of term limitations. Advocates claim that limits will promote a citizen legislature. Lloyd Noble consistently vocalized the goal of developing a citizen legislature, saying: "We want greater turnover so we can have a greater citizen legislature," and "If we can achieve a citizen legislature, then we will have citizens of all walks of life who will go to serve their constituents."

Many term-limit proponents believe that the increase in turnover within the context of a citizen legislature will motivate individuals to consider seeking public office when they otherwise might not. Likewise, those with a potential for political ambition may avoid the state legislature as a dead end or even abandon their political ambitions altogether. At first blush, that argument has some credibility, but under careful scrutiny it unravels, primarily because of the lengthy limit placed on Oklahoma's legislators.

The first fallacy of the argument is the assumption that the turnover rate will be drastically affected by term limitations. Very few people will be forced to leave their legislative post. Oklahoma house speaker Glen Johnson argued that there is "an inaccurate perception that there are lots of senior people in our legislature. When I was elected speaker, a majority of our body had served three terms or less." In fact, the opposite may occur with term limits: turnover may decline. First, as suggested by a lobbyist, some members may begin to feel that they actually have a twelve-year term (as opposed to twelve years' maximum service) and therefore feel compelled to serve the entire twelve years. That is, they may not retire as early as they would without term limits. Second, after several terms incumbents may be given a free ride, facing little or no electoral competition in their last or second-to-last bid for reelection.

The second shortcoming in the logic of term-limit advocates is found in the fact that few professional politicians with upward (or progressive) ambition serve more than twelve years in the Oklahoma state legislature. There are no recent examples of a state legislator with at least twelve years of service seeking election to the U.S. Congress or to another statewide office.

Finally, my interviews uncovered a resounding consensus that people do not run for the Oklahoma state legislature expecting to be seeking reelection a decade later. I interviewed only one member whose initial election followed the passage of term limits. He had filed for election and gained his party's nomination prior to the addition of term limitations to Oklahoma's constitution, but the amendment had been proposed and "everyone I talked to knew it was a cinch," but he claimed that it did not influence his decision. A member with a few years of service confidently proclaimed that term limits would not influence others' decisions to run for the state legislature because:

> the term is long enough to do what most want to do. There are also a myriad of other factors and considerations to take into account. With shorter terms it may be more of a problem, but it is hard to plan twelve or fourteen years in advance. I don't even buy green bananas.

Nevertheless, there seemed to be some doubt in the minds of those I interviewed even if they did not admit it. I heard comments like, "A guy's got to think twice before getting into politics . . . even more so with term limits," or "There may be a qualitative difference . . . more people with an ax to grind." Even the freshman who professed not to care about term limits simultaneously confessed to checking out the likelihood of passage with a number of people.

Still, what we know about Schlesinger's three types of ambition suggests that regardless of type, ambitious people will not be seriously affected by term limits as long as Oklahoma's. Those with discrete ambition will not be dissuaded by the knowledge that they can only serve a discrete amount of time. Few Oklahoma legislators display static ambition, as reflected by the very small numbers with more than twelve years of service. Finally, the evidence is clear that those with progressive ambition do not wait twelve years before exercising that ambition. In short, historical patterns show that only a handful of people will be forced from legislative office in any given election.

"Should I Stay?" Those who are sitting in a legislative seat face the same decision every two or four years. Incumbents have three choices: go home (leave public office), stay and continue doing what they have been doing, or seek another position. Term limits will affect only the second option and only after twelve years of service. From the previous discussion it is clear that very few people serve long enough to be affected in that direct manner.

The question of whether external career decisions will be affected indirectly at other stages of an individual's political progress is more interesting. Interviews suggested two reasons why legislators might serve longer and two reasons why their tenure might grow shorter over time.

As noted above, some members might come to see the normal period of service as twelve years and, after eight or ten years, decide reluctantly to serve out the entire twelve. Most interviewees, however, did not expect that situation to develop; if it did, they believed, it would be a very long time before it became the norm. The second factor that might increase the average tenure is the reluctance of strong challengers to confront incumbents before the expiration of their maximum term. As one legislator indicated, wishfully, "Challengers may just wait for there to be an open seat."

The possibility that members might opt to retire earlier under term limits than under the current situation was also raised. One longstanding member said that leadership may be reluctant to appoint lame ducks to important positions leading some members to retire earlier than the required twelve years rather than serve the last few years with decreased influence. Another possibility is that incumbents with progressive ambition might become more likely to exercise that ambition earlier rather than face the prospect of having no viable options for higher office after twelve years and no opportunity to return to the legislature one more time. For those with progressive ambition, timing becomes both more important and more difficult under term limits.

"Now I Have to Go." A few people will confront a forced end to their service in the state legislature. The options for a person who has spent twelve years in the state legislature include returning to private life, seeking higher elective office, seeking a nonelective political position (in the private or the public sector), or seeking lower elective office.

Proponents of term limits hope that legislators will return home to the private sector when they reach the limit of their service. That expectation is reasonable because it reflects what most people do currently when they leave the legislature. But most people who left the legislature before term limits did so before twelve years had expired. It may be difficult for individuals who have invested twelve years in public service and developed policy and political expertise to return to their previous endeavors full time. Those individuals may well opt to seek higher office at the end of their term because the relative cost of seeking higher office declines with the imminent loss of the current office. Research on progressive ambition offers models of the calculations politicians make of the costs and benefits of pursuing election to a higher office. Under term limits the benefits will be unaffected (unless limits have been imposed for higher offices also), but costs will decrease as the end of the term approaches or is reached. Ambitious politicians should be more inclined to take the risk of seeking higher office.[11]

According to these models, anyone running for an office of any stature pays a price or incurs costs. The cost may be financial or it may lie in the sacrifice of time that might otherwise be allocated to other activities, or opportunities. Term limits affect those costs by decreasing the value of continuing to hold office (or by completely preventing continuation in office when the limit has been reached). Moreover, that happens just when the benefits of continued time in office should be at their greatest; that is, when one has achieved some seniority. With constant benefits and decreased costs, there should be a greater propensity to take the risk of seeking higher office.[12]

A third possible career decision by those forced to retire from the state legislature is to stay in the business of governance but to step away from elective office. The opportunities are as great and as varied as the personalities and ambitions of legislators. When forced from office, former members might seek an appointed position in either the executive or legislative branch, the opportunity to serve on public boards, employment with interest groups, or any number of forums in which to continue to advocate valued positions.

A final response of those leaving the legislature is regressive ambition. Previously unexplored, regressive ambition is the pursuit of lower office. While most of my subjects doubted that much of this practice would occur, some felt that certain people might find returning "home" to become mayor or to serve as a county commissioner desirable to some of their colleagues. One long-standing legislator concluded, "If someone wants to stay in an elected environment that's what they'll have to do. You can't beat an incumbent for Congress. . . ." Many, however, felt that financial considerations would limit the likelihood that regressive ambition will be commonly practiced. Oklahoma's legislators are relatively generously compensated for part-time work; mayors and county commissioners are not. Still, the concept of mixing progressive and regressive ambition raises some interesting possibilities regarding the consequences of rotation in office.

Summary. What do we expect to see in the year 2002 when the first group of Oklahoma legislators bow to term limitations? First, we should see very few people forced from office. Most will have retired long before. Some will have moved to other political positions. Of those few who are being shown the door, some will seek higher or lower office, some other positions in or related to government. Most of the legislators that I interviewed did not want to see all legislators put in the same box: "It will just depend on what the individual wants," and "Each person will have to decide what's right for them," are typical comments. Even proponents of limits disliked the notion that all representatives were alike and would follow the same course.

If we have learned anything in our studies of political ambition it is that ambition is a very personal matter and the choice of how to exercise it is an intensely personal one. The parameters surrounding those decisions may be affected by term limitations, but the process remains largely the same. Further, the participants in the process are not pawns but active participants who can shape the process, their own opportunities, and the outcomes. In Oklahoma, we may see little impact on the careers of politicians because of the length of the limit and the ability of office holders to adapt to the minor changes. In other states, ambitious politicians may have to be more aggressive in shaping the more drastic new rules to their advantage. If history has taught us anything, though, we should not doubt their ability to do so.

Ambition and the Internal Career

Just as ambitious politicians have career goals outside the legislature, they also have goals as legislators—for what might be called their internal or legislative career. Legislators are as individualistic when it comes to their internal careers as they are regarding their external ambitions. In order to bring some order to the consideration of how term limits will influence the legislature and legislators we need to consider what ambitions members have. A reasonable framework, developed by Richard Fenno, suggests five goals for members: reelection, influence within the body, good public policy, a career beyond, and private gain.[13] If term limitations are going to have an influence on the legislature or on the exercise of members' internal ambitions (or goals, as Fenno calls them) then either the balance among them or how they are approached by legislators must change. This section will consider first the relative balance among the goals of legislators. Following that discussion we will consider how attempts to achieve those ambitions will be affected by term limits.

The Importance of Member Goals under Term Limitations. Fenno does not accept that legislators are single-minded seekers of reelection, but he does recognize that reelection is an important goal and that success in other areas is contingent upon success in the electoral arena.[14] One of the explicit goals of term limitations is to decrease the value or importance of reelection. Legislators will know that the number of times they can be reelected is finite. As the limit approaches the value of reelection will diminish. In Oklahoma, the value of reelection will diminish slowly and gradually. In states with shorter limits, the consequences will be more obvious and occur more rapidly. Regardless, the pursuit of reelection should decline relative to other goals.

In a similar vein, the value of influence in the legislature may decline and become less sought by some members. In Oklahoma, power traditionally begins to fall to members only after a number of years of service—seven to nine years, perhaps. Therefore, just as members begin to gain power and prestige term limits will force them to begin to think about closing their legislative careers. Again, the problem is more acute with shorter limits, but regardless of term length members will be removed from office just as they reach the pinnacle of power. Astute members may seek to fulfill other ambitions rather than strive for power and prestige only to hold it for a short while.

Pursuit of policy goals is unlikely to be affected by the imposition of term limitations. Some elected officials are more concerned with policy matters, both generally and narrowly, than are others, but there is no reason to expect that term limitations will influence that predisposition directly. There may be an indirect influence on the pursuit of policy goals by way of the fourth goal identified by Fenno— life after the legislature.

Term limits should make legislators more concerned about their career following legislative service. One vehicle, to be elaborated below, is the development of policy expertise that can be parlayed into a more enduring career. Concern about the future career may be irrational given Oklahoma's long limits—because few would stay more than twelve years even if they could—but the legislators I interviewed indicated that term limitations would hang over their heads anyway. Comments such as, "It's got to get some people thinking," and "Everyone will know that their time is coming," were common. As a result, legislators felt that incumbents would be more concerned about life after the legislature.

The fifth member goal, personal gain, is generally considered to be held by only a small minority. Most of my interview subjects admitted that some legislators are so motivated ("Graft is part of our political system"), but that the numbers are small ("No more than 3 to 5 percent are there purely for self-aggrandizement"). Only one legislator suggested that term limits might directly affect the pursuit of this goal, saying, "Term limits may change the balance between whether you choose seeking power over financial gain." Others shared some concern that the gray area that surrounds the fourth ambition, the career beyond the legislature, might become blurred when it comes to interaction with interest groups. Legislators and lobbyists indicated that it is reasonable for legislators to have career concerns, but worried that such concern might be translated into influence peddling for personal gain either while serving in the legislature or afterwards.

The Pursuit of Member Goals under Term Limitations. Representatives operating under the constraints of term limits but still seeking reelection are likely to do so in the same way as those not constrained by limitations. Incumbents pursuing a return to office will continue to engage in all the activities that we are used to seeing from incumbents—constituency service, representing policy interests of constituents, self-promotion, fund-raising, and so on. While the goal of reelection may become less important, the method of pursuing it should remain as we have come to expect.

How one pursues the fifth goal, private gain, is also unlikely to be seriously affected by term limitations. Some concern was expressed in two areas related to the pursuit of private gain under term limits. One institutionally oriented legislator fretted about the consequences of disconnecting the electoral connection. Short of explicit legal violations, he worried, anything goes for a person approaching the end of his or her term. The same person noted, though, that "higher ambition may temper that type of action." The second concern was that the truly corrupt might become more aggressive as term limits shortened their opportunity to fleece the public.

How legislators pursue good public policy and influence within the body *are* likely to be affected by term limits. Both are likely to be pursued more aggressively and earlier in legislators' careers. If goals are not achieved within twelve years, members cannot decide to come back for just one more term to complete the reform of their pet project. Nor can they be content to stand patiently in line for leadership positions. If a legislator waits too long it may be too late.

Policy aggressiveness began before term limits and most expect it to accelerate. One member said, "Freshmen already insist on seeing the speaker and the leadership." Speaker Glen Johnson also indicated that term limits would serve to increase the tendency whereby

> Junior members, those with less seniority, will be more aggressive, but that has already started. Since I've been here freshmen have been more aggressive—I mean that in a positive sense—involved in the process. They don't sit around and say nothing for two years. They are active and bring their ideas forward.

Policy ambition may also be influenced in practice by term limits in that they may encourage members to focus their policy interest more narrowly. Members may be forced to concentrate on the core of their own agenda. Complicated issues may attract less attention under term limits because they take time and because: "The young are less effective on complicated issues." Overall, then, policy ambitions may find themselves expressed through narrow and straightforward issues to the detriment of complicated and time consuming issues.

More aggressive pursuit of leadership positions is also seen as an acceleration of a recent tendency. One member speculated that term limits

> will magnify a trend that already is in place. Until recently it was required that a [house] speaker have longevity. Seniority was important. But, the last two speakers had shorter periods of service. I think term limits will only reinforce that pattern.

Another simply explained, "There'll be more jockeying. . . . They will be more aggressive because they cannot wait for their time."

The final internal ambition of members is a career after service in the legislature. As this goal becomes more important, how it is pursued calls for our attention. Legislators operating under term limits are more likely consciously to pursue the establishment of a record that will serve them after their legislative career. Those who desire to return to their previous occupation or to seek higher office are unlikely to be affected by term limits, but those who want to stay in public life or government affairs may react differently. One response might be to carve a policy niche in which to develop expertise and a network to be used after leaving the legislature. Various public- and private-sector opportunities are open to those with expertise, particularly if it is coupled with familiarity with the legislative process. But concern about one's career after the legislature might take a less noble turn for some members. Some may choose to use their time in the legislature to peddle influence and gain acceptance in groups who might offer employment after legislative service. Chits may be garnered to be cashed in for a new career. Most members value their reputation and are unlikely to engage in such activities, but as one member delicately expressed it, "Others may seek a close working relationship with interest groups as their term approaches an end."

In review, it is quite likely that term limits will affect which member goals will be pursued. How these differences will affect the legislature is the subject of the remainder of this chapter.

The Legislature under Term Limitations

Term limitations will clearly influence how members define and pursue their external and internal career ambitions. The consequences may not be as great in Oklahoma as in other states because of the length of the term, but they will be found. In the preceding section we reviewed the thoughts of legislative scholars and practitioners of our legislative process. Below we address the broader consequences of the changes to which they pointed. Specifically we will consider whether, how, and how well the legislature will accomplish its tasks as term limits take effect.

Before considering how the operations of the Oklahoma legislature will be influenced by term limitations, it is useful to consider the *status quo ante.* Powerful leaders in the Oklahoma legislature control committee appointments, chairmanships, other leadership positions, and appointments to the General Conference Committee on Appropriations. The latter committee is a powerful one that meets at the end of the session to reconcile differences between house and senate versions of appropriations legislation. In so doing, committee members must occasionally venture into substantive areas. Because most important matters come before the committee it is not unreasonable to call it a legislature within the legislature. Traditionally, candidates for leadership positions freely trade positions of responsibility for support of both their candidacy and their initiatives.[15]

During the second half of the 1980s power became increasingly consolidated in the hands of the leadership—a pattern particularly pronounced in the lower house. Speaker Jim Barker instituted the pledge-card system and freely rewarded his supporters and punished his adversaries. When he began to punish supporters, too, he ran into trouble. After his mid-session removal from the speakership in 1989, he was replaced by more progressive leadership. Under speakers Steve Lewis (who completed Barker's term prior to campaigning for governor) and Glen Johnson, legislators have been accorded more respect; junior members have been allowed more freedom and placed in positions of responsibility. Still, leadership remains important and strong. Committees remain relatively weak; rotation of membership is common.[16]

A number of changes are likely to accompany term limitations. Committees, already weak, will become weaker and the leadership will become less effective and more factionalized. Decision making will be made more difficult and influence is likely to flow away from the legislature.

As already noted, committees in the Oklahoma house and senate are not traditionally powerful. They lack expertise and cannot control the flow of legislation. The lack of expertise and the power of the leadership have traditionally limited the degree of deference to committee recommendations. Under term limits, there is likely to be even less expertise and, therefore, even less deference. Members, knowing their time is limited, are likely to move on their own. One representative explained, "People will have their own agenda and pursue it." Another legislator offered the possibility that committees with strong leaders may be circumvented by members or interest groups waiting for the inevitable turnover and, perhaps, a more favorable leader of the committee.

Formal leadership is a logical source of direction in a body with fewer senior members. Interviewees felt that good leaders would prosper under term limits. Most believed that future leaders would be more aggressive once in position and much more aggressive in pursuing leadership positions, a possibility that concerned a number of people for its potential to increase factionalization within the body. A veteran legislator speculated that aggressive pursuit of the leadership "will probably lead to an increase in the building of factions, making it more difficult to get things done." Several voiced the more obvious concern that lack of experience will show, that mistakes will be made, that direction will be lacking, and that procedural irregularities may become commonplace. Speaker Johnson explained his concerns:

> I became speaker without much seniority. I had only eight years, but if term limits had been in effect I could only serve four more years as speaker. In the leadership experience is important. Someone with short seniority may lack adequate preparation for the position. These positions take seasoning and time.

A third problem that might confront the legislature and hamper its ability to serve as an independent decision maker is a decline in expertise. States with short-term limits will be affected more than

Oklahoma, but even with long limits changes are likely. In a state like Oklahoma, the few people who have expertise on complicated issues are those few who have served for a long time. Therefore, even the loss of the handful of very experienced members may force the legislature to look elsewhere for cues. Nearly every legislator and lobbyist that I interviewed concurred in that judgment.[17] Lobbyists made comments such as: "It will make my job more difficult. There will be no historical reference." Or, "We're going to have to spend all of our time educating people just to bring them up to speed." But they also made comments such as: "It's easier to influence a freshman," and "They won't know the ropes. I'll be able to say I was there." In short, lobbyists see the task of influencing legislators becoming less efficient but more effective under term limits.

Legislators see the same outcome. Speaker Johnson discussed his concern for the institution in these terms:

> Entrenched interests will gain from term limits. Entrenched interests such as the bureaucracy may gain. They'll always be there. The elected officials will be limited so the sphere of influence for elected officials may be diminished. Someone else, like the bureaucracy, will pick it up.
>
> Interest groups, special interests, organized interests are a steady source of influence and that influence will increase. They [the bureaucracy and interest groups] will be there and the legislature will not. Those who stay around will have more influence than those who are new to the scene.

Others expressed the same concern in their own words, but proponents and opponents of term limits alike believed the influence of the legislature would be diminished and that others would fill the void left behind.

Finally, many legislators felt that the legislature would miss the steadying hand of the few who now bring considerable experience to the body. They fret about the loss of institutional memory and the transmission of legislative norms. One legislator said it well:

> Long-term members provide an anchor. Younger members tend to have a wolf pack mentality, but some of the veterans can calm them down. . . . They just have the experience and sense of the institution that is important. Representative X and others have an overwhelming understanding of the house and state that is indispensable.

Another said:

> When I first got to the capitol I chose to sit behind Senator Y. He knows a whole lot about politics. He has an institutional memory. We sat together for eight or ten years now and I understand why he

is respected; he knows what's going on. I've learned a lot from watching him. It also explains why he is disliked—he is effective. People go to him.

One of the house leaders explained:

When I first came in former speaker William Willis was still in the legislature. He was an invaluable resource. He understood how things worked and had a great memory for what had happened before. He was respected. Now there's Representative Z. . . . He is a tremendous resource; he has lots of information.

One freshman observed:

The "deans" carry a lot of tradition with them at various meetings—party, committee, whatever—they discuss topics that are taken very seriously. Term limits may erode that tradition and the legislative tradition may degenerate. Tradition needs to be nurtured. Institutions need to take care of themselves.

My interviews suggest that members of Oklahoma's state legislature appreciate their senior members. Of course, the context is that there are few of them and the few do not dominate the two bodies. In fact, all four of the legislators quoted above also discussed the value of junior members. One of the veterans, for example, continued:

Older legislators have been through all the battles and will tell the younger guys why their proposal won't work. But, sometimes the young turks work hard on something and it gets done.

Another added:

By the same token, new members bring new ideas and get involved, involved in bills and decision making. That is healthy for the process.

Within the context of the Oklahoma legislature, losing the most senior members is likely to be the most notable outcome of term limits.

Conclusion

It is obvious that term limitations will affect how the Oklahoma legislature operates. The discussion presented above suggests that the changes in the career paths of individual members and in the functioning of the legislature will be widespread but not particularly profound. The discussion also presents a generally negative interpretation of the changes; most observers will probably conclude that the changes outlined above are, on balance, more negative than positive. Before putting those conclusions into a permanent memory bank, though, three caveats need to be considered. First, much of what is presented is speculation—informed speculation, hopefully, but in the absence of experience with term limits it remains speculation. Second, most of those engaging in the speculation are insiders who carry their particular biases with them. Mr. Noble's speculation sounds quite different from that of Speaker Johnson. Finally, the limit on the length of the term that can be served in Oklahoma is so generous as to make it nearly irrelevant. States that enact shorter term limits will encounter similar, but more extreme consequences—for better or for worse.

Notes

The author would like to thank J. David Rausch for his help and intellectual companionship in the development of this chapter. In particular his work in our jointly authored "The End of Professionalism: The Dynamics of Term Limitations" (a paper delivered at the annual meeting of the Southwestern Political Science Association, San Antonio, Texas, March 27-30, 1991) is reflected in the section on the Oklahoma initiative in this chapter.

1. The author would like to thank Noble for sharing his polling results. For more detail see Patrick B. McGuigan, "Better Sooner than Later: How the Oklahoma Term Limitation Initiative Came to Pass" (Paper delivered at the annual meeting of the Western Political Science Association, Seattle, Washington, March 21-23, 1991).
2. Examples of Mitchell's view can be found in Mitchell, "Insider Tales of an Honorable Ex-Legislator," *Wall Street Journal,* October 11, 1990, or "Congressional Debate: Limit Terms? Yes!" *Extensions,* Spring 1991 (Carl Albert Congressional Research and Studies Center, University of Oklahoma, Norman).
3. McGuigan, "Better Sooner than Later," 11.
4. As a basis for comparison, about 650,000 people cast a vote on the issue when it appeared on the ballot.
5. McGuigan, "Better Sooner than Later."
6. John Greiner, "Term Limit Opponents Organize," *Daily Oklahoman,* September 14, 1990.
7. John Greiner, "Lawmaker Says Term Limit Plan Will Limit Voters' Rights," *Daily Oklahoman,* September 11, 1990.
8. This and all other quotes not attributed to a published source are based on personal and telephone interviews conducted by the author with more than twenty-five public officials, lobbyists, and term-limit activists following the vote in Oklahoma. The interviews were confidential and open ended. The house member quoted here suggests that the number of individuals who had served more than ten years was only about three. A more typical number would be five to seven in each house.

9. Joseph Schlesinger, *Ambition and Politics: Political Careers in the United States* (Chicago: Rand McNally, 1966). For further discussion see Linda L. Fowler and Robert D. McClure, *Political Ambition: Who Decides to Run for Congress* (New Haven: Yale University Press, 1989) and John R. Hibbing, *Congressional Careers: Contours of Life in the U.S. House of Representatives* (Chapel Hill: The University of North Carolina Press, 1991). It has been argued, convincingly, that "almost all elected officials ... are progressively ambitious" in Paul R. Abramson, John H. Aldrich, and David W. Rohde, "Progressive Ambition among United States Senators: 1972-1988," *Journal of Politics* 49 (February 1987): 5. See also David W. Rohde, "Risk-Bearing and Progressive Ambition: The Case of Members of the United States House of Representatives," *American Journal of Political Science* 23 (February 1979): 1-26.

10. James R. Scales and Danney Goble, *Oklahoma Politics: A History* (Norman: The University of Oklahoma Press, 1982), especially Chapter 2.

11. For examples, see Rohde, "Risk-Bearing and Progressive Ambition," William Bianco, "Strategic Decisions on Candidacy in U.S. Congressional Districts," *Legislative Studies Quarterly* 9 (May 1984): 351-364; and Paul Brace, "Progressive Ambition in the House: A Probabilistic Approach," *Journal of Politics* 46 (May 1984): 556-571.

12. Fowler and McClure, *Political Ambition*, discuss why, absent term limits, state legislators are unlikely to take the risk of seeking higher office (see especially pages 89-100).

13. Richard F. Fenno, Jr., *Congressmen in Committees* (Boston: Little, Brown, 1973), 1. The latter two goals are usually forgotten because of the focus of the remainder of Fenno's work.

14. For a discussion of reelection as the primary determinant of legislators' behavior, see David R. Mayhew, *Congress: The Electoral Connection* (New Haven: Yale University Press, 1974).

15. For good discussions of the Oklahoma legislature see Samuel A. Kirkpatrick, *The Legislative Process in Oklahoma* (Norman: The University of Oklahoma Press, 1978) and David R. Morgan, Robert E. England, and George G. Humphreys, *Oklahoma Politics and Policies: Governing the Sooner State* (Lincoln: The University of Nebraska Press, 1991).

16. Routine committee assignments are so unimportant to most representatives that they were unable to fathom why people might seek different assignments under term limits. I commonly heard comments such as: "Maybe in the U.S. House it would make a difference, but here capability is more important."

17. See also Hibbing, *Congressional Careers*, chap. 5.

8. TERM LIMITS IN THE STATE EXECUTIVE BRANCH

Thad L. Beyle

Limitations on gubernatorial terms based upon fear of excessive executive power have always been fundamental to the constitutional design of state governments. Where used, these limits have followed two general patterns. The first is very short terms with frequent reelections but no limit on the number of terms a person might serve. The "limit" in such a system arises from the shortness of the term and the regular return to the electorate. The second allows longer terms but limits the number of terms served or requires a break in service. The unlimited model, similar to that found in the original U.S. Constitution, allowed relatively long terms and no limit on service.

The early state constitutions focused authority in legislatures and allowed governors little or no real power. Often selected by the legislature itself, the first governors frequently served a one-year term. Though not the same as formal limits, very short terms were enacted to "cut the governor down to subservient size." [1]

Table 8-1 shows that the average gubernatorial term has gradually lengthened. Since 1955, with so much reform afoot in the states, the number of governors serving two-year terms has decreased from nineteen to three, while the number of states with four-year terms has risen from twenty-nine to forty-seven. Only the New England states of New Hampshire, Rhode Island, and Vermont still adhere to the shorter two-year terms.

Among the large number of states with four-year terms, there are some significant differences in the number of terms a governor may serve. The number limited to a single four-year term has declined from seventeen to two since 1955, while those limited to two four-year terms has risen from six to twenty-nine. Only Kentucky and Virginia still restrict their governors to a single term. Sixteen states have no constitutional limits on gubernatorial service.

There are two regions in which states are most restrictive of the terms of their elected chief executives (Table 8-2). Three small New England states still hold on to the two-year term limit and two southern

TABLE 8-1 Length of the Term of Governors, 1780-1991

Year	No. of states	One year	Two years	Three years	Four years
1780	13	10	1	2	0
1800	16	9	3	3	1
1820	24	10	6	4	4
1860	34	5	16	2	11
1900	45	2	22	1	20
1925	48	0	25	1	22
1940	48	0	24	1	23
1955	48	0	19	0	29
1964	50	0	15	0	35
1975	50	0	4	0	46
1991	50	0	3	0	47

Sources: Joseph E. Kallenbach, *The American Chief Executive: The Presidency and the Governorship* (New York: Harper and Row, 1966), 187; Larry Sabato, *Goodbye to Good-Time Charlie* (Lexington, Mass.: Lexington Books, 1978), 102; Advisory Commission on Intergovernmental Relations, *The Question of State Government Capability* (Washington, D.C.: ACIR, 1985), 129; *The Book of the States, 1990-91* (Lexington, Ky.: The Council of State Governments, 1990), 62-63; and Mark E. Tompkins, "Changing the Terms: Gubernatorial Term Reform in the Modern Era" (a paper presented at the annual meeting of the Southern Political Science Association, Tampa, Fla., 1991), 12.

states restrict their governors to one four-year term. Of the other southern states only Texas allows four-year terms with no term limitation.

Developments in the states over more than two centuries of history have thus left us with considerable variation in provisions for gubernatorial terms and term limits. Clearly the movement has been toward permitting longer service, but in many states the trend is away from unlimited service. The modal pattern in the states is similar to the current provision for the presidency in the national constitution: a four-year term with a two-term limit.

The reasons for the changes in the states concerning term limits were several, but the essential element was the reformers' belief that states needed governors to serve longer terms in order "to learn the job and to demonstrate leadership ability." [2] Tied to this belief was the argument that by limiting the tenure of an incumbent governor, the people were denied the opportunity to vote for a candidate who might be the best person for the job.[3] The Advisory Commission on Intergovernmental Relations made the case this way:

TABLE 8-2   Term Limitations on Governors in the Fifty States

Two years, unlimited terms (N = 3)	Four years, one-term limitation (N = 2)	Four years, two-term limitation (N = 29)	Four years, no term limitation (N = 16)
New Hampshire	Kentucky	Alabama	Arizona
Rhode Island	Virginia	Alaska	Connecticut
Vermont		Arkansas	Idaho
		California [a]	Illinois
		Colorado [b]	Iowa
		Delaware [c]	Massachusetts
		Florida	Michigan
		Georgia	Minnesota
		Hawaii	Montana
		Indiana	New York
		Kansas	North Dakota
		Louisiana	Texas
		Maine	Utah
		Maryland	Washington
		Mississippi	Wisconsin
		Missouri	Wyoming
		Nebraska	
		Nevada	
		New Jersey	
		New Mexico	
		North Carolina	
		Ohio	
		Oklahoma	
		Oregon [d]	
		Pennsylvania	
		South Carolina	
		South Dakota	
		Tennessee	
		West Virginia [e]	

Sources: Virginia Gray, Herbert Jacob, and Robert Albritton, eds., *Politics in the American States,* 5th ed. (Glenview, Ill.: Scott-Foresman, 1990), 568; unpublished data from The Rockefeller Institute of Government, August 1991.

Notes:

[a] Two-consecutive-term limit, lifetime limit of three terms.

[b] Two-consecutive-term limit; may serve again after break.

[c] Absolute two-term limit, whether or not consecutive.

[d] Prohibited from serving more than eight years in any twelve-year period.

[e] Prohibited from serving in the term immediately following two consecutive terms regardless of whether terms were filled in whole or in part.

Tenure reputedly constitutes an important factor in gubernatorial power. The argument goes that a governor serving only a two-year term or who cannot be reelected immediately is weaker than one who does not suffer these limitations. Because of a short term, programs requiring much time cannot be brought to fruition. Remodeling of state policies is also hampered because new governors must operate for a time under their predecessors' budgets. Restrictions on succession can destroy influence with the legislature and control over the bureaucracy because the incumbent is not in office long enough to build the necessary political coalitions or establish routines that serve as sources of political influence. Moreover, any reelection campaign must begin immediately although the public has had no real basis for approving or condemning an administration.[4]

The Effect of Constitutional Term Limits

It is hard to determine exactly what effect changing term limits have had on state governments and policies. But as Mark Tompkins suggests, the impact on who holds the office of governor is clear. Looking at the 1932-1990 period, he concludes that "the effort to buffer the gubernatorial office does, in important ways, seem to buffer it [by] reducing participation in gubernatorial elections and often making the outcomes of these elections more stable." [5]

Table 8-3 gives an indication of the effect of tenure and term limits on the governorship in the states. It examines (a) the overall tenure of state governors over ten decades; (b) the number of new governors either elected or who became governor due to the death, removal, or resignation of the incumbent governor during that decade; and (c) the number of states which had tenure or term limitations at the outset of the decade. Over the ten selected decades several patterns are evident:

1. The number of short gubernatorial tenures (one to two years) steadily declined over the past century from a high of 53 percent in the 1850s to only one governor in the 1980s (Evan Mecham, R-Ariz., 1987-1988, who was impeached and removed from office by the state legislature). This is no surprise. The gradual elimination of two-year terms could be expected to lead to this result.

2. The number of longer gubernatorial tenures (five or more years) has continued to increase in the twentieth century from a low of 10 percent at the outset to a high of 67 percent in the 1970s and to 51 percent in the 1980s. This drop for the 1980s will probably disappear as some of the new 1980s governors win

reelection in the 1990s. For example, seventeen of the twenty-three incumbents seeking reelection in 1990 won (but the two incumbents seeking reelection in 1991 were defeated). Six of the other nine incumbents are eligible for reelection in 1992 and 1993.

3. There has been a real shift in the actual numbers of newly elected individuals who have served as governor over the period. Up through the 1920s, there was an average of at least three new governors per state per decade and in some periods more than four new governors per state per decade. In the second half of this century, the average has dropped from slightly more than two new governors per state per decade to just slightly more than one per state per decade. Sabato also argues that more than constitutional tenure and term limits are involved in these longer gubernatorial terms, specifically "the [declining] death rate, which attests both to the greater health of the population as a whole and to the election of younger governors."[6]

Figure 8-1 depicts the changes since 1800 in the number of states with unlimited terms and with four-year terms. For a good portion of the time period, changes in the number of states with unlimited terms and with four-year terms had little apparent impact upon the average number of governors serving. But beginning in the 1920s and 1950s, as the number of states with unlimited terms topped out at 29 and began declining, and the number of states with four-year terms began escalating rapidly, the average number of governors serving per state per decade also dropped rapidly.

Clearly, we have fewer people serving as governor now than at any time in the past. Once a person is elected governor, he or she will tend to stay in that office for a longer period of time. Additionally, some governors do leave office for a period only to run successfully and serve again. These include Cecil Andrus (D-Idaho), Henry Bellmon (R-Okla.), Bill Clinton (D-Ark.), Michael Dukakis (D-Mass.), Rudy Perpich (D-Minn.), and George Wallace (D-Ala.). Tompkins indicates that although this may "provide stability in administration and consistency in policy"—the goal of the reformers—it does so at the expense of making "the office less 'responsive' . . . to expressions of the desires of the electorate."[7]

However, this conclusion assumes that a person serving a longer term as governor is doing so in a way that has excluded the electorate as part of the process. This is not so. What it really means is that other potential candidates for governor are at a considerable political disadvantage in trying to achieve the office due to the advantages tenure

TABLE 8-3 Tenure of Governors in Selected Decades, 1800-1989

	1800-1809	1820-1829	1850-1859	1870-1879	1900-1909	1920-1929	1950-1959	1960-1969[b]	1970-1979[c]	1980-1989
Tenure of Governors[a]										
10 +	14%	4%	1%	0%	1%	1%	5%	12%	8%	2%
5-9	16	14	6	12	9	15	24	24	59	49
3-4	30	40	40	49	54	54	50	46	27	47
1-2	39	42	53	39	36	30	21	19	6	2
Number of Governors and States Per Decade										
Governors	56	92	124	154	154	185	108	102	93	55
States	17	24	31	37	46	48	48	50	50	50
Avg. governors per state	3.3	3.8	4.0	4.2	3.3	3.9	2.3	2.0	1.9	1.1
Tenure and Term Limitations of Governors by State[d]										
Unlimited	7	10	13	25	31	29	29	28	26	21
4 years	1	3	8	16	20	22	27	32	38	46

Sources: Gerald Benjamin, "The Diffusion of Executive Power in American State Constitutions: Tenure and Tenure Limitations," *Publius* 15 (Fall 1985): 80-81; Joseph A. Schlesinger, "The Governor's Place in American Politics," *Public Administration Review* 30:1 (January/February 1970): 4; Larry Sabato, *Goodbye to Good-time Charlie* (Washington, D.C.: CQ Press, 1983), 104; and the author.

Notes: The figures in the table include only those governors who were elected to their first terms during each time span listed. The tenures of those who succeeded to the office of governor are included in the tabulations.

[a]Governors elected in the 1980s and still serving are counted for tenure to the end of their current elected term.

[b]Two changes were made in Sabato's data because of the reelection of two 1960s governors in the 1980s.

[c]Changes were made in Sabato's data because of additional terms won in the 1980s by governors who were first elected in the 1970s.

[d]Numbers represent states with either unlimited terms or four-year terms at the outset of the decade involved.

provides incumbents. The electorate is still part of the process; it just does not have the variety of choices it may have had in the past. But more on this later.

Table 8-4 provides a state-by-state picture of the effect of the trend toward fewer new governors in the states by looking at a single decade, the 1980s. Shown in boldface are the new governors selected either by election or succession to the office during the decade; the others are governors who either completed terms begun in the 1970s or former governors who had served previously and were reelected after a period out of office.

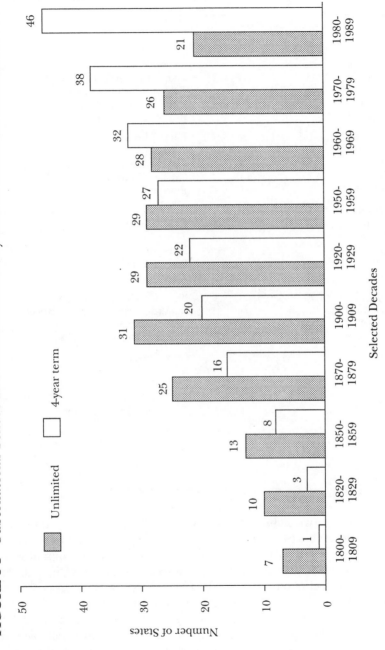

FIGURE 8-1 Gubernatorial Tenure and Term Limitations by State in Selected Decades, 1800-1989

Source: Table 8-3

TABLE 8-4   The 1980s: New Governors Serving in the Fifty States

State	Governors
Alabama	James, Wallace, **Hunt**
Alaska	Hammond, **Sheffield, Cowper**
Arizona	Babbitt, **Mecham, Mofford**
Arkansas	Clinton, **White,** Clinton
California	Brown, **Deukmejian**
Colorado	Lamm, **Romer**
Connecticut	**O'Neill**
Delaware	DuPont, **Castle**
Florida	Graham, **Martinez**
Georgia	Busbee, **Harris**
Hawaii	Ariyoshi, **Waihee**
Idaho	Evans, Andrus
Illinois	Thompson
Indiana	Bowen, **Orr, Bayh**
Iowa	Ray, **Branstad**
Kansas	Carlin, **Orr**
Kentucky	**Brown, Collins, Wilkinson**
Louisiana	Edwards, **Treen,** Edwards, **Roemer**
Maine	Brennan, **McKernan**
Maryland	Hughes, **Schaefer**
Massachusetts	King, Dukakis
Michigan	Milliken, **Blanchard**
Minnesota	Quie, Perpich
Mississippi	**Winter, Allain, Maupus**
Missouri	Teasdale, Bond, **Ashcroft**

(Continued on next page)

There are several points of note in the table:

1. Only two states (Kentucky and Mississippi) had three new governors over the decade. This level of turnover was clearly the result of their limit of one four-year term. (Mississippi has since removed this limitation.) Because of the timing of its gubernatorial elections (1977-1981-1987), Virginia is not in this group, although in any ten-year period it has three new governors.
2. Four states (Idaho, Massachusetts, Minnesota and Oklahoma) did not see a new face in the governor's mansion over the decade. Gubernatorial tenure was unlimited in all of these states but Oklahoma, which has a two-term rule. A change in

TABLE 8-4   *(Continued)*

State	Governors
Montana	Judge, **Schwinden, Stephens**
Nebraska	Thone, **Kerrey, Orr**
Nevada	List, **Bryan, Miller**
New Hampshire	Gallen, **Sununu, Gregg**
New Jersey	Byrne, **Kean**
New Mexico	King, **Anaya, Carruthers**
New York	Carey, **Cuomo**
North Carolina	Hunt, **Martin**
North Dakota	Link, **Olson, Sinner**
Ohio	Rhodes, **Celeste**
Oklahoma	Nigh, Bellmon
Oregon	Atiyeh, **Goldschmidt**
Pennsylvania	Thornburgh, **Casey**
Rhode Island	Garrahy, **DiPrete**
South Carolina	Riley, **Campbell**
South Dakota	Janklow, **Mickelson**
Tennessee	Alexander, **McWherter**
Texas	Clements, **White,** Clements
Utah	Mathewson, **Bangerter**
Vermont	Snelling, **Kunin**
Virginia	Dalton, **Robb, Baliles**
Washington	Ray, **Spellman, Gardner**
West Virginia	Rockefeller, Moore, **Caperton**
Wisconsin	Dreyfus, **Earl, Thompson**
Wyoming	Herschler, **Sullivan**

Note: Names in **bold** were new to the governor's chair in the 1980s either by election or by succession.

governor occurred in the decade, but it was a former governor returning to office after an enforced vacation.

3. Two states had one governor over the whole decade—William O'Neill (D, 1980-1991) in Connecticut and James Thompson (R, 1977-1991) in Illinois. This points to the longevity that several states without limits on service have experienced in the past few decades. For instance, the Midwest has been a safe haven for several governors: Bill Milliken (R-Mich., 1969-1983); Bob Ray (R-Iowa, 1969-1983); James Rhodes (R-Ohio, 1963-71, 1975-1983), who had to wait out a term because of a two-term limit; and Thompson. In 1983, Bob Ray was succeeded by his lieutenant governor, Terry Branstad, in a transi-

tion where only the person in the governor's chair changed—virtually the entire personal staff and most major department and agency appointments stayed on.[8] Thus, Iowa has had essentially the same administration since 1969.

4. The remaining forty-one states either had one new governor over the decade who had not served previously (twenty-eight states) or two new governors (thirteen states). Interestingly, almost half of the states (six) with higher turnovers during this period had no term limits. In the case of Bill Clinton in Arkansas (D, 1979-1981, 1983-) and Edwin Edwards in Louisiana (D, 1972-1980, 1984-1988, 1992-) one of the new governors only served to split the tenure of a governor who later came back to serve once again, and in Edwards's case twice again after winning the highly visible 1991 election against Republican David Duke.

State Political Limits

Despite constitutional changes leading to longer stays in office by governors, politics still can cut short gubernatorial careers. Voters may refuse to renominate or reelect an incumbent governor, or, for a variety of reasons, an incumbent governor may decide not to seek another term.

Table 8-5 presents the results of 312 gubernatorial elections between 1970 and 1991. There was considerable turnover in the governorship during this time; only 42 percent of the incumbent governors were reelected to serve another term (131 of 312). Of the 81 governors who did not receive another term, sixty-nine (38 percent) were not eligible due to constitutional term limits, sixty-three (35 percent) decided not to seek reelection for other reasons, and forty-nine (27 percent) tried and lost. In sum, constitutional term limits stopped three out of eight of these governors from being reelected; their own decisions and politics stopped the other five.[9]

Looking just at the fifty-three elections in the last election cycle (1988-1991) and adding those who could not seek reelection for constitutional reasons (nine) to those who decided not to run although eligible (ten) and those who were beaten at the ballot box (nine), we find that the states had a 53 percent rate of turnover (twenty-eight of fifty-three).

Often these wounds are self-inflicted. Some incumbents who decide not to seek reelection read the political tea leaves—political polls—and realize that they may not be successful.

Others do not read the situation correctly, and are beaten in their attempt to serve another term. An example is Bill Clinton (D-Ark., 1979-1981, 1983-) who fell victim to the wrath of Arkansas voters.

TABLE 8-5 Vulnerability of Incumbent Governors Seeking Reelection, 1970-1991

		Incumbents						
		Eligible to run		Running		Winning		Losing	
Year	Elections held	No.	(%)	No.	(%)	No.	(%)	No.	(%)
---	---	---	---	---	---	---	---	---	---
1970	34	30	(88)	22	(73)	14	(64)	8	(36)
1971	3	0	—	—	—	—	—	—	—
1972	19	15	(79)	8	(53)	7	(88)	1	(13)
1973	2	1	(50)	1	(100)	—	—	1	(100)
1974	35	29	(83)	21	(72)	16	(76)	5	(24)
1975	3	1	(33)	1	(100)	1	(100)	—	—
1976	14	12	(86)	7	(58)	5	(71)	2	(29)
1977	2	1	(50)	1	(100)	1	(100)	—	—
1978	36	29	(81)	22	(76)	16	(73)	6	(27)
1979	3	0	—	—	—	—	—	—	—
1980	13	12	(92)	12	(100)	7	(58)	5	(42)
1981	2	0	—	—	—	—	—	—	—
1982	36	33	(92)	25	(76)	19	(76)	6	(24)
1983	3	0	—	—	—	—	—	—	—
1984	13	9	(69)	6	(67)	4	(67)	2	(33)
1985	2	1	(50)	1	(100)	1	(100)	—	—
1986	36	24	(67)	18	(75)	15	(83)	3	(18)
1987	3	2	(67)	1	(50)	—	—	1	(100)
1988	12	9	(75)	9	(100)	8	(89)	1	(11)
1989	2	0	—	—	—	—	—	—	—
1990	36	33	(92)	23	(70)	17	(74)	6	(26)
1991	3	2	(67)	2	(100)	0	(0)	2	(100)
By Banks of Elections									
1972-75	59	46	(78)	31	(67)	24	(77)	7	(23)
1976-79	55	42	(76)	30	(71)	22	(73)	8	(27)
1980-83	54	45	(83)	37	(82)	26	(70)	11	(30)
1984-87	54	34	(63)	26	(76)	20	(77)	6	(23)
1988-91	53	44	(83)	34	(77)	25	(74)	9	(26)
Totals									
1970-91	312	243	(78)	180	(74)	131	(73)	49	(27)

Sources: Sarah McCally Morehouse, *State Politics, Parties and Policy* (New York: Holt, Rinehart and Winston, 1982), 207; and Thad L. Beyle, *State Government: CQ's Guide to Current Issues and Activities, 1992-93* (Washington, D.C.: CQ Press, 1992), 12.

There were a variety of reasons for the voters' anger including unpopular policy innovations and Clinton's remoteness from the state as he sought national acclaim. There was also the Carter administration's decision to use Fort Chaffee in Arkansas as a place to relocate "undesirable Cuban refugees." [10]

The latter point indicates that not all the politics that end a gubernatorial career occur within the state's boundaries. Another example, in 1990, was the declining regional (soon to be national) economic situation facing the incumbent governors in New England. Three decided not to seek reelection; a fourth lost his bid for reelection.[11] Earlier, in 1982, when six governors lost their reelection bids, an economic downturn had caused political problems. At that time some long-serving governors (William Milliken in Michigan and Bob Ray in Iowa) decided not to seek reelection, in part due to the deteriorating economic conditions in their states.

Looking at gubernatorial vulnerability by type of election year—presidential election year vs. off-year; even year vs. odd year—some distinct differences emerge, tied in part to the impact of gubernatorial term limitations.

1. In even nonpresidential years, when most gubernatorial elections are held,[12] there is an amazingly stable percentage of incumbents whose terms are ending and who seek reelection (about 75 percent). And, equally consistent, about three-quarters of them are successful. During these years, there are no presidential coattails to ride on or hide from. State issues—including the incumbent's own record—are usually the major issues in the campaign.

2. In the odd nonpresidential years, when few gubernatorial elections are held, the rate of incumbents seeking reelection is very low. Most of these states have had or still do have term limitations for their governors. Incumbents do not run because they are not allowed to.[13]

3. In the presidential years, when around a dozen states hold their gubernatorial elections, the percentage of governors seeking reelection varies greatly (from 58 percent in 1976 to 100 percent in 1980 and 1988). The explanation is that although seven of these states have no term limits, in four of the five states with two-term limitations those terms expire at the same time. So there were mandatory turnover elections in 1976 and 1984 in Delaware, Missouri, North Carolina, and West Virginia; reelection campaigns were waged in those states in 1980 and 1988.

Other Constitutionally Elected
Executive-Branch Offices

In many states, constitutional and political term limitations on those at the top of the political ballot are not replicated further down the ballot. Recently, there have been some notable retirements of other elected state executive officials that make the point well.

Those "Heart-Beat Away" Offices

John A. Cherberg, the long-time lieutenant governor of Washington State, retired in 1989 after serving for thirty-two years. He had succeeded Vic Meyers, who served from 1933 to 1953. Between them, Washington had but two lieutenant governors over the sixty-two-year period, during which time nine governors were elected.[14] Although no constitutional term limits applied to governors in the state, there obviously were political limits, but not for those two lieutenant governors.

In fact, only eight of the forty-two states with an office of lieutenant governor placed term limits on their lieutenant governors as of 1986. In every case, the state had a four-year term and there was a two-term limit.[15] As a result of the 1990 referenda in California and Colorado, those states now impose two-term limits on their lieutenant governors. In five other states, the next in line to succeed the governor is a legislative leader whose tenure is limited politically by the continued votes of the members of his or her legislative party, the votes of the electorate who keep the party as a majority in the legislature, and by the voters in his or her own home district. For some of these leaders, redistricting in the wake of the 1990 census may add another limit.

Secretaries of State

In 1989, Secretary of State Thad Eure of North Carolina decided to step down after serving in that office since 1937. In his fifty-two years of service, he watched twelve separate governors come and go.[16] For most of this period, the state's governor was restricted to a single four-year term, but beginning in 1977 the governor could seek reelection for an additional four-year term.

Across the fifty states, thirty-nine secretaries of state are elected by the voters; in thirty-three of these states there is no limit on the number of terms that can be served.[17] Five of the other six elective states restrict their secretaries of state either to two consecutive terms or to eight years in any twelve-year period.[18] Kentucky has a one-term restriction. The remaining eleven secretaries of state are either appointed by the governor (nine states) or by the legislature (two states). Their terms, of course, are politically determined.[19]

Other Offices

The office of attorney general in the states is even less restricted than are those just discussed. Forty-four attorneys general are elected by the people; all states but Kentucky allow them to serve successive, unlimited terms. In five states the governor appoints the attorney general; in Tennessee the state supreme court appoints this official.[20]

Finally in a rather strange paradox, the term-limitation amendment adopted by California voters in 1990 will not apply to John Garamendi who won his race to become the state's first elected insurance commissioner. The language of the term-limitation amendment did not mention the office, so Garamendi can serve as long as he wishes to run and the electorate votes him into office.[21]

Term Limits and Political Ambition
Ladders in the States

A most important question concerns how a state's political ambition ladder is affected by allowing longer service at the top of the ticket. If the governorship is the ultimate or penultimate office on the state political ladder, then the frequency with which it is actually and realistically attainable can have great impact on politics in the state.

The argument is straightforward: consistent turnover at the top of a political system allows new faces and "fresh ideas" to move up as the old faces and stale ideas move on. Conversely, if turnover at the top of the system is restricted or even blocked for a period of time, the opportunity for advancement is lessened. In Joseph Schlesinger's terms, if and as the governor's office becomes "a career office" in a state, political opportunities are restricted, and the entire political opportunity structure changes.[22]

This analysis requires an understanding of the concept of "political time," that moment in an individual's career when he or she can or should move to run for higher office. It is hard to define exactly when that political time occurs, how long it lasts, or for whom it really does exist. It is much easier to determine when it is not the right political time for people to try to move upward: they may be too young and their time will come; they may be too old and it is past their time. For some, there never will be a time for this type of political move. Clearly, the concept of political time varies from system to system or, for the purposes of this essay, from state to state.

Generally, political time is relatively short from the individual's perspective. There are several reasons for this. Term limits, where they exist, create periodic openings for those seeking an office and time between those openings is increasing for the reasons noted earlier. In addition, others on the ladder are calculating their own political time, which may conflict. Finally, with the new calculus that money politics (rather than party politics) brings to the political ladder, political interlopers can interrupt any "ordered" process of political advancement by buying their way into the political system at the very top.

Is the concept of political time a real factor? Yes. Just ask any political consultant and most savvy politicians. I once asked former North Carolina governor Terry Sanford (1961-1965) why the 1972 Democratic candidate lost the state's gubernatorial election, the first to do so in this century. His answer was very simple and to the point: "It wasn't his turn." Why? The Democratic candidate, Hargrove "Skipper" Bowles, who had held no previous elective office, had won the gubernatorial nomination by defeating incumbent lieutenant governor Pat Taylor in the Democratic primary. Because he pushed Taylor out of line, Bowles lost critical support from members of his own party and was beaten by Republican Jim Holshouser in the general election.

Although political time is relatively short for any one individual, it becomes prohibitively long for legislators and others aspiring to higher office when gubernatorial terms are lengthened. What do ambitious politicians do when this happens? Most probably move their ambitions elsewhere, even if it means leaving the political system. If this is true, the reformers' objective to give governors longer terms in which to achieve their goals may have led to the unanticipated result of shunting off into other careers individuals who might have vied for the governorship or who might have stayed in the state's political ambition system and tried to move up the political ladder. This ambition shift is hard to measure, but the cries that there are too few good candidates in many states suggests that something like this could be afoot.

Experience suggests that a one-term limit combined with a four-year term can open up the governorship more frequently, thus potentially retaining in the system a greater number of those with ambition. Clearly, however, a two-year term limit combined with a four-year term has not had this effect.

Gubernatorial Career Paths

If the opportunity structure at the top of the ballot changes in the states, the paths to the governorship may change also. Taking the concept of political time and reduced opportunities due to term limits— both lodged in constitutions and in politics—as givens, the route to the governorship is being reduced to those who can "bide their time" in meaningful political positions and be ready to strike when the political time is right for them.

To examine this hypothesis, I explored Schlesinger's analysis of the penultimate office held in the path to the governorship. Table 8-6 presents those last-step positions for three separate periods: 1900-1958, 1970-1991, and the last cycle of gubernatorial elections, 1988-1991. The first period (1900-1958) immediately precedes the spate of state government reform beginning in the 1960s; the second (1970-1991) can be said to show the effects of that reform, if any. The final period (1988-1991) tells us what has happened most recently in the last full cycle of gubernatorial elections.

Overall, there was greater diversity in the last step on the gubernatorial career ladder in the first half of the twentieth century than there has been in the last two decades. Some offices have decreased in stature (law enforcement and state administrative), while others have increased in stature (statewide elective) or stayed about the same (state legislature, federal elective, and no prior office). The last category of no prior office indicates those who, in effect, start at the top.

The most recent cycle of gubernatorial elections (1988-1991) shows a rather stark pattern. There were three major penultimate positions for these newly elected governors: statewide elective (46 percent), those with no prior office experience (21 percent), and federal elective (18 percent). These categories account for twenty-four of the twenty-eight new governors (86 percent) over the four-year period.

Among those thirteen whose last step was a statewide elective office are four former governors, three each of lieutenant governors and secretaries of state, two treasurers and one auditor. Among those five whose last step was a federal elective office are three former U.S. senators and two former U.S. representatives. The six with no prior office still had fairly high name recognition in the state or sufficient funds to create that recognition. The winning race for two was preceded by an unsuccessful attempt at the office that helped in developing name recognition.[23]

If this most recent cycle of gubernatorial election results is a preview for the 1990s and beyond, we can guess the future calculus of those seeking the governorship. First, winning and holding a major statewide office is of paramount importance on the ladder to the top. Second, rather than using the state career ladder to reach top positions in the U.S. Congress, winning and holding a national legislative position for a period of time can be a most important step in seeking the top state elective position. Finally, if one has the drive and money to do so, it is possible to start at the top rather than climbing the political ladder.

TABLE 8-6   Changes in Gubernatorial Career Patterns, 1900-1991

Office held just prior to becoming governor	Number and percentage of governors					
	1900-1958		1970-1991		1988-1991	
	No.	%	No.	%	No.	%
Statewide elective	128	20	60	28	13	46
Law enforcement	124	19	30	14	1	4
State legislative	121	19	43	20	2	7
State administrative	85	13	13	6	0	0
Federal elective	61	10	26	12	5	18
No prior office	52	8	17	8	6	21
Local elective	44	7	11	5	1	4
Other	26	4	16	7	0	0
Totals	641	100	216	100	28	100

Sources: Joseph A. Schlesinger, *Ambition and Politics* (Chicago: Rand McNally, 1966), 91; and Thad L. Beyle, "Governors," in *Politics in the American States*, 5th ed., ed. Virginia Gray, Herbert Jacob and Robert B. Albritton (Glenview, Ill.: Scott Foresman, 1990), 206; and Michael Barone and Grant Ujifusa, *The Almanac of American Politics, 1992* (Washington, D.C.: National Journal, 1991).

Note: Newly elected governors only, not incumbents, are included.

We must be wary of drawing too much from the results of the last four elections in the cycle; they may be unique and prove not to be precursors. Further, other important influences on state politics at this level must be kept in mind. One is the shift from party politics to the politics of money and media, a trend founded on the decline of traditional political parties and their ability to structure political activities.

However, there is a ring of truth to the trends outlined above, which match the nature and style of politics of the day. The magic of name recognition leads to electoral success. Holding statewide office, being a federal office holder, or having considerable wealth or notoriety can create that magic.

Some Other Unintended Consequences: The Case of North Carolina

The recent political changes in tenure in North Carolina indicate another consequence of imposing limits on the term of governor. For most of the twentieth century there was a single four-year term limit for governors and lieutenant governors which led to constant movement at the very top of the state's political ladder. No governor came back after sitting out a term; and no former governor ran for or held one of the eight lesser offices filled by statewide election. Mobility was an up-and-out proposition.

Similarly, legislative leadership in the state house turned over every two years, creating movement there, up through the chairs. With the lieutenant governor serving as the chief legislative officer in the state senate, the leadership of that house turned over every four years. There has not been as much turnover in the other eight statewide elected executive offices, which tended to become career offices, held until an individual decided to retire or died. An extreme example was the fifty-two-year tenure of Thad Eure as North Carolina's secretary of state.

In 1977, Democratic governor Jim Hunt (1977-1985) proposed and received legislative approval to place a constitutional amendment on the ballot to allow governors and lieutenant governors to serve a second four-year term, effective immediately. This allowed Hunt to seek and win a second term in 1990. In fact, Hunt won legislative approval of the measure because he tied it to his own political future and the value of the promises that could be made to individual legislators by a long-serving governor.

Since then North Carolina has had only two governors—Hunt and Republican Jim Martin (1985-), both for two terms. And now Jim Hunt is seeking his third term in the office in the 1992 elections. If he wins, Hunt could seek reelection in 1996 and serve out the rest of the twentieth century.

Since 1976, gubernatorial politics in North Carolina have involved only two incumbents. It is very possible that they will be the only governors serving the state for the last quarter of the twentieth century. In contrast, between 1900 and 1976 twenty individuals served in the office. In response to this change in tenure on the executive side, the legislature changed its process of selecting leaders. In the state house, speakers began to hold multiple two-year terms. The first to do so was Carl Stewart of the western Piedmont, who left after two terms to run unsuccessfully for governor in 1980. Stewart was followed by Liston Ramsey, from the mountains, who stayed for four terms and left only after a 1989 coup d'etat led by twenty dissident Democrats and all of the Republicans except one, a close friend of Ramsey.

His successor, Josephus Mavretic from the eastern part of the state and a key actor in the coup, was able to hold on for just one term as the Democratic side of the coalition fell apart. He was succeeded in 1991 by Dan Blue of Raleigh, who received broad support among all Democrats. It is not clear whether the many-term pattern has been changed back to a shorter stay, involving more people in the process, or whether Blue will reinstate the multiterm pattern by seeking a second term in 1993 and additional terms thereafter.

In the state senate, leadership also changed as the lieutenant governor could now serve a second four-year term as the chief presiding officer. The second-term possibility has been realized only once. In 1980 Lieutenant Governor Jimmy Green, elected in 1976, was able to win reelection and thus served eight years as presiding officer. The other two lieutenant governors elected since the change in tenure limits have sought the governorship after serving one term. Not insignificantly, the senate's rules have been changed to reduce the power of the lieutenant governor in that body.

Some observers argue that one of the major effects of the prolongation of gubernatorial service has been the loss of the candidacies of some who could not afford to wait around for the chance to run for governor. Under the changed limits, there are just too few opportunities. These observers fear that the state has lost the services of some fine potential leaders who have turned elsewhere to seek fame and fortune. Certainly, the change has shaken up some tidy patterns of selecting legislative leadership.

Conclusion

On average, and in accord with the explicit goals of state government reformers, constitutional changes in the states over the last third of this century have permitted longer tenure in office for recent governors. The vast institutional differences between the executive and legislative branches dictate great caution in applying lessons drawn from one to the other. However, the correlation in recent years between the extension of term limits for governor and longer, not shorter, service by individuals in the governorship, does suggest that, in considering the potential effect of term limits for legislators, analysts need to carefully weigh the precise nature of the provisions by which limits are imposed and the context in which they will apply. Term limits cannot be assessed in isolation. The way they work in any system is linked to a number of other factors; for example, term length, the length of the limits, the manner in which personal ambitions are structured by the political system, and the competitiveness of the system.

Term limits on governors—constitutional, personal, and political—can be effective in bringing in new people with "fresh ideas." But because of the reform-driven move to longer gubernatorial terms (two four-year terms), these new faces and "fresh ideas" appear less often than in the past and enter by different paths.

Should we argue for shorter terms and tighter restrictions on how many terms an individual can serve as governor of a state? No, for the very reasons adduced by those who have backed the reforms to give governors more authority. But we should be aware of the basic trade-offs we create when adopting these reforms: fewer gubernatorial elections of real moment, fewer new individuals in the governor's chair, and a reduced pool of potential candidates for the position. The more important questions may revolve around how we can widen the sources of gubernatorial candidates and the pools from which they come.

Notes

1. Terry Sanford, *Storm Over the States* (New York: McGraw-Hill, 1967), 190.
2. Advisory Commission on Intergovernmental Relations, *The Question of State Government Capability* (Washington, D.C.: ACIR, 1985), 128-129.
3. Sanford, 191.
4. Advisory Commission on Intergovernmental Relations, 128-129.
5. Mark E. Tompkins, "Changing the Terms: Gubernatorial Term Reform in the Modern Era" (paper presented to 1991 annual meeting of the Southern Political Science Association, Tampa, Fla., November 1991), 17.
6. Larry Sabato, *Goodbye to Good-time Charlie: The American Governorship Transformed,* 2d ed. (Washington, D.C.: CQ Press, 1983), 105.
7. Tompkins, "Changing the Terms," 6. Andrus left office to serve as U.S. secretary of the interior in the Carter administration and Bellmon served two terms as a U.S. senator. Wallace was reelected to office after complying with term limits in that state's constitution. Clinton, Dukakis, and Perpich were reelected to office after having been defeated in an earlier attempt for reelection.
8. Russell M. Ross, "The Gubernatorial Transition in Iowa, 1982-83," in *Gubernatorial Transitions: The 1982 Elections,* ed. Thad L. Beyle (Durham, N.C.: Duke University Press, 1985), 184-185.
9. For similar rates for other offices, see Gerald Benjamin, "The Power of Incumbency," *Empire State Report* (April 1987): 33-37; Rich Jones, "Legislative Elections in Six States Barely Change Partisan Makeup," *State Legislatures* 14:1 (January 1988), 20-21; and Karl Kurtz, "No Change—For a Change," *State Legislatures* 15:1 (January 1989), 29.
10. Diane D. Blair, "Two Transitions in Arkansas, 1978 and 1982," in Beyle, *Gubernatorial Transitions: The 1982 Elections,* 96.
11. Those deciding not to seek reelection were Dukakis in Massachusetts, O'Neill in Connecticut, and Madeleine Kunin in Vermont (D, 1985-1991). Edward DiPrete (R-R.I.) lost his bid for a fourth term.
12. Thirty-six gubernatorial elections have been held in each of the even nonpresidential years of 1970, 1974, 1978, 1982, 1986, and 1990.
13. Only New Jersey and Virginia held elections in 1973, 1977, 1981, 1985, and 1989. Kentucky, Louisiana, and Mississippi held their gubernatorial

elections in 1971, 1975, 1979, 1983, 1987, and 1991. Kentucky, Mississippi, and Virginia have a one-term limitation, although beginning with the 1987 election Mississippi governors could seek a second term. New Jersey has a two-term limitation.

14. Hugh A. Bone, "Record Setting Incumbent Retires in Washington State," *Comparative State Politics Newsletter* 9:6 (December 1988), 2-3.

15. The states with these limits were Alabama, Hawaii, Kansas, New Mexico, North Carolina, Ohio, Pennsylvania, and South Dakota. *The Book of the States, 1990-91* (Lexington, Ky.: The Council of State Governments, 1990), 96. See also Gail B. Manning and Edward F. Feigenbaum, *The Lieutenant Governor: The Office and Its Powers* (Lexington, Ky.: The Council of State Governments, 1987), 3-4.

16. Jack Betts, "The Department of the Secretary of State: Which Way Now?" *North Carolina Insight* 11:4 (August 1989), 5.

17. As of 1991, there are actually thirty-two states with unlimited terms, but the winner of the 1994 election in Colorado will be able to serve with no limit.

18. Alaska, Hawaii, New Mexico as of the 1990 election, and Oregon permit two consecutive terms. Indiana limits service to eight years in twelve.

19. Kathy Tyson, ed., *Secretary of State: The Office and Duties* (Lexington, Ky.: The Council of State Governments, 1991), Table 1.2.

20. Lynne M. Ross, ed., *State Attorneys General: Power and Responsibilities* (Washington, D.C.: Bureau of National Affairs, 1990), Table 1.

21. Rob Gurwitt, "California's John Garamendi: Insurance Commissioner for Life?" *Governing* 4:4 (January 1991), 13.

22. Joseph A. Schlesinger, *Ambition and Politics: Political Careers in the United States* (Chicago: Rand McNally, 1966).

23. The former governors are Walter Hickel (R-Alaska, 1966-1969, 1991-), Edwin Edwards (D-La.), Bruce King (D-N.M., 1971-1975, 1979-83, 1991-), and Richard Snelling (R-Vt., 1977-1985, 1991). The three lieutenant governors are Brereton Jones (D-Ky., 1991-), Bob Miller (D-Nev., 1989-) and Douglas Wilder (D-Va., 1990-); and the secretaries of state are Jim Edgar (R-Ill., 1991-), Evan Bayh (D-Ind., 1989-), and Barbara Roberts (D-Ore., 1991-). The two treasurers are Joan Finney (D-Kan., 1991-) and Ann Richards (D-Texas, 1991), and the auditor is Arne Carlson (R-Minn., 1991-). One other secretary of state was elected to the governorship (Rose Mofford, D-Ariz., 1988-1991) upon the impeachment of Governor Evan Mecham; she is not included here as she did not seek election to the office. The three U.S. senators are Pete Wilson (R-Calif., 1991-), Lowell Weiker (I-Conn., 1991), and Lawton Chiles (D-Fla., 1991-). The two representatives are Judd Gregg (R-New Hamp., 1989-) and Jim Florio (D-N.J., 1990-). Those with no prior state elective experience are Fife Symington (R-Ariz., 1991-), Kirk Fordice (R-Miss., 1992-), Ben Nelson (D-Neb., 1991-), David Walters (D-Okla., 1991-), Bruce Sundlin (D-R.I., 1991-), and Gasper Caperton (D-W.Va., 1989-). The two who failed once before succeeding were David Walters (D-Okla.) and Bruce Sundlin (D-R.I.).

9. A COMMENT ON COMPETITION AND CAREERS

Linda L. Fowler

The message of the previous chapters is that it is extremely difficult to generalize about the consequences of term limitations. Clearly, the impact is going to be highly variable by state and by the level of office. What happens in the nonprofessionalized legislature of Colorado will be very different from what is likely to occur in the highly professionalized legislature of New York, and both results will be dissimilar from what happens in the U.S. Congress. But I think it is possible to step back a bit and examine the assumptions about politicians and elections that guide the advocates of term limitations. My comments, therefore, will focus on two questions: Will term limitations really bring a different kind of person into office? And will they foster more electoral competition?

I would answer "no" to both of these questions because I believe that the reform proposals are being put forward in a political vacuum. We are talking about changing one part of the political system and leaving the rest untouched. Term limitations will do nothing to alter voters' expectations about their elected representatives, nor will they create a political context that is more conducive to competitive elections. At best, the proposal is misguided and at worst it will probably leave legislatures in worse shape.

First, term limitations do not address voters' desire to have attentive representatives—particularly their expectation for access, casework, and concern for local interests. All of these aspects of the lawmakers' job are mentioned by term-limitation advocates as being part of the corruption associated with a professionalized legislature. But they are also a big part of what citizens say they think their legislators should be doing. Without changing these expectations, it is not clear to me that reformers will get a sensible match between the voters' desire for someone to bring home the bacon and the incentives confronting legislators to be responsive.

Moreover, as long as we have entrepreneurial, candidate-based politics in this country, it seems unreasonable to think that term limitations will do anything to spur electoral competition. We will still have media-dominated campaigns, weak party organizations, and candidates who are forced to rely on their own skills in selling their personal attributes to the electorate.

This situation should make people stop and think, because skillful political entrepreneurs need incentives to take electoral risks, just as skillful business entrepreneurs need incentives in the private marketplace. What you do when you impose term limitations, however, is to remove the most fundamental incentive for people to engage in political entrepreneurship by saying to potential candidates: "You can take all these risks, but there will be no payoff. You will not be in a position to capitalize on your investment." So, it seems to me that one of the fundamental matters we have to think about is the political context in which these reforms are being introduced. If we do not change that context by changing the other variables affecting competition, then some rather perverse and unintended consequences are likely to flow from term limits.

Let me suggest what some of these consequences might be. First, will a different *kind* of politician run for legislative office? I think not. If you look at an historical analysis of the backgrounds of lawmakers throughout the nineteenth century[1]—when we had norms of voluntary term limitation that were often reinforced by party fiat—you will see that the country basically had the same political class of legislators as it has now. Members of Congress were lawyers or otherwise well-educated, higher-status, white males, just as they are today. When I look at two hundred years of data and see that we have always drawn our lawmakers from the same social stratum, it is hard for me to believe that term limitations are going to alter the composition of the legislature very much.

There is one possible exception to what I have just said, however. I do think that women will benefit selectively from term limits. In states such as New York, Pennsylvania, and Massachusetts, where you have a real mismatch between the pool of women in lower-level offices and the number of congressional seats available, it is very difficult for women to gain entry into the state legislature, from which they might subsequently run for Congress. In states with lots of House seats but few eligible women to run, term limits might encourage the emergence of female candidates. But women are not going to gain by this reform across the board, however, because the more basic problem remains: too few women run in most states—in either primaries or open seat races—to produce significant increases in the number of female office holders.

What I do see happening as a consequence of term limits is that the gatekeepers to political resources will have a disproportionate say in who gets nominated—even more than they have now. As long as we still have entrepreneurial politics, the potential candidates who can raise early money—particularly preemptive money that keeps other contestants from entering a primary—will emerge on top. And they will be the candidates who are most closely involved with the keepers of political capital—the well-endowed interest groups or affluent corporations. I can easily see a situation in which we would have the representative from Exxon or the National Education Association, because people with those kinds of ties would have an extraordinary advantage during the initial stages of a campaign, when the emphasis is on gaining recognition, gathering endorsements, creating a volunteer organization to get on the ballot, getting seed money for polling, and so forth. Thus, under term limits, the financial gatekeepers will in all probability be more rather than less important in elections, particularly at the congressional level.

These gatekeepers will not be interested in getting "average citizens"—people like you and me—to run for Congress. Rather, they will be drawn to politicians who have their own money or who are already plugged into the existing interest group structure. What is more troubling is the fact that backers will have the opportunity to demand more from the politicians who do get elected. Having gotten their own kind into office, they will be in a position to offer them positions out of office—after the term limits take effect. Look at what happens now to members of Congress and to state legislators when they leave office. Do they go home? No, they stay in Washington or the state capital. And what do they do? They use their knowledge of the legislative system, as well as their contacts inside the legislature and bureaucracy, to make a living. Viewed from this perspective, I think term limits could mean even more, rather than less, influence peddling in the national and state capitals because both the recruitment process and the "de-recruitment" process for legislators would create perverse incentives.

Will term limits lead to more competition? Although there is a notion among reformers that lots of people are out in the community just waiting for public office if only the incumbents would get out of the way, I think this view is naive.

First, we know from looking at nineteenth century data that incumbents have always had an advantage in running for election. Indeed, 80 percent of them were reelected in that period, if they chose to run. The big source of turnover in the good old days came from voluntary retirement and party-imposed rotation, not defeat at the polls. It is fair to say, therefore, that whenever an incumbent runs, he or she will still have an enormous advantage. And presumably under term limits, most districts will still have an incumbent running. With mandatory retirement looming, potential challengers will have every reason to wait for an open seat, just as they do now. Thus, term limits could end up decreasing the average level of competition for those incumbents who are eligible to seek reelection.

Second, much of my research has been on the supply of candidates in House districts and how various structural, community-level variables affect whether or not people think they can run successfully for a seat in Congress. These influences include the shape of the district and the range of offices that provide potential candidates with a natural political base inside the district. Certainly, as the country continues to reapportion seats after each census, fewer and fewer districts bear any resemblance to natural political communities. And as long as we continue to draw lines purely on the basis of numerical equality, it is hard to see how term limits will induce more politicians to look at these districts and say: "That district has my name on it. That is a place where I can run and win."

Furthermore, other aspects of a district's political geography untouched by the reform will continue to affect the supply of candidates. One important factor, for example, is whether or not there are affordable and efficient media markets in the district that candidates can use to make themselves known to the voters. Another factor is the existence of a party grass-roots organization—particularly on the Republican side. In fact, I think that Republicans will pay a heavy price under term limits because they do not have strong party organizations at the local level. Lacking such networks to identify and encourage political talent, the GOP is going to have difficulty sustaining the constant stream of candidates that will be needed once term limits are in effect.

Lastly, I think we have to consider how the personal costs of running for office affect the supply of prospective candidates. Potential lawmakers will still have the burden of losing their privacy and time with their families if they run for office. But these drawbacks will not be offset by any gains in power or prestige over the long run. So much investment with so little prospect of return is bound to turn off many good candidates.

In the presence of these structural influences on the supply of would-be office seekers, which advocates of term limitations ignore, I can only conclude that increased electoral competition is not their only purpose. I have to look, therefore, for their hidden agenda. What I see are Republicans attempting to legislate Democrats out of office because they have not been able to dislodge them in head-to-head competition. Yet, here too, the effort is misplaced, because incumbency is far from being the Republicans' only electoral obstacle. They have not fared well over the past decade in open seat races at either the state or federal level. Therefore, proponents of term limits who think they will help the GOP carry out its partisan program are probably misguided.

Perhaps there is one other agenda at the bottom of the term-limitation movement—the promotion of a strong executive at the expense of the legislative branch. Here, I am reminded of Thad Beyle's suggestion that term limitations for governors were initiated in order to weaken state executives and subordinate them to the legislative branch. It seems likely, therefore, that reformers hope to cut the members of Congress and state legislatures down to size so that they will have to do what presidents and governors want. Because I believe that legislatures ultimately are what make democracies work, I simply cannot support a reform whose likely consequence is to turn legislators into obedient puppets.

Note

1. Allan G. Bogue, Jerome M. Clubb, Carroll R. McKibbin, and Santa Traugott, "Members of the House of Representatives and the Process of Modernization: 1789-1960," *Journal of American History* 63 (1976): 275-302.

Part IV

THE LIKELY EFFECTS ON LEGISLATURES AND ON GOVERNMENT

10. THE IMPACT OF TERM LIMITATIONS ON THE STATES: CUTTING THE UNDERBRUSH OR CHOPPING DOWN THE TALL TIMBER?

David H. Everson

Fewer than thirty years ago excessive membership turnover in state legislatures was considered to be a significant problem, the source of far too much amateurism in the legislative process. The remedy prescribed by political scientists? Make the job of the state legislator a more attractive career through legislative modernization and professionalization. The reformers of that era sought to do this by altering the incentives for service to recruit lawmakers who would stay around long enough to become seasoned professionals.

To a significant degree, the reformers achieved their objectives. Beginning in the 1960s, a great wave of legislative reform swept the states. By the 1980s it had clearly produced its intended effects: more professionalized state legislators and greater stability in the membership of state legislatures. Ironically, that very stability has led some critics of contemporary legislatures to conclude that legislative careerism is now a serious problem and that state legislators (along with members of Congress) have become obsessed with perpetuating themselves in office at the expense of the public.

In 1990, limiting congressional and state legislative terms suddenly became the political reform of choice. The cry went up to restore the citizen legislature by booting out career politicians at the national and state levels and keeping them out by enforcing term limits. The state legislative world had turned full circle. And, ironically, the reforms of the earlier period helped to bring about the very conditions which bred the current clamor for term limits.

Consequences of Term Limits: Heaven or Hell?

Discussions of the consequences of term limits have been largely conjectural to date.[1] Despite the lack of empirical analysis, there is no dearth of contradictory predictions about what will happen. The world after term limits is usually pictured in black or white terms.

The lack of empirical analysis undoubtedly stems from the absence of direct experience with legislative term limits. The limits passed in California, Colorado, and Oklahoma in 1990 were not retroactive, and

their full consequences may not be known for years. However, whatever
the predictions, unanticipated consequences of term limits are almost
certain, as Robert K. Merton warned us with respect to political reform
long ago.[2] And there is a corollary to the law of unanticipated
consequences: unanticipated nonconsequences. Political reform usually
fails to achieve either the heaven on earth described by its proponents or
the hell feared by its opponents. One reason for this is that the conditions
reformers wish to alter are usually the product of multiple causes and
reform usually focuses on a single factor. For example, in 1980, Illinois
voters reduced the size of the Illinois house of representatives by one third
(bringing the terms of fifty-nine state legislators to an abrupt halt),
abolished multimember districts, and ended cumulative voting. Proponents claimed the cutback would increase electoral competition and
legislative efficiency, and reduce legislative costs. Opponents argued that
it would decrease the representation of women and minorities. Neither
set of expectations has been fulfilled.[3]

This chapter will take a first cut at closing the empirical gap. Its
focus is the impact of term limits on state legislative membership and
leadership, with leadership broadly defined to include committee chairs.
The burden of my argument is that the effects of term limits will vary
from state to state depending upon at least two factors: the length of the
term limit imposed and the type of state legislature in which it is
imposed.

It seems obvious that differing lengths will have differing impacts,
yet the discussion of the effect of term limits has proceeded without
much attention to that factor. Moreover, some states have moved much
farther along the path of professionalism and have lower levels of
turnover than other states. We would expect term limits to have their
greatest effects in states that are highly professionalized and that
experience low turnover. Limits should have the least effect in states
with the opposite characteristics.

What would the state legislative world look like if term limits
were put into effect retroactively? Answering this question should give
us a rough sense of the likely effects of term limits, with at least two
caveats. To date, no states have adopted retroactive term limits.
Moreover, it is likely that in states that have adopted limits to take
effect some time in the future, legislators and legislatures will alter their
behavior in ways not yet predictable.

This study will not survey all states. Rather, three states—Illinois,
Minnesota, and West Virginia—have been selected for scrutiny because they represent different degrees of legislative professionalism and
different rates of turnover. For purposes of further simplification, this
preliminary analysis will be limited to lower houses.

Before turning to the analysis, it is instructive to review the recent history of legislative turnover in the state legislatures.

The Era of De Facto Term Limits

As noted above, there is a certain irony to the current drive for term limitations. We once had de facto term limits and deliberately got rid of them. By de facto, I mean that natural legislative turnover in the states continuously circulated new blood into the legislature and pumped out the old, one important goal of the current advocates of term limits.

The consequences of high membership turnover were deemed by many to be negative. Beginning in the late 1930s, many students of state legislatures deplored excessive instability in state legislative membership, with its presumed negative effects on the legislative process and policy outputs, while noting that involuntary retirement by electoral defeat was not the major problem. In his classic study of legislative turnover, Charles Hyneman argued:

> The real task is to find why so many [state] legislators . . . choose not to run again. Devices and arrangements which reduce the hazards of an election year to a minimum will still not give us a body of lawmakers rich in the experience of their trade. The state legislator must be made more happy in his career. . . . The key to rehabilitation of the legislative branch is in the nature of the legislator's job and his attitude toward it.[4]

Hyneman concluded that low pay and adverse working conditions were major causes of membership instability.

How much instability was there? As an extreme example of the high level of turnover under de facto term limits, the percentage of first termers in the Wisconsin senate in 1893 was eighty-five.[5] During the 1930s, the average turnover from session to session in all state legislatures was such that in every session about one of every two members in both chambers was a novice.[6] In 1957, over half of the Tennessee house had no prior legislative experience and the same was true for the Kentucky house in 1960.[7] In 1965, James David Barber reported that "the rate of turnover among state legislators is very high. More than half of the approximately 7,800 members must be replaced every other year."[8] As late as the 1960s, two of five state legislators were newcomers.[9]

In the view of the legislative modernizers, making the job of legislator more attractive by professionalizing it would entice talented, promising people into seeking legislative careers. The modernizers valued legislative careerism because it would provide the experience necessary for making informed legislative decisions. The underlying premise: an inexperienced legislator is a less effective legislator than the career professional. One is reminded of the college basketball coach's aphorism: the best thing about freshmen is that they become sophomores.

The basic reform critique of high turnover was quite simple: "It is difficult for any organization to function with a sizable portion of its membership being replaced every two years, as has been the case in many state legislatures during this century." [10] "Excessive" turnover in the legislature was deplored by those who wished to see state legislatures increase their capability: "Beginning with Hyneman's . . . initial study of the problem, most political scientists and journalists have expounded the idea that more stable memberships are necessary to produce less amateur legislatures and consequently better public policy." [11] As recently as twenty years ago, with turnover down substantially from prior levels, reformers still argued that "it is still hard to attract and then hold the most able men in legislative service. . . . After an average election, perhaps one-third of the members are replaced by newcomers. Nor is it certain that the best members make the legislature their career or stay long enough to make a real difference." [12]

A cornerstone of the reform argument was that time in service was needed for members to master the legislative process and to develop the specialized grasp of policy complexities necessary for legislative effectiveness. "Charles Hyneman's estimate is that three or four sessions are necessary for a legislator to learn enough background to participate effectively." [13] Hyneman argued that if Americans wanted better state legislatures, "they had better attract a substantial number of individuals to the legislative chamber for session after session of service." [14]

Reformers believed that modernizing the legislature would attract legislative craftsmen. Indeed, it was even argued that a modernized legislature was something like a graduate school for training public-policy experts. California was presented as an ideal type by William K. Muir: "It was a posh school, this California legislature, a special kind of school where the students were important . . . with the unmistakable air of the East Coast prep school to which the sons and daughters of the well-to-do went." Muir described the California legislators as learning by imitating their more experienced "tutors" and then by active participation in legislating. In his view, legislative experience was equivalent to getting an advanced degree in legislative process and public policy. In his conclusion, Muir rejected reform proposals that "legislative seats should be turned over more frequently" and argued against the theory that fresh blood is necessarily the most invigorating:

"While some freshmen were quick learners and achieved legislative recognition of their competence, the most resourceful legislators were likely to have been reelected from safe districts. . . . In fact it took years for legislators to become truly competent. And the more competent they became, the more they bubbled over with ideas." [15] Ironically, what Muir called the "best legislature" in the United States in the 1970s has now adopted the most severe term limits and reduced legislative professionalization by slashing staff.[16]

Beyond creating better legislators, the modernizers had another goal: to restore a perceived imbalance in the separation of powers in the states. Governors had become too dominant. The reformers wanted to reestablish the state legislature as a branch coequal with the executive.

The modernizers did not want state legislatures to be stable for the sake of stability. Their interest was in promoting the effectiveness of the legislative institution by encouraging more "lawmakers." This argument was logically extended to the absence of an effective legislative committee system in many states. The contention was that the capability of a committee system to play its role in the legislative process was heavily determined by the degree of stability in committee membership and continuity of committee leadership. Effective committees require members with experience in the subject matter of the committee. Explicitly or implicitly, the congressional model of strong committees was the standard against which state legislatures were compared.

Writing in the mid-1970s, Alan Rosenthal noted that "if state legislative committees seldom achieve expertness and influence comparable to that of their congressional counterparts, a principal reason is the high turnover of committee members." In Rosenthal's view, high turnover on committees had the undesirable consequences of impeding "specialization," preventing the "development of a stable leadership group," and undermining "committee influence." Rosenthal noted that "not only do committee members in state legislatures change frequently, but chairmen rotate rapidly as well." [17] This confirmed what Hyneman had found in his study of legislative turnover: only 30 percent of committee chairs had as much as four terms' experience in the legislature and nearly 20 percent were in their first session.[18]

An empirical link was established between turnover in the legislature as a whole and committee inexperience. Rosenthal identified "legislative membership change" as the factor of "greatest importance" in producing the variations "in the rates of turnover of committee members and chairmen in legislatures throughout the states." His analysis showed that "legislator turnover and change in chairmen vary together, [although] they are by no means perfectly associated." [19]

Further research by Basehart substantiated the finding of the relationship of membership stability and committee stability. He examined legislative membership stability and the continuity of the members and chairmen of state legislative committees. In general, he found that legislative "membership stability is closely associated with the other indicators of [committee] experience and stability." He also found that the relationships were weakened by partisan changes and legislature size so that "increases in membership stability will have the greatest effect in state legislatures that have few partisan changes and a small membership." [20]

Triumph of the Modernizers

As we now know, the legislative modernizers carried the day. Many, if not most, state legislatures took steps in the direction of legislative professionalization and modernization in the 1960s, 1970s, and 1980s. These steps included providing professional staff, legislative offices and secretarial support, higher salaries, and legislative pensions.

> In 1988, there were over 33,000 staffers working in state legislatures, 40 percent of them full-time professionals. In 1990, all but seven states met in annual sessions. Legislative compensation has been increased in most states . . . and legislators in 42 states are eligible for retirement benefits.[21]

Rich Jones groups the states into three categories based on their level of professionalization: full-time professional, purely part-time, and states whose legislatures have some full-time characteristics but not all.[22]

Even prior to the full impact of state legislative reform, Ray's research on three legislatures showed a steady increase in various indicators of legislative stability in this century.[23] Recently, turnover has continued to decline. In the first half of the 1980s, average membership turnover in all state legislatures was around 25 percent, compared to the 50 percent figure of the 1930s and the 30 percent figure of the 1960s.[24] In the second half of the decade, turnover appears to have dipped even more. In 1988, average turnover was about 20 percent in state houses.[25]

Nonetheless, two additional points need to be made here. First, turnover varies substantially among the states. Contrast, for example, the Pennsylvania and West Virginia houses in 1988: 13 percent versus 45 percent. Second, the cumulative effect of turnover even in states with relatively low session-to-session turnover is substantial. In the three states that have adopted term limits to date—Colorado, California, and Oklahoma—house membership has turned over "89 percent or more in the twelve-year period from 1977 to 1989." [26] Pennsylvania, a professionalized state legislature with one of the lower rates of session-to-session turnover in its lower house, still had a 68 percent turnover rate in the decade of the 1980s. At the other end of the spectrum, West Virginia, a citizen legislature with high session-to-session turnover, had 90 percent turnover for the decade—legal term limits could hardly do a better job of "house cleaning." [27]

At this point, it is important to note that a high level of natural turnover from session to session does not necessarily produce the precise equivalent of the effects of mandatory term limitations, which affect every legislator and every district. The fact that one of every two members of a state legislature is new in every session is not inconsistent with a high level of stability in some portion of the membership: "Two legislatures could have the same turnover rate and have different average years of consecutive service—for instance, if one body has the same seats turning over each election and the other body loses members from a different set of districts each time." [28] As David Ray discovered in his historical examination of membership stability in three state legislatures, "average prior service sometimes varies directly and sometimes inversely with the number of freshman legislators." [29] This is an important caveat and suggests the need to examine whether the leadership of a state legislature might be quite stable while the membership is fluid. It also suggests that natural as opposed to enforced turnover might combine a mix of experience and youth in the same body.

Effects of Term Limits

Types of States

It seems reasonable to assume that the effects of term limits will vary depending on the degree to which states already have high turnover. The consequences for members and leaders in low-turnover states should be greater. In high-turnover states, we may discover that "natural" term limits currently produce results substantially similar to those that formal limits would produce. However, we must also ask whether, even in high-turnover states, there is an entrenched legislative leadership that may be the actual target of the limiters.

In addition to the rate of turnover, we would expect that states that have moved along the path from citizen legislatures to legislative modernization and professionalization would be more affected than states that have not. "If the intended consequence of term limitations is to open more seats by substantially reducing the number of 'old timers,' it will achieve this goal primarily in the professional state legislatures." [30] These two characteristics—low turnover and high professionalization—tend to overlap but do not do so completely.

Lengths of Term Limits

A second factor, length of the limits, should make a significant difference in the impact of term limits. Research suggests that, on average, a little under half of the state house members have left the legislature after serving six years, the length of the California limits; just under 75 percent have left after twelve years, the Oklahoma limits.[31] The impact of the stringent California-style limits, then, should affect many more legislators than would the relatively lenient limits of Oklahoma.

Our analysis will use the three different term limits that have been adopted to illustrate the consequences of the differences.

Again, the three legislative bodies chosen for analysis are the lower houses of Illinois, Minnesota, and West Virginia. The three share two similarities. First, they are approximately the same size: 118, 134, and 100 members respectively. Second, they have been dominated by Democratic party majorities in recent years. However, with regard to legislative turnover and the degree of professionalization of the state legislature the states provide sharp contrasts.

Illinois can lay some claim to being a representative state. It has often been called the political microcosm of the nation, largely because voting in presidential elections in Illinois closely parallels national trends.[32] More directly to the point, it may well represent one end of a continuum of state legislative membership stability and professionalization. Illinois has one of the most professionalized state legislatures in the nation. In the mid- to late 1960s, there was a strong legislative modernization movement in Illinois.[33] As early as 1971, Illinois was ranked as one of the three most capable state legislatures.[34] In 1990, Burdett A. Loomis reported that "the Illinois Legislature ranks in the top ten among the fifty states in each of three categories: professionalism . . . percentage of full-time legislators, and low turnover of membership." [35] In quantity of professional staff, the Illinois General Assembly ranks sixth in the nation.[36]

Illinois has annual legislative sessions, although the off-year session is theoretically confined to budgetary and emergency legislation. In 1991, the legislature met for at least one day in eight months of the year. Nearly half of the members of the general assembly consider themselves to be full-time legislators.

Hyneman argued that the state legislative career needed to be made more attractive. Illinois legislators are well-compensated. "In 1990 they received salaries that ranged from a base of $35,600 annually to $51,600, increasing with committee and party leadership roles; four-fifths of all lawmakers received a 'leadership' stipend of at least $6,000." In addition, Illinois legislators "receive $65 per day in expenses when the legislature is in session, health insurance, a generous pension plan and $47,000 per year for district offices." [37] Moreover, if Illinois state legislators serve twenty years, they receive a pension of $2,500 per month.

Turnover was low even before the legislative modernization movement took hold in the state:

> What the record shows ... is that from 1931 to 1978, Illinois ranked third among the states in terms of stability of combined House and Senate membership, behind only New York and California. During that period, the overall turnover in the Illinois General Assembly averaged 25.2 percent as compared to a composite average of 40.4 percent for all the fifty state legislatures. [38]

More recently, turnover has declined further. In 1988, for example, turnover in the Illinois house was 8 percent. However, as noted above, one must be careful not to equate low turnover per election to a low level of turnover over time. Of the thirty-eight new Illinois house members seated in 1978-1979, only eleven remained in 1989-1990, a mere 30 percent. [39] Thus, even in a professionalized and low-turnover state such as Illinois, the cumulative effect of election-to-election turnover and reapportionment/redistricting can be quite substantial.

In contrast to that of Illinois, the Minnesota legislature has been classified as mixed, or hybrid, in terms of its degree of modernization. [40] As a practical matter, the Minnesota legislature meets in annual sessions from January to mid-May. The legislators have a substantial staff. However, annual legislative salaries in Minnesota run almost ten thousand dollars below those in Illinois and pensions after twenty years are less than half of those in Illinois. Turnover in the Minnesota house from 1981 to 1985 was close to the national average and significantly higher than in Illinois. [41] More recently, in 1988, turnover in the Minnesota house was 13 percent compared to 8 percent in Illinois. Of the forty-two new members of the Minnesota house in 1979-1980, exactly one-quarter were left twelve years later, slightly lower than the national average. [42]

West Virginia's lower house is classified as a citizen legislature, for good reason. [43] It meets in annual sessions for sixty days. Legislative staff support is minimal. Few West Virginia legislators regard the

TABLE 10-1 Impact of Retroactive Term Limits on House Membership in Illinois, Minnesota, and West Virginia—Percentage of Current Membership Excluded on the Basis of Retroactive Term Limits

Type of state legislature	*6-term limit*	*4-term limit*	*3-term limit*	*Difference between high and low figures*
Professionalized (Ill.) (n = 118)	29%	52%	63%	34%
Hybrid (Minn.) (n = 134)	22	37	54	32
Citizen (W.Va.) (n = 100)	14	28	40	26
All three states (n = 352)	22	37	53	31
Difference between high and low figures	15	24	23	

Sources: Handbook of the Illinois Legislature, 1990; Official Directory of the Minnesota Legislature, 1989-1990; West Virginia Manual of the Senate and House of Delegates, 1989-1990.

legislature as a career. The annual legislative salary in West Virginia is $6,500 per year, and the pension after 20 years is $217 per month. Session-to-session and cumulative turnover is extremely high. After twelve years, three of the thirty-four members of the 1978-1979 cohort in the West Virginia house remained in office. In the West Virginia house, truly, "the term limit bell will toll for few." [44]

Effects of Retroactive Limits on Membership

What impact would retroactive term limits of differing lengths have on the full house membership in the three types of states? Table 10-1 examines this question. First, consider the impact in the three states combined. Twenty-two percent of all house members in the three states would be affected by retroactive six-term (twelve-year) limits. This is very close to the 23 percent figure taken from a similar analysis based on twenty-one states, giving us some confidence that the data from these three states are not hopelessly out of line with those of other states.[45] With limits half as long (three terms or six years), more than twice as many of the members in the three states, over half, would be affected.

The breakdown by length of terms strongly confirms our expectations about the impact of the various term lengths on the various types of state legislatures. In each case, the length of term is a significant factor. The percentage of members affected increases as the limits for each state contract. The cumulative difference between six-term limits and three-term limits for the three states is 31 percent. The importance of the length of the limits can be illustrated in this way: six-term limits would retroactively affect only 29 percent of the professionalized Illinois house members, but three-term limits would affect 40 percent of the West Virginia citizen house. Although not unexpected, this finding adds to our understanding of the likely impact of various lengths of limits.

Notice also that the impact of limits is always greatest—no matter what the term length—in professional Illinois and least in citizen West Virginia, with Minnesota in between. The average difference for the three different term length limits proposed between Illinois and West Virginia is 21 percent. However, at the opposite extreme, six-term limits would affect only 14 percent of the West Virginia house membership and three-term limits, 63 percent of the Illinois house membership. Again, the hybrid, Minnesota, falls neatly in the middle, the percentages for it almost duplicating the three-state averages.

Table 10-1 permits us to conclude that (1) varying the length of term limits will have a substantial impact in all three types of states, and (2) any term limits will have greater effects in professionalized states, lesser effects in hybrid states, and minimal effects in citizen states.

Effects on Leadership

The most obvious effects of term limits would seem to be in the area of legislative leadership, broadly construed. As Florida house speaker T. K. Wetherell put it: "Term limits are like clear-cutting old forests. They don't bother the underbrush much, but they're hell on the tall timber." [46] Moncrief and Thompson agree: "We expect term limitations to affect those presently in leadership positions." [47] Their research on twenty-one states strongly supported that proposition: "More than half ... of the major house leadership positions are occupied by legislators with more than twelve years of experience. Almost 38 percent of all committees are chaired by legislators with more than twelve years of service." [48]

We would expect, however, that the effects on leadership would be even greater in professional states like Illinois and less in citizen states like West Virginia. Moncrief and Thompson found that legislators in professional legislatures did tend to stay around longer; it is a straightforward extension to assume this should apply to leaders as well. For example, in Illinois, House Speaker Michael J. Madigan was first elected in 1970; his counterpart, Minority Leader Lee Daniels, was first elected in 1974.

TABLE 10-2   Impact of Retroactive Term Limits on Leaders of the Lower House in Illinois, Minnesota, and West Virginia

Type of state legislature	6-term limit	4-term limit	3-term limit	Difference between high and low figures
Professionalized (Ill.) (n = 40)	73%	73%	93%	20%
Hybrid (Minn.) (n = 33)	59	85	90	31
Citizen (W. Va.) (n = 19)	16	27	52	36
Difference between high and low figures	57	58	41	

Sources: *Handbook of the Illinois Legislature*, 1990; *Official Directory of the Minnesota Legislature*, 1989-1990; *West Virginia Manual of the Senate and House of Delegates*, 1989-1990.

There are now eighteen party "leaders" in the Illinois house. A second arena of legislative leadership is in the committee system. There are twenty-two committees in the Illinois house.

For purposes of this analysis, two types of leaders—party leaders and committee chairs—have been combined in Table 10-2 for the three states. The table compares the impact of the various term limits on leadership in the three legislatures. As before, the impact of the length of the limits can be observed: there is an average difference of 29 percent for the three states. Again, the type of state makes a difference: The average difference between professional Illinois and citizen West Virginia is 51 percent. However, the first irregularity in the data appears at the four-term limit, where the impact on leadership is greater in Minnesota than in Illinois. This may, in fact, be due to the recent expansion of the leadership ranks in Illinois. Overall, the impact of term limits on leadership in hybrid Minnesota is nearly as great as it is in professional Illinois.

Table 10-2 confirms the expectation that the impact of term limits on leadership in a state like West Virginia will be minimal, especially at the six-term (twelve-year) and four-term (eight-year) marks. In fact, at these limits, there is little more impact on West Virginia leadership than there is on the membership (see Table 10-1).

As a final and extreme contrast, consider that whereas six-term limits would affect just 14 percent of the house's entire membership in West Virginia, three-term limits would affect 93 percent of the leaders in Illinois.

Hypotheses, Not Conclusions

These findings from three states provide examples of anticipated consequences, unanticipated consequences, and nonconsequences of term limits. It seems appropriate to be modest about conclusions from research based on just three states. The "conclusions" are more appropriately stated as hypotheses. Four seem warranted at this point:

1. **Anticipated consequences.** The data on these three states— representing three types of legislature ranging from the professionalized legislature with low turnover to the citizen legislature with high turnover—confirm the expectation that the impact of term limits on the general membership of the chamber is significantly greater in the professionalized legislature and quite minimal in the citizen legislature, with hybrid legislatures coming out in the middle.

2. **Anticipated consequences.** In addition, the data support the supposition that the length of term limits imposed will make a significant difference, regardless of the type of legislature. Consider the column data in Table 10-1. In terms of the impact of three-term versus six-term limits, the average percentage differences in the three types of states are 34 percent (Illinois), 32 percent (Minnesota), and 26 percent (West Virginia). To put it another way, the impact of six-term limits in professionalized Illinois is relatively modest, affecting fewer than 30 percent of house members. However, three-term limits in citizen West Virginia would affect 40 percent of the membership.

3. **Unanticipated consequences.** In terms of the impact on leadership, the most important finding is that a hybrid legislature—Minnesota's—can be affected as much as a professionalized one—Illinois's. This finding—as well as the impact of the length of the limits noted above—elaborates the conclusion that "except in the most professional state legislatures, the term limit bell will toll for few." The key question is: which few? The answer in both Illinois and Minnesota: the leaders.

4. **Nonconsequences.** Finally, it should be noted that the impact of term limits in a state like West Virginia will be quite limited, even on the leadership, because high turnover results in "natural term limits." There just is not much tall timber to be cut in such a state.

Notes

1. Two important exceptions: Gary F. Moncrief and Joel A. Thompson, "The Term Limitation Movement: Assessing the Consequences for Female (and Other) State Legislators" (Paper delivered to the annual meeting of the Western Political Science Association, Seattle, Washington, March 20-23, 1991); and Gary F. Moncrief et al., "For Whom the Bell Tolls: Term Limits and State Legislatures," *Legislative Studies Quarterly*, forthcoming.

2. See Robert K. Merton, "The Unanticipated Consequences of Purposive Social Action," *American Sociological Review* 1 (1936): 894-904.

3. David H. Everson, "The Cutback at 10: Illinois House without Cumulative Voting and 59 Members," *Illinois Issues*, July 1991, 13-15.

4. Charles S. Hyneman, "Tenure and Turnover of Legislative Personnel," *Annals of the Academy of Political and Social Science* 23 (1938): 30-31.

5. David Ray, "Membership Stability in Three State Legislatures: 1893-1969," *American Political Science Review* 68 (1974): 108.

6. Richard G. Niemi and Laura R. Winski, "Membership Turnover in U.S. State Legislatures: Trends and Effects of Districting," *Legislative Studies Quarterly* 12 (1987): 118.

7. John C. Wahlke et al., *The Legislative System* (New York: Wiley, 1962), 491. Malcolm E. Jewell and Penny M. Miller, *The Kentucky Legislature* (Lexington: The University of Kentucky Press, 1988), 57.

8. James David Barber, *The Lawmakers* (New Haven: Yale University Press, 1965), 8.

9. Niemi and Winsky, "Membership Turnover," 118.

10. Peverill Squire, "Membership Stability in Legislatures," *Legislative Studies Quarterly* 13 (1988): 65.

11. Ibid., 65.

12. Alan Rosenthal, "The Scope of Legislative Reform," in *Strengthening the States: Essays on Legislative Reform*, ed. Donald G. Herzberg and Alan Rosenthal (Garden City, New York: Doubleday, 1972), 5.

13. Barber, *The Lawmakers*, 8.

14. Hyneman, "Tenure and Turnover of Legislative Personnel," 3.

15. William K. Muir, *Legislature* (Chicago: The University of Chicago Press, 1982), 16, 197.

16. See Chapter 6 of this volume and Richard C. Paddock, "Disaster or Democracy?" *State Legislatures* (July 1991): 22-26.

17. Alan Rosenthal, *Legislative Performance in the States* (New York: Free Press, 1974), 169, 170, 174.

18. Hyneman, "Tenure and Turnover of Legislative Personnel," 25.

19. Rosenthal, *Legislative Performance in the States*, 180-181.

20. Hubert Harry Basehart, "U.S. State Legislative Committees," *Legislative Studies Quarterly* 5 (February 1980): 66.

21. Rich Jones, "The Legislature 2010: Which Direction?" *State Legislatures* (July 1991): 23-24.

22. Ibid., 24.
23. Ray, "Membership Stability in Three State Legislatures," 111.
24. Niemi and Winsky, "Membership Turnover," 118.
25. Moncrief et al., "For Whom the Bell Tolls," 9.
26. Paddock, "Disaster or Democracy," 26.
27. Moncrief et al., "For Whom the Bell Tolls," Table 1.
28. Squire, "Membership Stability in Legislatures," 66.
29. Ray, "Membership Stability in Three State Legislatures," 110.
30. Moncrief et al., "For Whom the Bell Tolls," 7.
31. Ibid., Table 1.
32. David H. Everson, "Illinois: A Bellwether?" in *Almanac of Illinois Politics—1990,* ed. Jack R. Van Der Slik (Springfield, Illinois: Illinois Issues, 1990), 1-5.
33. Illinois Commission on the Organization of the General Assembly, *Improving the State Legislature* (Urbana: University of Illinois Press, 1967).
34. Citizens Conference on State Legislatures, *The Sometimes Governments: A Critical Study of Fifty American Legislatures* (New York: Bantam, 1973).
35. James D. Nowlan and Phillip M. Gonet, "The Legislature," in *Inside State Government in Illinois,* ed. James D. Nowlan (Chicago: Neltnor House, 1991), 65.
36. Van Der Slik, ed., *Almanac of Illinois Politics—1990,* 368.
37. Nowlan and Gonet, "The Legislature," 65.
38. Kwang S. Shin and David H. Everson, "What's the Turnover Rate in the Illinois Legislature?" *Illinois Issues* (May 1979): 18.
39. Moncrief et al., "For Whom the Bell Tolls," Table 1. This estimate may be slightly distorted by the fact that in 1980, just prior to the 1982 election, a constitutional initiative was adopted by Illinois voters that reduced the size of the Illinois house by one-third and abolished multi-member districts with cumulative voting. Several minority party representatives retired because they despaired of gaining reelection in the absence of cumulative voting. Many incumbents had to run against their incumbents in the new districts. Consequently, fourteen of the twenty-seven drop-outs from the class of 1978-1979 fell by the wayside in that one unusual election.
40. Ibid., Table 2.
41. Niemi and Winski, "Membership Turnover," 116-117.
42. Moncrief et al., "For Whom the Bell Tolls," Table 1.
43. Ibid., Table 2.
44. Ibid., 10.
45. Moncrief and Thompson, "The Term Limitation Movement," 4.
46. *The Gainesville Sun,* August 11, 1991, 4b.
47. Moncrief and Thompson, "The Term Limitation Movement," 2.
48. Ibid., 5.

11. THE EFFECTS OF TERM LIMITS ON LEGISLATURES: A COMMENT

Alan Rosenthal

Term limitations might have several effects on the legislature as an institution. The observations that follow are limited to state legislatures and are not meant to refer to Congress. Although my remarks will be general, it must be remembered that there are real differences among the states.

Parenthetically, I do not think there is any relationship between present conditions in the individual state legislatures and the desire to have term limits. That desire stems from a variety of motives, including anger at Congress. It would not be surprising if a term-limit movement began in New Hampshire, where the citizen legislature model is the strongest, not because such a movement was called for by legislative conditions but because it reflected the public's anger.

The first point to examine concerns what difference there will be in the kinds of people who serve in the legislature. There is good reason to doubt that the people will be very different from the members of today. People who go into politics do not think in terms of ten or fifteen years; they think in terms of what they want now and do not worry about tomorrow. Their time perspective has to be short, because they are subject to so many uncertainties.

Second, will there be a difference in the way people adjust to legislative life? I doubt there will be much difference in that either. Legislatures today are fairly malleable institutions. Of course, in New York, New Jersey, or Pennsylvania, it is better to be in the majority than the minority. Aside from that, nobody serves an apprenticeship anywhere. If you come in with an education program or a feminist agenda, you can accomplish a lot in a very short span of time. Legislators do not come in thinking "I have twenty years to do it." They want it now. They want instant gratification of their programmatic needs. It will be the same with term limits. The limits will not change the members' time perspectives significantly because the perspectives already are short.

A third subject would be in the members' information networks and the sources of their behavioral cues. There, the effects of term limits might be subtle, especially if a reduction in staff accompanies the limitation on terms, as is happening in California. If there are no senior members with more than six or seven years of service to serve as a repository of knowledge, then members may have to rely more on somebody like the old-time director of the office of legislative counsel, the nonpartisan staff agency in many states. The director, who typically had years of service, was powerful in the period before there were many staff or senior legislators specializing in policy domains. In Arkansas, for example, everyone would come to Marcus Holbrook and ask what to do. Holbrook, who prided himself on not making policy, advised them—and he gave good advice. Maybe lobbyists will play that role; I do not know. What develops will vary from state to state and the differences will be extraordinarily subtle.

Fourth, will term limits bring about any differences in the level of specialization or expertise? I doubt it. If there are any differences, they would also be subtle. Members already jump from committee to committee in order to get a chairmanship or vice-chairmanship, or to get from a minor committee to judiciary, or from judiciary to appropriations. We political scientists have a congressional picture in our heads in which the committee is a repository of expertise. That is not the way it is in state legislatures, nor should it be. There are a few expert legislators in each area, but only a few.

Even though we may not be cutting down on expertise and specialized knowledge with term limits, we will be reducing the level of general knowledge. In my opinion, the longer members are in, the more they learn. This is not true of everyone, but it is probably true of those who are skillful and like what they are doing. They get more savvy and more knowledgeable over time. Their judgment improves, too. But a lot of what they learn is political knowledge, not substantive knowledge about policy. That kind of knowledge is going to dissipate with term limits, and I do not know what will substitute for it. In addition, members today have time to build up their reputations and the respect they are accorded for their political knowledge and skills. Other members, therefore, turn to them for cues. Term limits afford legislators less time to develop such reputations. That is bound to affect the way members pick up their cues within the legislature. Consequently, it is also bound to affect the legislature's informal networks of leadership.

The fifth area is one where I do foresee significant change in a relatively short time: the internal distribution of power within the legislative body. Term limitations will accelerate the ongoing dispersion of power. For ten or twenty years, members have been becoming more individualistic as a result of the weakening of parties and the development of candidate-centered campaigns. Legislative reform and modernization have facilitated this by spreading the resources around. In the good old days, only a few people got to read the bills. They just were not available. Everybody can read bills now. Leaders had more control then. Today, resources are much more widely distributed, members put in more time, and the knowledge gap between the leaders and members is shrinking.

In addition, there have been a number of assaults made on leadership over the last five or ten years; for example, in North Carolina, Connecticut, Oklahoma, and, unsuccessfully, in California. With term limits, the tenure of leaders is naturally going to be extremely short, because members will not be willing to wait around. They will have little time to achieve a leadership position. One reason Speaker Tom Loftus ran for governor in Wisconsin was that he felt the hot breath of the Democratic caucus on him. He had been in for eight years. Some of the members wanted him out of the speakership because they wanted their turns.

There are still some strong leaders around—in New York, for instance. But even in New York, the leaders are not as strong as they were ten years ago. I would expect that this generation of strong leaders—Tom Murphy in Georgia, Phil Rock in Illinois, Vern Riffe in Ohio, and John Martin in Maine—will be succeeded by a generation of weaker leaders. With term limits, members are not going to tolerate anyone serving six, eight, ten, or twelve years as leader. The rest of the members will have very little time to wait for their own chances. No leader will be able to serve very long, and certainly not long enough to become even vaguely familiar with the job. Leadership will have to rotate—maybe even annually if the members have six-year term limits. Chairmanships will also rotate until committees mean very little. From some point of view this may be a dream to hope for; from another it is a horror story. But it is a real possibility.

So, term limits will mean that leaders' powers will be weakened still further. They will not have control over committee appointments; committees will generate on a rotational system. They will not control bills; members will manage their own bills. Calendaring will become automatic. The term-limited legislature will resemble the Indiana legislature when it was tied, with a Republican speaker one day and a Democratic speaker the next day. Everything passed in the house, although a lot of it was stopped in the senate. The little bills, the special-interest bills, probably will go through a kind of logrolling process, but the tough ones may well be stalemated.

My final point concerns the power of the legislature vis-a-vis the executive. A legislature needs some sort of responsible leadership to deal with the executive. Without effective legislative leaders, a governor can knock off the members one by one, buying them cheaply and easily. What you are going to see with term limits is a shift, generally speaking, back to executive dominance. Maybe that is good. Maybe that is what we need, but I doubt it. If that is what you want, term limits will get you there.

Gubernatorial dominance will be accompanied by bureaucratic dominance as well. The government will be ruled by bureaucrats building up their programs and their budgets without having to contend with strong legislatures. That will be a splendid irony for those advocates of term limits who prefer a small government.

12. LEGISLATURES AFTER TERM LIMITS

Michael J. Malbin and Gerald Benjamin

Most people support or oppose term limits because they believe that placing mandatory limits on terms will affect the way legislatures work and the policies they produce. Proponents and opponents fill the air with predictions, unconstrained by empirical evidence. In one respect, they are clearly right. Term limitations will make a difference. But what will that difference be?

To address that question, we have to begin by disabusing ourselves of the notion that prediction is easy. For one thing, we have already seen—in the introductory chapter to this volume—that term limitations come in many varieties. In addition, no statewide legislative term limit has yet taken effect. It is tough enough to untangle the effects of a structural change after the fact. To feel confident of one's predictions at this stage would be a sure sign of foolhardiness.

Nevertheless, it is important to try, for two reasons. First, the voters in a large number of states are being asked to change, or not change, their governing institutions on the basis of speculations that are already quoted in the political marketplace. We may not be able to settle the debate, but perhaps we can help inform it by giving the predictions on both sides a critical look.

Our second reason is more academic. The potential effects of term limits can be divided into two rough categories: the effects on the career choices of individual legislators and the institutional effects on legislatures. Obviously, these two sets of effects will be intertwined. However, we make the distinction as a way of putting forward a research agenda.

Term limits have been adopted in three states so far—California, Colorado, and Oklahoma—where the individual-level effects are already beginning to be felt. Even though the limits have yet to be applied formally, individual politicians can anticipate the likely effect on their own career choices and adjust their behavior accordingly. We already have seen this in California's reapportionment politics, where a six-year limit prevails. Thus, our speculations about the effects of term limits on individuals at least can be informed by, and tested against, interviews with actual legislators. The first steps in that process can be seen in the contributions to this volume by Charles Price and Gary Copeland.

In contrast, the institutional impacts generally will not be felt until term limits actually go into effect. However, we do know exactly when this will be in some states. Therefore, we have the opportunity for a rare natural experiment. We can test our ideas about the way institutions work by putting our expectations on paper so we can check back later to see how the predictions stand up. We go through this exercise not because we want to be able to pat ourselves on the back should our predictions be borne out, but as a way to invite our colleagues to develop an agenda for comparative research on the actual impact of an important structural change.

As we see it, a research agenda on term limitations would move from the effects on the individual legislator, to the effects on the legislative institution and, finally, to the effects on the institution's role in the political system. To some extent, we have already talked about individual-level effects in the introductory chapter. There, we argued that the effects a term-limit provision would have on the kinds of people who became legislators would vary with the specific content of the provision in question. Broadly speaking, the proposals so far have had two basic tendencies. Less common are the lifetime limits, or combined limits with long break periods, that would produce real amateur legislators. More common are the limits on continuous service in one chamber that would give experienced politicians every reason to remain active in politics, as long as they were willing to run for a new office every few terms. Both situations would be very different from the status quo, but they also would be very different from each other. For example, we argued in the introductory chapter that if legislative service were attractive only to amateurs, the level of electoral competition might well decline instead of increase. In contrast, a system that encouraged political professionals to play musical chairs might have the opposite effect. In this chapter, we take a similar look at the effects of different kinds of term limits on the internal operations of legislatures and on the relationship between the legislature and other institutions in its political environment—the chief executive (president or governor), bureaucracy, interest groups, and political parties.

Inside the Legislature

If term limits are to affect the distribution of power inside the legislature, they must first alter the incentives, norms, and expectations of individual legislators. Therefore, we shall consider norms and incentives before turning to leadership and structure.

Incentives and Norms

Advocates of term limits believe that under a new system members will be more motivated than current members by a desire to "do the right thing" for its own sake, and less by a constant seeking after reelection. Perhaps amateur politicians would be willing to ignore reelection concerns. If so, term limits that produce amateurs *might* also produce legislatures filled with members who act out of their pure commitment to the merits of a proposal, unsullied by any concerns about how their support or opposition might affect their careers. Before anyone begins dancing with joy at this prospect, however, it should be noted that a desire to do the right thing does not guarantee success. For example, although many commentators have argued that stalemate results when politicians are too cowardly to make tough decisions, stalemate occurs at least as often among members who are quite willing to do the right thing but disagree sharply over just what the right thing *is*.

But however one thinks amateur legislators would behave under term limits, it is clear that a completely different kind of analysis is necessary for those term-limit proposals that would encourage musical chairs by professional politicians. For one thing, such limits would mean that politicians could never rest content with maintaining a safe constituency. Perhaps they would, in fact, *be* safe in their current office. But they could never be content with that. If they wanted to remain active in politics, they would have to plan ahead for a future run for another office. As a result, far from seeing term limits decrease the members' feeling of dependence, the limits might well make some members feel even less free to take policy risks than they do now. The difference is that the members' focus might shift from their current to their potential constituencies. If so, the members would simply replace reelection behavior with preelection behavior.

That would be a change of some consequence. We can predict at least some of the effects by looking at how members behave now when they start positioning themselves to seek another office on the political career ladder. The difference would be that most members would be positioning themselves, instead of just a few.

When members plan a run for another office, the new constituency will almost always be different from, and usually larger than, the present one. The members will not be able to reach it with newsletters or district office hours. Therefore, members who want to become known to their potential constituents probably will have to place a heavy emphasis on attracting favorable media coverage. Some members may get regular coverage within the current constituency, but any who want to be recognized across the broader geographical sweep of a potential constituency will have to work at it. They will have to gear their behavior toward activities that will gain the attention of the regional, statewide, or national media.

All of this clearly would affect legislatures internally. Many scholars have noted that the declining importance of the party in the electorate has been associated with a more individualistic style of behavior inside the legislature. More members play to the press galleries today than a few decades ago. But that is not all they do.

The U.S. House and Senate, and most state legislatures, still have many mechanisms for rewarding members who do the unpublicized but crucial kind of work that goes under the heading of "institutional maintenance." Members get nothing politically out of serving on an ethics committee, but they do gain credit and prestige with their colleagues. A job well done today can mean more internal power later. Similarly, the role of the chairman of the budget committee can be a political negative during a time of fiscal constraint, but it is important for the institution and therefore important for the chairman's long-term power inside the institution.[1]

Clearly, term limits would reduce the incentives for individual members to engage in long-term strategies for increasing their power inside the institution. Similarly, they would make members less likely to put any of their personal emphasis on maintaining the power or prestige of their current institution as a whole. When combined with the incentives for media attention, the net effect of term limits therefore probably would intensify the individualism that has marked Congress and many state legislatures in recent decades.

Leadership and Internal Organization

The effect of term limits on incentives and norms in turn would spill over to affect every other aspect of institutional life. For example, it almost goes without saying that term limits would make seniority all but untenable as a basis for allocating power within the legislature. The shorter the limit, the more untenable seniority would be.

It is possible, as some have argued, that this could strengthen the hand of party leaders by weakening the independence of committee and subcommittee chairmen.[2] In the late nineteenth through early twentieth centuries, party leaders lost power in Congress as legislative careerism took hold and members with long-term stakes in the institution revolted against putting their internal power in arbitrary hands. That, in part, was what the 1910 uprising against Speaker Joseph Cannon was about. After the 1910 revolt, seniority became all but inviolate, reducing leaders to the role of brokers and facilitators.[3]

There can be no question that eliminating seniority, perhaps even eliminating the presumption of reappointment, would weaken the independent power of committees and subcommittees. And there is some historical plausibility to the assumption that weakening committees would increase the power of party leaders. The problem with the assumption, however, is that it presupposes that the same members who refuse to tolerate seniority would be willing to grant their party leaders an independent power base. The shorter the term limit, the less likely this would be. Remember that these would be the very same members just described as having every reason to behave as media-oriented individualists. There is no reason for them to turn the reins of power over to anyone else.

On the contrary, we expect that members with defined term limits will be unlikely to let strong party leadership develop. In fact, we would not be surprised to see a more fluid party leadership, with leaders changing every few years. Members would trade their votes for favorable committee positions, as the potential leaders seek to put together majority coalitions for their leadership races. In addition, because the leaders would have no ability to impose sanctions that pinch over the long term, there is every possibility that the resulting factionalism would encourage leadership fights in an increasing number of states to become cross-party factional contests.

Thus, even if term limits do away with seniority, it should not simply be assumed that the average member of Congress, or of a state legislature, will follow somebody else. If the term limits produce amateur legislators, the amateur might be more inclined than contemporary careerists to follow their personal convictions. On the other hand, if the limits merely encourage professionals to run for new offices periodically, the professionals would become more entrepreneurial. In neither case would most members be likely to feel a long-term, institutionally based incentive for following a collective institutional leadership.

Legislatures and Executives

Many of the same dynamics that affect the relationships between leaders and followers would also affect relationships between the legislative and executive branches of government. Thad Beyle, Linda Fowler, and Alan Rosenthal suggest elsewhere in this volume that term limits would increase the power of presidents and governors. We agree that term limits would diminish certain legislative capacities. However, to say that the legislature's capacities would be altered is not the same as to say that a president's or governor's policy objectives would be more easily achieved.

During the first six or so decades of the twentieth century, executives came to the forefront of American political life at every level. This was no haphazard development. The growth of executive power was facilitated by a broad set of institutional reforms that had their origins in the Progressive Era. By 1970, however, the pendulum had begun to swing back. Legislatures at the state and national levels focused their efforts—as David Everson's chapter explains—on developing the professionalism, institutional capacity, and will to reclaim an independent role. On the national level, a major 1981 book was plausibly entitled *The Decline and Resurgence of Congress*. And on the state level, Alan Rosenthal wrote in 1990 that "in most states today, although the governor may have an advantage, the two branches are in rough balance." [4]

Opponents of term limitations believe a hard-won institutional balance between the legislative and executive branches would be lost if the term-limit movement were successful. In contrast, many term-limit advocates believe that the chief result of legislative professionalization has not been more deliberation or a better legislative product but electoral safety for individual incumbents. They reject the idea that the reform movement of the 1970s has in fact brought about a healthy balance between the branches. Instead, they maintain that professionalism ultimately promotes individualism, and individualism makes cooperation more difficult—whether cooperation among members, between members and followers, or between legislators and executives. This makes it harder for governors and presidents to lead, they conclude, but does not systematically give legislatures the will or ability to take the lead by themselves.

Thus, both the advocates and opponents of term limits agree that limiting legislative terms will bring about a major shift in the balance between the legislative and executive branches of government. The two sides differ over what is desirable, but both seem to assume that term limits will produce a legislature that is more inclined to vote yes to whatever the governor or president might want. In our view, there is no reason to make this assumption.

To explain why, it is first necessary to do some backtracking. We assume that some members in any legislature will be inclined to cooperate with or resist a chief executive simply because they agree or disagree with a particular proposal on the merits. What we want to do is consider how term limits might affect the political incentives—as distinct from the policy inclinations—that incline members to cooperate or resist. There are three logically different possibilities. One would be a set of conditions under which the legislators felt a strong incentive to cooperate with the executive. The second would be a situation in which the personal political incentives were more or less neutral. In the third situation, the members would have an incentive *not* to cooperate.

Historically, governors—and, to a lesser extent, presidents—have been at their strongest when they sat at the top of electorally important party organizations. The executive's party before the 1960s was generally the majority party in the legislature. Party members would support the executive's program not only out of conviction, but because they felt a sense of common political fate before the electorate, linked as they were to the executive through the political party.[5] That is the situation we look to, therefore, for examples in which legislators feel a positive political incentive to cooperate.

For the typical contemporary member, by comparison, the political party has become less important in elections. Most incumbents more or less control their own fates. To the extent the members think about making common cause with their president or governor for electoral reasons, they are thinking more about building up their party in the legislature or retaining control over the government than about their personal reelection. As a result, the incentives for cooperation are more mixed for today's members than was true for their counterparts of decades ago. Cooperation is not important for the member's personal reelection, but it can be important for the effective power the members exercise inside the legislature.

Strictly speaking, therefore, the contemporary legislature does not quite fit any of our three ideal types. The incentives do not leave the members neutral, for reasons that will become clear when we look at the amateur legislature. Rather, they are felt strongly, but create cross-pressures. Some political incentives will strongly incline the contemporary legislator to cooperate. Others will incline the members toward showing their independence. The ones that prevail at any given moment will vary with the member and with the circumstances.

Now let us imagine how term limits might alter the current mixture of incentives for cooperation or resistance. In doing so, let us also remember that some term limits will produce amateur legislatures; others will produce legislatures of itinerant political professionals. First let us consider the amateur legislature.

To the extent that a legislature tends toward the purely amateur, then—almost by definition—the members will have no personal electoral motivation for supporting or resisting the chief executive. (Legislators who are on leave from an interest group—the possibility raised by Linda Fowler—will not have the same incentives as a pure amateur because they are political professionals in another institution.) The amateur will have no personal, career-based reason to help make the chief executive look good, and there is little an executive or legislative leader can do to hurt the amateur's career. Therefore, the amateur legislature is our best example of the middle of our three logical possibilities. The members' personal political incentives leave them more or less neutral between cooperating with or resisting the executive because, by definition, the true amateur will not have a long-term political career inside or outside the legislature.

The situation will be different for professionals facing term limits. Professionals cannot afford to let their futures depend solely upon a governor's or president's popularity. If they want to remain in politics, they will have to try to stand out from the crowd. Their career interests will lead them to promote legislation in their own names, conduct oversight, or, perhaps, become gadflies to the governor and legislative party leaders. No professional faced with a term limit could afford to accept a governor's or a president's lead passively. If anything, the incentives run in the opposite direction. (For example, contrary to those who predict term limits will produce an unchecked bureaucracy, we believe the political incentives for high-visibility oversight would increase under term limits.) The term-limited legislature of itinerant professionals thus is the kind most likely to fit our third logical possibility; neither cooperative nor neutral, this will be a legislature whose members have a personal stake in opposing the executive.

So far, we have concentrated on incentives. However, term-limit supporters and opponents seem to base their predictions about a shift in legislative-executive relations more upon capacity than incentives. If legislatures lose their most experienced members, the reasoning goes, then the institution will be less able to withstand the executive. We are not convinced that legislatures will suffer a major loss in technical competence under all term-limit proposals—for example, we do not believe that term limits need do away with competent legislative staff or that politically capable members with a year or two of experience need be captives of their staffs—but we concede that a net loss of competence is more likely than a gain.

If a legislature does suffer a significant loss in technical skill or experience, that in turn would compromise its ability to substitute its considered judgment for the executive's. That is, it would probably be less able to pass a fully developed legislative package on its own initiative. But a lack of capacity does not automatically imply a lack of incentive. If legislators are less able to develop intricate packages on their own, it does not mean they will stop trying. If the incentives are strong, they can draw upon lobbyists or simply ignore some of the technical details. Of course, a legislature that ignores details would also lose some of its control over how policy is implemented. In other words, it would be a weakened legislature in some respects, and the content of policy would be affected. But the crucial point for legislative-executive relations is this: governors and presidents are *not* automatically made stronger when the legislatures they face are made weaker. Legislators will let their political interests and goals dictate whether to resist the executive, whatever their technical capacities. In that respect, as in so many others, interbranch politics are not a zero-sum game.[6]

This point is seen even more graphically if we move away from the subject of technical competence to one we believe will be more important for legislative-executive relations: legislative leadership. We have already mentioned that leaders in term-limited legislatures are likely to change rapidly and to have a relatively weak set of resources at their disposal. That means, among other things, that the leaders will have less ability to set agendas and mobilize majorities. This could be interpreted as a sign of a weakened institutional capacity. At the same time, however, it would probably cause problems for chief executives.

Many opponents of term limits have argued that the loss of experienced, long-serving leaders would weaken the legislature in its negotiations with the executive over policy. Our point in some ways is just the opposite: the governor has a stake in strong legislative leadership. It is easier for the chief executive to develop a relationship with a few leaders in each house who can deliver majorities on a range of tough issues—including leaders of the opposite party—than it is to assemble separate majorities on each issue. Insofar as term limitations weaken the capacity of legislative leaders to provide disciplined majorities, they are likely to make it harder, not easier, for governors to achieve their objectives.

Governors could, in theory, try to turn themselves into legislative leaders. With term-limited legislatures, they may have to try. The question is, what resources could they bring to bear to counter the members' individualistic incentives? One possibility might be for governors (it would be harder for presidents) to try to recreate state party organizations to provide resources to candidates—as they run for their next office. There is no hope that the party organizations of fifty years ago will be revived in the political environment of today. However, one opening may present itself. Over the past two decades, legislative party leaders in Congress and at least thirty-five states have established or strengthened their leadership campaign funds or legislative campaign committees.[7] These efforts have all but displaced traditional party organizations as the main sources of party funds for legislative candidates. If legislative leaders become weaker after term limits—and particularly if they rotate quickly—the leaders probably will not have the time to build or maintain strong campaign committees. Facing term limits themselves, they would be less inclined to devote themselves to building collective organizations for the long haul. That would create a vacuum into which governors might well try to move.

The odds against a governor's succeeding in such an effort would be long. With politics even further fragmented by term limitations, collective campaign activities are more likely to be abandoned than to be assumed by the governor. However, even though the odds would be long, the stakes would be high.

Strong legislative leadership and collective party campaign activities, including fund-raising, can help insulate legislators in their relationship with interest groups. If term limitations strip away this insulation, they will make the relationships between members and organized interests even more direct. Despite the opposition of large corporations and labor unions to the term-limit initiatives in California and Washington, we do not believe term limits are likely to weaken interest group influence in the legislature. Groups with compelling legislative agendas will adapt to their new environment, as they have already adapted to the decentralization of power in Congress and many state legislatures. If anything, some groups may become more powerful. Specifically, large and politically well organized groups that have the capacity and resources to organize majorities and provide major assistance to election campaigns, will become more important in an environment in which legislative party leaders and governors are even less able to perform these activities than they are now.

Therefore, if term limits should be adopted, the precise effects of such limits on the role of interest groups—and therefore on the content of public policy—will depend upon the ability of governors and other leaders to organize new coordinating mechanisms, in an unpromising environment, to replace the ones that would be lost.

Time Perspectives

So far we have explored the likely effects of different kinds of term limitations on:

- The legislative career
- The competitiveness of legislative elections
- Internal legislative norms, organization, and leadership
- Relations between the legislative and executive branches of government.

There has been a common thread running through these topics. At bottom, what term limits are about is an effort to alter the time perspectives of legislators. In this final section, therefore, we shall focus explicitly on time.

An analogy between U.S. legislators and corporate executives may be helpful here. Both groups are extremely sensitive to the immediate environment: legislators to opinion in their districts as expressed in polls and elections, executives to opinion in the marketplace as expressed in sales or the movement of stock prices. This is because both are likely to be evaluated on short-term performance. Consequently, both are inclined to stress short-term performance and short-term gains—quarterly reports, this year's achievements for the district—at the risk of the long-term interests of the institutions they serve.

In corporations, time perspectives may be changed in a number of ways. One is by making managers owners—replacing salary or performance bonuses with stock to be held for a minimum time period—thus giving the managers a financial stake in the company's long-term success. In legislatures, a similar effect is achieved by giving members the chance to stay longer and exercise the responsibilities of leadership. Elected leaders and committee chairs come to understand and value the institutional stakes of the legislature and to forge an identity between these and their own personal stakes. In addition, these members are in a position to pursue their larger policy goals in session after session, providing the continuity of effort necessary for bringing major legislation to the top of the agenda and, ultimately, seeing it through to adoption.

Term limitations would reinforce the inclination of legislators to think and act in the short term, without sufficient consideration of long-term institutional consequences. They would reduce the incentives for persistence in pursuing large-scale policy changes by reducing the likelihood that a member would be "in on the kill." Even those term limitations that would not end political careers would weaken the identity between the interests of legislators and the specific institution in which they were currently serving.

We can consider what this might mean by returning to the subject of legislative-executive relations. Presidents and governors, like legislators, are elected for fixed terms and therefore are driven to seek measurable achievements within a finite amount of time. This is a reality even in the nineteen states where gubernatorial terms are not limited. Visibility and electoral vulnerability make executives far more conscious of their time limits than a safe legislator needs to be. The one countervailing consideration for presidents is that they tend to wonder how they will be judged by history. However, that does not alter the finitude of the time period they must keep in mind as they plan their policies. Projects involving a great deal of personal political investment will not be undertaken unless there is a reasonable chance to alter policy during the course of a term in office.

Without legislative term limitations, even though most legislators are present-oriented, leaders can afford to think beyond a single-term cycle. They have incentives to resist a governor's or president's immediate agenda, and to offer members an alternative legislative perspective. The twin realities of high reelection rates and increasing rates of average service bolster the argument that they have time while the executive may not. With term limits, this would no longer be the case.

Our point here is not to defend contemporary legislatures as embodiments of the public will or public interest, but to emphasize the importance of rewarding some people in the political system for keeping their eyes on the long term. Even now, finite terms for the executive mean that career staff often have a better understanding of institutional issues than do their elected superiors. People who plan careers in an institution have personal stakes that lead them to worry about the implications of today's decisions for the day after tomorrow.

In one of his best known statements, James Madison said,"The interest of the man must be connected to the constitutional rights of the place." [8] Our point is similar to Madison's. We also believe ambition and performance to be linked. Limiting terms will not do away with ambition but will channel or divert it. The public is disillusioned and angry. The question is whether using term limits to shift legislative time frameworks will serve the country's best interests.

Notes

1. Richard F. Fenno, Jr., *Pete Domenici: Portrait of a Senate Leader* (Washington, D.C.: CQ Press, 1991).
2. See, for example, David W. Brady and Douglas Rivers, "Term Limits Make Sense," *The New York Times,* October 5, 1991, 21.
3. Nelson Polsby, "The Institutionalization of the U.S. House of Representatives," *American Political Science Review* 62 (1968): 144-168. Nelson Polsby, Miriam Gallagher and Barry S. Rundquist, "The Growth of the Seniority System in the U.S. House of Representatives," *American Political Science Review* 63 (1969): 787-807. Ronald M. Peters, Jr., *The American Speakership: The Office in Historical Perspective* (Baltimore: Johns Hopkins University Press, 1990). Joseph Cooper and David W. Brady, "Institutional Context and Leadership Style: The House from Cannon to Rayburn," *American Political Science Review* 75 (1981): 411-425.
4. James L. Sundquist, *The Decline and Resurgence of Congress* (Washington, D.C.: The Brookings Institution, 1981). Alan Rosenthal, *Governors and Legislators: Contending Powers* (Washington, D.C.: CQ Press, 1990), 197.

5. Morris P. Fiorina, "Divided Government in the States," in *The Politics of Divided Government,* ed. Gary W. Cox and Samuel Kernell (Boulder, Colo.: Westview, 1991), 179-202. The major exception to this rule would be Democrats in the one-party South, where factions were more important than parties in state politics.
6. For use of this phrase to make a similar institutional point in a different policy context, see Michael J. Malbin, "Legislative-Executive Lessons From the Iran-Contra Affair," in *Congress Reconsidered,* 4th ed., ed. Lawrence D. Dodd and Bruce I. Oppenheimer (Washington, D.C.: C.Q. Press, 1989), 387.
7. Daniel M. Shea, "The Myth of Party Adaptation: Linkages between Legislative Campaign Committees and Party" (paper presented to the annual meeting of the New York State Political Science Association, April 12-13, 1991).
8. Alexander Hamilton, James Madison, and John Jay, *The Federalist* (New York: World, 1961), 349.

Appendix A

THE PROS AND THE CONS REPRINTED

Editors' note: The main body of this book consists of original essays analyzing the history, the politics, and the potential effects of legislative term limits. Even though most of the authors have stated their own support or opposition to term limits publicly—and some of them do so in the course of their essays here—none of them is a straightforward presentation of the pro and the con arguments.

We made this editorial decision because some excellent pro and con statements were already in print. However, because some of these appeared in sources that are not readily available, we decided to include four sets of arguments here. We have chosen these sets to illustrate two points: first, that the debate takes place on different levels in different arenas, and second, that there are liberals and conservatives, Republicans and Democrats, on both sides of the issue.

The first pair of essays are thoughtful statements published by two conservative Washington, D.C., think tanks. John H. Fund is an editorial page writer for the *Wall Street Journal* whose "Term Limits: An Idea Whose Time Has Come" was written for the Cato Institute. Cato has also published pro-term-limit essays by Mark Petracca. The organization's president, Edward Crane—who helped found the Libertarian party in the 1970s—is a prominent national spokesman for term limits. Crane participated in an October 11, 1991, public debate with former Senator William Proxmire as part of our Albany conference.

The essay in opposition to term limits was written by Charles R. Kesler, who teaches political science at Claremont McKenna College in California. Kesler's essay appeared in *Policy Review,* a journal published by the Heritage Foundation. (Heritage has also published articles in favor of term limits.)

The second set of selections presents the arguments as they appeared in the law courts. The French aristocrat, Alexis de Tocqueville, remarked in his 1835-1840 classic, *Democracy in America,* that "there is hardly a political question in the United States which does not sooner or later turn into a judicial one." Term limits are no exception. The selections in this volume come from attorneys' briefs filed in the

Florida Supreme Court on whether states may impose term limits on members of the U.S. Congress. The attorneys—Cleta Deatherage Mitchell for the Term Limits Legal Institute, and Steven R. Ross and Charles Tiefer for U.S. Rep. Larry Smith—are all liberal Democrats. Following the Florida briefs are a California Opinion of the Court and a dissent on some of the more basic constitutional issues raised by limitations on legislative terms.

The final selections are good examples of the arguments as they appear in the heat of an election campaign. As explained in an editors' note below, the selections were written by interest groups for the official California Ballot Pamphlet.

A-1. TERM LIMITATION: AN IDEA WHOSE TIME HAS COME

John H. Fund

Not since Proposition 13 created a nationwide tidal wave of tax protest has a political idea caught on with such speed. Polls show that over 70 percent of Americans back a limit on terms for elected officials, and by next month [November 1990] voters in states where one of every seven Americans live may have voted some form of term limits into law.

Elected officials from city council members to President Bush are scrambling to get to the front of the term-limit parade. As Mike Kelley of Colorado's Independence Institute writes, "Term limitation could become in the 1990s what tax limitation was in the 1970s—a popular movement politicians abhor, but one to which they must respond." [1]

The gulf between legislators and the American people has never been greater than on the issue of term limits. A Gallup survey found that 66 percent of U.S. House members oppose limiting the number of congressional terms, while opinion polls show two-to-one support among all demographic groups.[2] (See Table A-1.) The idea is overwhelmingly popular with Americans regardless of party, ideology, or income. Blacks favor it even more than whites, women more than men. Martin Plissner, political director for CBS News, says he has "never seen an issue on which there was so little demographic variation." [3]

Term limits were a part of the nation's first governing document, the Articles of Confederation, and were left out of the Constitution largely because they were thought of as "entering too much into detail" for a short document. Nonetheless, self-imposed limits on officeholders were long a part of America's public-service ethic; members of Congress returned to private life after a couple of terms. With the rise of the modern superstate, term limitation, once the accepted American tradition, has been replaced by congressional careerism. That is why

In October 1990 the Cato Institute published this article as *Policy Analysis No. 141.* It is reprinted here with permission.

the voluntary service limitations of the past must now be made part of the nation's laws.

Where Does the Term-Limit Idea Come From?

Term limitation is not a new idea, just one that the realities of modern politics have made necessary. Something must be done to help repair the damage caused by the "permanent government" of career politicians that now dominates the U.S. Congress and most state legislatures.

Over the years, term limits for Congress have been endorsed by the likes of Thomas Jefferson, Abraham Lincoln, Harry Truman, Dwight Eisenhower, and John F. Kennedy. Many political scientists have supported the idea since the 1951 constitutional amendment limiting presidents to two terms began creating an imbalance of power in favor of the legislative branch.

The promotion of turnover in the legislative branch predates the Constitution. The Pennsylvania constitution of 1776, the most radical constitution of the revolutionary era, had a strict limit of four years on legislative service. In 1777 the Continental Congress, the direct predecessor of today's Congress, allowed delegates to serve a maximum of three years.[4] The primary motivation was to ensure that legislators reflected the makeup and outlook of the citizenry they claimed to represent.

However, the first attempt to enforce term limits met with understandable resistance from the incumbent delegates. In 1784 an attempt to deny certain delegates their seats led to a near-rebellion on the floor of the Continental Congress. James Monroe commented, "I never saw more indecent conduct in any assembly before."[5]

When the Constitution was debated in 1787, the sour experience with term limits in the Continental Congress led delegates to hesitate to propose them for the nation's new charter. But there is no doubt that encouraging turnover of legislators was popular at the Constitutional Convention. A proposal by James Madison for three-year elections to the House of Representatives was attacked by Massachusetts delegate Elbridge Gerry as a form of "limited monarchy." Eventually, a proposal for two-year terms was adopted unanimously.[6]

Roger Sherman of Rhode Island summed up the feeling of many delegates when he commented that Congress should be made up of "citizen-legislators" who through the principle of rotation in office would "return home and mix with the people. By remaining at the seat of government, they would acquire the habits of the place, which might differ from those of their constituents."[7]

While mandatory term limits were not included in the final draft of the Constitution, many delegates assumed that voluntary term limits

TABLE A-1   Survey—Cross-Section of Electorate Considers Term
Limits for U.S. Representatives

*Question: Do you think there should be a limit to the number of times a
member of the House of Representatives can be elected to a two-year term?*

Respondents	*Yes*	*No*
Total sample	61%	21%
By party		
Republican	64	28
Democrat	60	30
Independent	58	33
By philosophy/ideology		
Liberal	58	34
Moderate	64	30
Conservative	63	29
By presidential preference		
Favored Bush	61	32
Opposed Bush	60	23
By race		
White	61	31
Black	61	27
By gender		
Men	57	35
Women	63	27

Source: New York Times/CBS survey of 1,515 adults, conducted March 30-April 2, 1990, with a
3 percent margin of error.

would be the norm. It was never thought that serving in Congress
would become a career. And indeed, in the first House election after
George Washington was elected president, 40 percent of incumbents
[did not return], allaying fears of an entrenched "government of
strangers." [8]

The practice through the first half of the 19th century was for
members to serve only four years in the House and six in the Senate; in
every election 40 to 50 percent of Congress left office.[9]

Abraham Lincoln, for example, had an informal rotation agreement with his political rivals. He served a single term in the House in
the 1840s and then moved back to Illinois, not to return to Washington
until he was elected president. Lincoln was a firm supporter of rotation
in office. He once wrote, "If our American society and United States
Government are overthrown, it will come from the voracious desire for

office, this wriggle to live without toil, work and labor—from which I am not free myself." [10]

As political scientist Charles Kesler notes, such rotation agreements were not uncommon; they were signs of a vigorous intraparty political life as well as keen competition between the parties. He noted that "the parties and the country enjoyed the best of both worlds, . . . a circulation of capable and experienced men through public office, with the possibility of keeping truly exceptional ones in office if circumstances demanded it." [11]

The conduct of the House's business also discouraged extended tenure in office. The House leadership was not driven by seniority, and party control frequently shifted. Members who wanted a career in politics were compelled to run for the Senate, seek a position in the executive branch, or return home and run for governor. Of the seven Speakers of the House elected between 1870 and 1894, for example, one was elected in his third term of service, two in their fourth, two in their fifth, one in his sixth, and one in his seventh. [12] In 1811 Henry Clay was elected Speaker of the House at the beginning of his first term. Contrast that with Jim Wright, elected Speaker in 1987 in his 17th term, or Thomas Foley, elected in 1989 in his 13th term!

House seniority began to rise after the turmoil of the Civil War and the establishment of standing committees made seniority important. Between 1860 and 1920, the average length of service doubled from four to eight years. According to Rep. Bill McCollum (R-Fla.), in 1901 when the 57th Congress convened, for the first time less than 30 percent of members were freshmen. [13] In 1981, when the 97th Congress convened, 17 percent of the members were newly elected. In 1989, when the 101st Congress convened, fewer than 8 percent were newly elected.

Another major change in Congress since the 19th century has been in the amount of time it meets. Even 60 years ago, Congress would meet for two months a year, and meeting for three months was considered unusual. A congressman was more or less compelled to be a citizen-legislator who would go home after a session and spend most of his time running a business or practicing law or whatever. Today the sheer size and scope of the federal government have made service in Congress a full-time job, and most who are elected have to give up their careers. With each passing year of congressional service, members are more reluctant to go back home and reenter the job market. In 1989 ethics legislation actually banned members of the U.S. House from practicing many professions and severely curtailed their power to earn any outside income.

The first popular movement for term limitation came in the 1940s, after President Franklin Roosevelt broke the two-term tradition started by George Washington. The Twenty-Second Amendment was introduced in 1947 by the new majority of Republicans in Congress. But despite its partisan origins, many members felt that since the two-term limit had been violated, it was necessary to put it into the Constitution. The amendment was ratified in 1951 with widespread support. The *Washington Post* editorialized that "power-grasping officials are common enough in both history and current world experience to warrant this safeguard." [14] However, members of Congress were horrified at any thought that the principle of term limits should extend to the legislative branch. During the 1947 debate on the Twenty-Second Amendment, Sen. W. Lee O'Daniel (D-Tex.) offered an amendment to limit the terms of all federal officials. His proposal was rejected 82 to 1, with O'Daniel's the only vote in favor. [15] In 1950 President Harry S Truman proposed a 12-year limit on service in each chamber of Congress, but his proposal got nowhere.

Executive-branch term limits are also common at the state level. The governors of 25 states are limited to two terms, and in Virginia, New Mexico, and Kentucky all statewide officials are limited to a single term. [16]

Attempts to revise the tradition of rotation in office for members of Congress surfaced in the late 1970s. Sens. William L. Armstrong (R-Colo.) and Gordon J. Humphrey (R-N.H.) both indicated that they would retire after two terms in the Senate and, to everyone's surprise, did precisely that. For others the addiction of higher office proved to be too much. As first-time candidates Sens. Dennis DeConcini (D-Ariz.), Malcolm Wallop (R-Wyo.), John C. Danforth (R-Mo.), and Nancy Landon Kassebaum (R-Kans.) all pledged to serve only 12 years in office. All are now in their third term or running for it. In 1988 DeConcini was running for a third term on the claim that he could better fight for a 12-year limitation if he was in the Senate for 18 years. Kassebaum announced her candidacy for a third term in 1989 by saying that she was convinced her seniority "could be put to good and worthwhile purposes." [17]

Is the Term-Limit Movement Bipartisan, or Is It Just Republicans Frustrated at Their Lack of Power in Congress?

Of the 35 former members of Congress on the advisory board of Americans to Limit Congressional Terms, eight are Democrats. [18] In California, Democratic attorney general John Van de Kamp has sponsored a ballot initiative that imposes a 12-year limit on state legislative service. He explains the need for the initiative: "Electoral competition has declined so dramatically that state officials, once elected, hold virtually a life-time lock on state office, with the result that citizen interest and participation in the political process have dropped to record lows." [19]

John Lindsay, a former Republican mayor of New York City, member of the House, and later contender for the Democratic presidential nomination, says the 98 percent reelection rate for House incumbents has convinced him that "you no longer have effective competition." A term limit would mean there was at least "some way to sweep out the old wood." [20]

His views were echoed by another New York Democrat, the late Ned Pattison, who died last August. A member of the 1974 "Watergate baby" class in Congress, Pattison became convinced after he left Congress that term limits were necessary. A major reason was to counteract the tendency of Congress to vote for bigger government merely for its ability to help legislators to bring pork-barrel projects home and to get credit for helping their constituents through the maze of federal regulations. "Some members actually enjoy creating bureaucracy," he said. "They then become more indispensable to their constituents, and thus more likely to be re-elected. The job becomes administrative rather than political." [21]

Cleta Mitchell, a self-described liberal Democrat who served for three years as chairman of the Oklahoma State House Appropriations Committee, says term limits will actually help her party. "Democrats have to show they offer the American people more than the simple powers of incumbency," she says. "We need to elect more idealistic newcomers and fewer cynical veterans." Her own experience is revealing. "When I first was elected in 1976, I wanted to rock the boat. I often told my colleagues that they should try something new. They would respond by rolling their eyes and saying, 'It's always been done this way.' Then one day I found myself saying the same things that they had. I knew it was time for me to go." [22]

Even savvy Democrats are surprised by the unrepresentative nature of Congress when they come into direct contact with it. Richard Phelan was an active Democrat and national convention delegate when he was named special counsel to the House Ethics Committee in the Jim Wright case. He returned to Chicago in 1989 with a new appreciation of what is wrong with Washington. His recent comments before the Federal Bar Association are worth quoting.

> In 1988, all but one of the incumbents who chose to run and [were] defeated had ethical problems. Now what that says to me is

that with the franking privilege, with the PACs, all of the other people had been scared off or weren't able to raise enough money. What we now have is a House of Lords instead of a popularly elected Congress. . . . It's difficult, if not impossible, for Members not to be reelected to it. I think that carries with it a great deal of problems. Lots and lots of people have suggested to me that one of the things Congress ought to do is to just limit their own terms.[23]

Objections to Term Limitation

Opponents of term limits raise several objections, both philosophical and practical, to the idea. Here are the most frequently cited, together with responses.

Won't Term Limits Restrict the Voters' Choices at the Ballot Box?

That implies that voters now have a choice at the ballot box. Common Cause reports that, as of September 30, of the 405 House incumbents seeking reelection this fall, 78 lack major-party opponents. Another 218 have opponents who have raised less than $25,000, and 86 have opponents who have raised more than $25,000 but less than half the amount the incumbents have raised. Only 23 races are remotely competitive. People don't vote for someone they've never heard of, and skewed campaign laws mean that almost all the contributions to House races flow to incumbents.

Voters are deciding that the only way they can ensure a real choice at the ballot box is to democratically guarantee that no one has a lifetime hold on an office. If term limits pass in, say, California, voters there will be freely choosing to open the political process to outsiders, women, and minorities who are often excluded by the presence of lifetime incumbents.

Won't Term Limits Disrupt the Way Congress Works?

Yes, and that is one of the best arguments for term limits. Congress has become an ossified structure that accomplishes little of value, wastes much, and impedes progress made by other sectors of society.

Limiting terms would limit abuse of the congressional seniority system by rotating power so it could not remain long enough with any one person for him or her to abuse it. Under the current seniority system, a handful of career-oriented congressmen chair key committees for years (for instance, Jamie Whitten, chairman of the House Appropriations Committee since 1979 and of its Agriculture Subcommittee since 1949; John Dingell, chairman of the Energy and Commerce Committee since 1981; and Dan Rostenkowski, chairman of the Ways and Means Committee since the same year) and control much of the legislative agenda, often preventing members from even voting on matters of national interest.

Rep. Jamie L. Whitten (D-Miss.), who was elected 33 days before Pearl Harbor, is the powerful chair of the House Appropriations Subcommittee on Agriculture. Eight presidents have left office during Whitten's tenure and with them 17 secretaries of agriculture. Those officials have only transitory control over policy; Whitten is the "permanent secretary of agriculture." [24]

Term limitation would create a climate in which talented men and women from businesses and professions would want to run for Congress, since they would know they would reach a position of significant influence in a few short years instead of having to make a career of politics if they wanted to play a major role in Congress. Citizen-legislators would come to government briefly, then many would return to private life and live with the consequences of the laws they had passed. George McGovern, a senator for 18 years, recently bought a hotel in Connecticut. "I wish that someone had told me about the problems of running a business," he told the *Washington Post*. "I have to pay taxes, meet a payroll—I wish I had had a better sense of what it took to do that when I was in Washington." [25] . . .

Isn't There a Lot of Turnover in Congress Now?

That view is propounded most forcefully by Rep. Mickey Edwards (R-Okla.), who has spent seven terms in office, and Rep. Pat Schroeder (D-Colo.), who has spent nine terms in office. "The image of a House top-heavy with long-term incumbents is false," says Schroeder. "Since 1980, more than half of the House has turned over due to defeat, resignation, retirement or death. The average length of service is 5.8 terms." [26] Many current members, of course, will go on to serve many more terms before choosing to retire.

But turnover in Congress should not come chiefly because members choose to leave on their own timetable. In a democratic society, some turnover should be caused at the polls.

The reelection rate for members of the U.S. House seeking new terms, about 90 percent in the generation after World War II, soared closer to 100 percent in the 1980s. In 1988 only 6 of the 405 members lost their reelection bids, and 5 of those were under some sort of ethical cloud. [27]

What's worse, the entrenched incumbency of Congress is trickling down to the state legislative level. In the 1960s and 1970s typically one-third of the membership of state legislatures changed every two years. In earlier decades turnover rates of 50 percent were common. In the

1980s turnover slowed to a crawl, and in 1988 an all-time low of only 16 percent of state legislators were newly elected.[28]

In California, the state with the professionalized legislature that most resembles Congress, only three incumbents lost in the last three legislative elections. More than 270 won. The turnover rate for assembly members has dropped by more than half since 1980.[29]

In Colorado no incumbent state senator has lost since 1982. In Pennsylvania 98 percent of incumbents in the state legislature won reelection in 1988.

Critics say the trend is even seeping down to the local level. "Entrenched incumbency is strangling local government, and the quality of life is suffering in many ways," says University of California at Los Angeles professor Laura Lake.[30]

Term limits work for many occupations in America. Why not for Congress? Presidents are limited, executive branch employees are limited, and nearly everyone in the private sector faces a "term limitation" of some kind—"65 and out" or whatever—no matter how respected, important, or powerful they are.

Won't Term Limits Deprive Us of the Services of Valuable and Experienced Legislators?

"Longevity promotes competence," says Nelson Polsby, a professor of political science at the University of California at Berkeley. "You have to actually advocate incompetent legislators to get the turnover some want." [31]

But, of course, term limits can still allow for long political careers. Senator Armstrong of Colorado has served in public office continuously since his 1962 election to the state legislature, but he has never served in any one office for more than 12 years.[32]

Some critics of term limits argue that even 12 years isn't enough time to become an expert legislator. But there are very few jobs that take that long to learn, and representing the public isn't one of them.

Besides, although term limits may shorten the congressional careers of the best members, those people will not have to withdraw from public life. Former congressmen will be available for service in the executive branch, in industry, in think tanks, and in the academy.

The Founding Fathers envisioned Congress and state legislatures as representative bodies, not the entrenched micro-managing monsters they have become. Their job is to make policy, not implement it. Considerable experience in government isn't necessary for that. Considerable experience in life is.

And what have our experienced lawmakers brought us? Certainly not innovative and bold public policy. Instead, they have brought us endemic compromise, institutional paralysis, and the Beltway mentality—a narrow, self-contained culture with addictive qualities. . . .

Wouldn't Term Limits Merely Shift Power to Staffers and Lobbyists?

The view that term limits would give more power to the "permanent" world of congressional and state capital staff aides, lobbyists, and journalists is expressed by Rep. Henry Hyde (R-Ill.). "A mandatory revolving door for elected officials would only strengthen the grip of the 'permanent bureaucracy' because lack of experience would make the legislators even more dependent on staff," he said.[33]

Of course, any Capitol Hill observer knows that it's the most senior members who are most dependent on staff and lobbyists, not the hot-shot young freshmen. And there is nothing to prevent a reduction in the mushrooming growth of staffers from accompanying term limits [as happened in California]. . . .

Critics also say that term limits might increase influence-peddling by putting pressure on members of Congress to curry favor with the interests that might reward them with future employment. But few members are likely to become lobbyists, because the turnover on Capitol Hill will quickly make their contacts obsolete and their influence limited.

In addition, the executive branch has successfully limited the revolving-door syndrome. Restricting post-congressional work should also be possible. Freed to some extent from the never-ending necessity for political fund-raising by term limits, legislators might actually find the time to lead rather than follow their staffs.

It is also difficult to see how the special interests will readily gain more access and influence than they have now. In a recent hearing on a California term-limit initiative, Democratic assemblyman Tom Bane argued with its sponsor, Pete Schabarum, that term limits would "turn this legislature over to big power special interests." Schabarum, a Los Angeles County supervisor and former three-term state assemblyman, shot back: "Special interests already run this legislature. Can I make that any clearer?" [34] . . .

The Case for Term Limitation

There are many practical benefits to be gained from imposing a limitation on terms.

Elections Would Be More Competitive

This year 78 House candidates—one-fifth of all members—will face no major-party opposition. Another 304 House incumbents hold prohibitive fund-raising leads over their opponents. In 1988, 56 of the 435 seats were uncontested; 20 winners got more than 90 percent of the vote; 70 percent (356) won 65 percent. Only 38 of 435 members won with less than 55 percent of the vote—the normal definition of a landslide.[35] The average incumbent won with 73.5 percent of the vote that year.[36]

Matters are not much better in the U.S. Senate. This year, for the first time since 1956, four senators have no major-party opponents. Another 12 face merely token opposition.[37]

Elections increasingly resemble sullen ratifications of the status quo, rather than competitive contests, and voter turnout is suffering as public interest in politics declines. Voter turnout in 1988 was 50 percent, down 3.4 percent from 1984. Only in Colorado, Nebraska, Nevada, and Utah was turnout up. In the last off-year election, voter turnout was only 37 percent, and it was only 27 percent in states without a contest for governor or U.S. senator.[38] Voter turnout to select new occupants for open seats for governor, U.S. senator, or U.S. representative is often much higher than it is for races in which an entrenched incumbent is running.

Term Limits Would Make Ability More Important Than Seniority

Term limits will encourage different people to run for office and pave the way for passage of other reforms—including rules to make legislative districts more competitive and reduce incumbent advantages in campaign financing.

"I believe that if we knew on Day One that we couldn't parlay this into a career, no matter how many carloads of pork we shipped home, there would be a fundamental change in attitudes," says retiring Senator Humphrey. "The whole idea of careerism would dissipate— and no single reform would do more good than that." [39]

Cleta Mitchell, a former Democratic legislator from Oklahoma, says that term limits would allow assignments such as committee chairmanships to be awarded more on the basis of talent and leadership qualities than on someone's staying power in office.[40]

"Professionalism and careerism [are] the bane of democratic governance," writes Mark Petracca, an assistant professor of politics at the University of California at Irvine. "Experience in government tends to produce legislators who are more interested in defending government than they are in solving serious public problems." [41]

Term Limits Would Improve the Quality of Candidates

One often-overlooked problem with unlimited legislative terms is that they create a situation in which a legislator must remain in office for 15 or 20 years in order to have significant influence. Such a situation attracts those, such as California assemblyman Mike Roos, whose lifelong ambition was to be a politician. Roos, who is in his 13th year as the sole assemblyman for 300,000 citizens, studied public administration in college and never has had to earn a living in the private sector.

Many worthy individuals, of the kind who would compose a truly representative citizen-legislature, find the concept of spending that much time in the legislature off-putting. They have their own jobs—as doctors, carpenters, lawyers, engineers, computer specialists, teachers—and have no interest at all in becoming career legislators. Nevertheless, as civic-minded individuals they would find it a worthwhile experience to represent their home districts in the legislature for two, four, or even six years. Much beyond that, however, would represent too great a break from their real careers back home. Why should we be denied the good sense and good judgment of such people?

Term Limits Would Counter the "Culture of Ruling"

Studies by such respected organizations as the National Taxpayers Union and Citizens for a Sound Economy have found that the longer a legislator is in office, the greater the number of special interests he or she becomes associated with. It is also a common observation that the longer a legislator works in Washington, D.C., or in a state capital, the more self-important that person seems to become. Obviously, that is not always true. But it would defy human nature if it weren't true much of the time. In a capital city one is surrounded by individuals whose daily routine involves setting rules and regulations for the rest of society—a kind of "culture of ruling."

And it is subtly corrupting to have microphones pushed in your face daily and to have reporters asking your opinion about every question under the sun. Eventually, one comes to believe that his or her opinion is more important than perhaps it really is. Worse, the legislator then has a tendency to want to codify those opinions on everything under the sun. A citizen-legislature would be likely to pass fewer laws, and those that were passed would reflect more level-headed judgment. . . .

Conclusion

Franking privileges, huge staffs, liberal travel funds, easy access to the news media, and unfair campaign finance laws have all provided incumbents with a grossly unfair advantage. A fifth of all congressional districts will elect unopposed incumbents this November because would-be challengers were unwilling and unable to spend the time and money required by the virtually impossible task of unseating those in power. The playing field must be made more level than it is now.

A limit on elected congressional and state legislative tenure would reduce the incentive for such abuses of power by eliminating congressional careerism. No longer would those political offices be held by longtime incumbents. They would be held by citizen-legislators, who would be more disposed to represent the will of the people and rein in the out-of-control bureaucracy that now substitutes for a federal government.

The idea of citizen-representatives serving a relatively short time is not new or radical. Although the writers of the Constitution did not see fit to include a term limitation, perhaps that was because the public-service norm of those days did not include careerist senators and representatives.[42] Instead, the attitude of that time can be seen in the decision of George Washington to voluntarily serve only two terms as president.

Term limitation is a traditional and uniquely American concept. Now it must be made mandatory instead of voluntary because the spirit of voluntary service limitation has obviously been lost.

Notes

1. Mike Kelley, "Limit Terms, Expand Democracy," Independence Institute, Denver, Colo., July 18, 1990, 1.
2. Gallup Organization, *Poll for the National Federation of Independent Business* (Princeton, N.J.: Gallup, January 1990), 6.
3. Interview with author, April 18, 1990.
4. Edmund C. Burnett, *The Continental Congress* (New York: Macmillan, 1941), 250.
5. Ibid., 605.
6. Charles O. Jones, *Every Second Year* (Washington, D.C.: Brookings Institution, 1968), 4.
7. Ibid., 4.
8. George F. Will, "Is 18 Years on the Hill Enough?" *Washington Post,* January 7, 1990, B7.
9. Charles R. Kesler, "The Case against Congressional Term Limitations," *Policy Review* (Summer 1990): 21.
10. Mike Klein, "Limiting Congressional Terms: An Historical Perspective," Americans to Limit Congressional Terms, 1990, 6.
11. Ibid.; Kesler, 22.
12. Nelson W. Polsby, *The Congressional Career* (New York: Random House, 1971), 23.

13. Bill McCollum, speech to the Conservative Political Action Conference, Washington, D.C., March 1, 1990.
14. "22nd Amendment," *Washington Post*, February 29, 1951.
15. Sula P. Richardson, *Congressional Tenure: A Review of Efforts to Limit House and Senate Service* (Washington, D.C.: Congressional Research Service, September 13, 1990), 5.
16. American Enterprise Institute, *How Long Should They Serve?* (Washington, D.C.: AEI, 1980), 20.
17. Janet Hook, "New Drive to Limit Tenure Revives an Old Proposal," *Congressional Quarterly* (February 24, 1990): 568.
18. News release, Americans to Limit Congressional Terms, February 14, 1990.
19. News conference, California attorney general John Van de Kamp, January 11, 1990, Los Angeles.
20. Interview with author, February 8, 1990.
21. Interview with author, February 11, 1990.
22. Cleta Deatherage Mitchell, "Insider Tales of an Honorable Ex-Legislator," *Wall Street Journal*, October 11, 1990, A14.
23. "Terms of Limitation," *Wall Street Journal*, December 11, 1989, A14.
24. Hook, 567.
25. *Washington Post*, December 1, 1989, F2.
26. Letter to constituent from Rep. Pat Schroeder of Colorado, June 12, 1990.
27. Bill McCollum, speech to the Conservative Political Action Conference, Washington, D.C., March 1, 1990.
28. Karl T. Kurtz, "No Change—For a Change," *State Legislatures*, January, 1989, 29.
29. Neal R. Pierce, "Zeroing in on Permanent Incumbency," *National Journal*, October 6, 1990, 2417.
30. Quoted in Pierce.
31. Nelson W. Polsby, "Congress Bashing for Beginners," *Public Interest* (Summer 1990): 18.
32. Kelley, 6.
33. Scripps Howard News Service, *Washington Times*, February 22, 1990, A8.
34. Quoted in Robert Reinhold, "California Voters' Ire Augurs Curbs," *New York Times*, September 30, 1990, 18.
35. "High-Tech Vote Grabbing," *Wall Street Journal*, May 12, 1989, A14.
36. Hendrik Hertzberg, "Twelve Is Enough," *New Republic*, May 14, 1990, 22.
37. Laurence I. Barrett, "Throw Some of the Bums Out!" *Time*, October 1, 1990, 42.
38. Hertzberg, 22.
39. Quoted in David Shribman, "Drive to Restrict Tenure in Congress," *Wall Street Journal*, March 12, 1990, A12.
40. Anna America, "Cap on Congressional Terms Pushed," *Tulsa Tribune*, February 19, 1990, A9.

41. Mark Petracca, "Political Careerism Is the Bane of True Democracy," *New York Times*, October 17, 1989, A16.
42. Thomas F. Hartnett, "Put Members of Congress on a Short Lease," *Wall Street Journal*, September 19, 1988, A14.

A-2. BAD HOUSEKEEPING: THE CASE AGAINST CONGRESSIONAL TERM LIMITS

Charles R. Kesler

Everyone complains about Congress, but nobody does anything about it. Frustration with our national legislature, which is by almost every measure widespread among the American public, is about to be explored by a national movement to throw the rascals out—the rascals, in this case, being incumbent congressmen and senators who have so mastered the art of reelection as to be thought unremovable by conventional means. The most widely touted solution to the problem is the extreme one of adding an amendment to the Constitution limiting the number of terms that members of the House and Senate can serve.

This notion appears to have been first circulated by the same informal network of radio talk-show hosts who were instrumental in rallying public opposition to last year's congressional pay raise. The idea has found support in public opinion polls and is being pressed by a new organization, Americans to Limit Congressional Terms (ALCT), that operates out of the offices of Republican political consultant Eddie Mahe and whose board includes both prominent Democrats and Republicans.

It is the latter party that stands to benefit most from limiting the years a congressman can serve, inasmuch as it is the Republicans who suffer under the rule of a more or less permanent Democratic majority in the House and Senate. In fact, term limitations were endorsed in the 1988 Republican platform. It is hardly surprising, therefore, that conservatives, too, are seizing the issue. In the symposium on conservatism for the 1990s featured in the Spring 1990 issue of *Policy Review,* almost a third of the contributors called for some sort of limitations on congressional terms.

This essay first appeared in the Summer 1990 issue of the Heritage Foundation's *Policy Review* and is reprinted here with permission. Copyright © The Heritage Foundation.

98-Percent Paradox

This movement builds on the public's mounting dissatisfaction with a Congress that is seen not only as unresponsive but also as incompetent and corrupt. Indeed, in light of the chronically unbalanced federal budget, Congress's reluctance to perform even its minimal duty of passing a budget (balanced or not) without resort to omnibus continuing resolutions and reconciliation acts, the 51 percent salary increase for its members that it tried to brazen through without a roll call vote, the generous privileges it extends to its members (large staffs, multiple offices, free travel allowances, frequent mailings at public expense, liberal pensions), the corruption-tinged resignations of former House Speaker Jim Wright and former Democratic Whip Tony Coelho, the metastasizing scandal of the Keating Five—in light of all these things, it is a wonder that congressmen get reelected at all.

And yet that is the paradox. Despite a deep dissatisfaction with Congress as an institution, the American people are reelecting their congressmen (that is, members of the House) at the highest rates in history. In the 1986 and 1988 elections, more than 98 percent of incumbent congressmen seeking reelection were returned to office. By now we have all heard the joke about there being more turnover in the British House of Lords or in the Soviet Politburo than in the U.S. House of Representatives. The interesting question is, Why? What has happened to transform what the Framers of the Constitution envisioned as the most democratic, turbulent, changeable branch of the national government into the least changeable, most stable of the elective branches? And to come around to the question of the moment, will limiting the number of terms a congressman or senator can serve do anything to remedy the problem?

Antifederalists: "Virtue Will Slumber"

This is not the first time in American history that a limit on the reeligibility of elected federal officials has been proposed. At the Constitutional Convention in 1787, whether the president ought to be eligible for reelection was extensively debated, although always in close connection with the related questions of his term of office and mode of election. With the invention of the electoral college and with his term fixed at four years, it was thought to be productive of good effects and consistent with his independence from the legislature to allow the president to be eligible for reelection indefinitely; and so it remained until the 22nd Amendment was added to the Constitution. But what is less well known is that the Constitutional Convention also considered limitations on the reeligibility of the lower house of the legislature. The so-called Virginia Plan, introduced by Edmund Randolph, would have rendered members of the House ineligible for reelection for an unspecified period after their term's end. The period was never specified because the Convention expunged the limitation less than a month after it had been proposed.

Nevertheless, the question of limiting congressional terms lived on. It was taken up vigorously by the Antifederalists, the opponents of the new Constitution, who urged that "rotation in office" be imposed not so much on House members as on senators, whose small number, long term of office, and multifaceted powers made them suspiciously undemocratic. The Antifederalists built upon the legacy of the Articles of Confederation, which required that members of Congress rotate out after serving three one-year terms within any five-year period. Quite a few critics of the Constitution attacked the unlimited reeligibility of the president, too, but the brunt of their criticism fell upon the Senate. In their view, it was a fatal mistake to neglect "rotation, that noble prerogative of liberty." As "An Office of the Late Continental Army" called it in a Philadelphia newspaper, rotation was the "noble prerogative" by which liberty secured itself, even as the Tudor and Stuart kings had ignobly wielded their "prerogative power" in defense of tyranny.

The current appeal for limits on congressional office-holding echoes the major themes of the Antifederalists 200 years ago. One of the most rigorous of the Constitution's critics, the writer who styled himself "The Federal Farmer," put it this way: "[I]n a government consisting of but a few members, elected for long periods, and far removed from the observation of the people, but few changes in the ordinary course of elections take place among the members; they become in some measure a fixed body, and often inattentive to the public good, callous, selfish, and the fountain of corruption." After serving several years in office, he continued, it will be expedient for a man "to return home, mix with the people, and reside some time with them; this will tend to reinstate him in the interests, feelings and views similar to theirs, and thereby confirm in him the essential qualifications of a legislator." Were the people watchful, they could recall him on their own and substitute a new representative at their discretion. But they are not sufficiently vigilant. As Patrick Henry warned at the Virginia ratifying convention, "Virtue will slumber. The wicked will be continually watching: Consequently you will be undone."

Federalists: The People Are Not Fools

The Antifederalist arguments were rejected by the advocates of the new Constitution. However, it is only for the presidency that the authors of the most authoritative defense of the Constitution, *The Federalist,* give a detailed refutation of the scheme of rotation in office. In *The Federalist*'s view, there is "an excess of refinement" in the notion of preventing the people from returning to office men who had proved worthy of their confidence. The people are not fools, at least not all of the time, and they can be trusted to keep a reasonably sharp eye on their representatives. So far as history can confirm such a proposition, it seems to pronounce in favor of *The Federalist.* Throughout the 19th and most of the 20th centuries, American politics was not characterized by a professional class of legislators insulated from the fluctuations, much less the deliberate changes, of public opinion. In the 19th century, it was not unusual for a majority of the membership of Congress to serve only one term; congressional turnover consistently averaged 40 to 50 percent every election. Occasionally it reached 60 or 70 percent.

The young Abraham Lincoln, for example, served only one term in the House of Representatives, in keeping with an informal rotation agreement he had negotiated with two Whig Party rivals in his district. Such agreements were not uncommon, and betokened a vigorous intraparty political life as well as keen competition between the parties: no party wanted its officeholders to betray an unrepublican ambition. But ambition was controlled informally by rotation within a party's bank of candidates so that the party and the country enjoyed the best of both worlds—a circulation of capable and experienced men through public office, with the possibility of keeping truly exceptional ones in office if circumstances demanded it.

Accordingly, even the most distinguished congressmen and senators of the 19th century pursued what by today's standards would be frenetic and irregular political careers. Henry Clay, famous as "the Great Compromiser," was sent thrice to the Senate to serve out someone else's term (the first time despite his being less than 30 years old); served two years in the Kentucky assembly, the second as its speaker; was elected seven times (not consecutively) to the House and three times was chosen Speaker, although he often resigned in midterm to take up a diplomatic post or run (unsuccessfully, three times) for president; and was elected twice to the Senate in his own right. Daniel Webster was elected to five terms in the House (not consecutively) and four terms in the Senate, in addition to running once (fruitlessly) for president and serving more than four nonconsecutive years as secretary of state under three presidents. John C. Calhoun was elected to four terms in the House, served seven years as secretary of war, was elected twice to the vice presidency, and then served two years of Robert Hayne's (of the Webster-Hayne debate) Senate term, two Senate terms in his own right, one year as secretary of state, and four more years in the Senate.

By the way, the ALCT's proposed constitutional amendment, which would limit members of Congress to 12 consecutive years in office (six terms for representatives, two for senators), would have had no impact on Clay's or Calhoun's career but would have disabled Webster, who was elected three times in a row to the Senate.

The Swing Era Ends

But the larger and more important point is that today's entrenched Congress is a product of the great changes in American politics that have occurred since the late 19th century, particularly the weakening of political parties and the great increase in the size and scope of the federal government. Serving in Congress has become a profession over the past 100 years. The average (continuous) career of congressmen hovered around five years at the turn of the century, already up significantly from its earlier levels; today, the figure has doubled again, with the average member of the House serving about 10 years. In the century after 1860, the proportion of freshmen in the House plummeted from nearly 60 percent to around 10 percent, about where it remains today. This gradual professionalization of Congress owes something to the gradual increase of power in Washington, which made it more attractive to hold office; and still more to the seniority system, introduced in the House after the famous revolt against the power of the Speaker around 1910. With the seniority system in place, districts had great incentives to keep their representatives serving continuously. But the contemporary problems of incumbency are something else again. Since 1971, when House Democrats voted in their caucus to elect committee chairmen by secret ballot rather than follow the rule of committee seniority, the perquisites of seniority have declined, in part. Yet congressional reelection rates have risen. If it is not the advantages of seniority that account for today's almost invulnerable incumbents, then what is it?

Since the Second World War, reelection rates have been very high, averaging more than 90 percent; they have risen even further recently, approaching 100 percent in the last few elections. The political scientist David Mayhew identified the key to the incumbency problem as "the vanishing marginals," that is, the decline over the past 40 years in the number of marginal or competitive House districts. (A victory margin of 50 to 55 percent makes a district marginal, that is, capable of being won by a challenger.) In 1948 most incumbents won narrowly, getting less than 55 percent of their district's vote. Twenty years later, three-fourths of the incumbents received 60 percent or more of their district's vote, making these essentially safe seats for the winning congressmen. So, not only are more incumbents than ever winning, they are winning by bigger margins than ever before.

Explanations for the decline in marginal districts have not been scarce. First, there is the effect of gerrymandered congressional districts, which tend to be drawn in such a fashion as to lock in incumbents of both parties. Researchers have shown, however, that marginal districts declined just as sharply in the 1960s in states that did *not* redistrict as in those that did; so gerrymandering cannot be the principal culprit. Then there is the effect of incumbency itself—the franking privilege, free publicity stemming from benefits delivered to the district, prodigious sums of money contributed by political action committees, all of which make possible the greater name recognition that is supposed to discourage unknown and underfunded challengers. As the rates of incumbent reelection have climbed, therefore, one would expect an increase in incumbent name recognition. But, as John Ferejohn and other analysts have shown, the data do not bear this out: incumbents are no better known now than they were before the marginal districts started vanishing. For all of the incumbents' advantages in name recognition, this factor cannot be the crucial one in explaining the decline in competitive House districts.

Faceless Bureaucracy's Friendly Face

In his arresting book *Congress: Keystone of the Washington Establishment,* the political scientist Morris Fiorina puts his finger on the nub of the problem. During the 1960s, congressmen began to put an unprecedented emphasis on casework or constituent service and pork-barrel activities as a way to ensure their reelection. The new emphasis was made possible precisely by "big government," the federal government's expansion of authority over state and local affairs that began dramatically with the New Deal and accelerated during the Great Society. As the federal bureaucracy expanded, more and more citizens found themselves dealing directly with federal agencies—the Social Security Administration, the Veterans Administration, the Equal Employment Opportunity Commission, the Environmental Protection Agency, and so on. To penetrate the mysteries of the administrative state, to find a friendly face amid the "faceless" bureaucrats and a helping hand among so many seemingly determined to do injustice in particular cases, citizens began increasingly to turn to their congressman for succor.

And they were encouraged to do so, particularly by the younger and more vulnerable congressmen who had come into office in the great Democratic waves of 1964 and 1974. Eventually, however, almost all congressmen caught on to the "new deal" made possible and necessary by the increased reach of Washington. The beauty of the new politics was that the same congressmen who were applauded for creating new federal agencies to tackle social problems also got credit for helping their constituents through the labyrinths of these impersonal bureaucracies. In Fiorina's words: "Congressmen take credit coming and going. They are the alpha and the omega." The more ambitious of them exploit the paradox shamelessly: The more bureaucracy they create, the more indispensable they are to their constituents. To which one must add: the longer they've been around Washington, the more plausible is their claim to know precisely how to aid their constituents with the bureaucracy.

It is clear that knowledge of these bureaucratic folkways is more important to voters than ever before. But it requires only a very small number of swing voters, perhaps only 5 percent or so, to transform a district from being marginal or competitive into being safe (thus increasing the incumbent's vote from, say, 53 to 58 percent). To explain the disappearing marginal districts it is therefore necessary only for a very small sector of the electorate to have been won over to the incumbent by the constituent service and pork-barrel opportunities opened up by an activist federal government. To this group of voters in particular, perhaps to most voters to one degree or another, the congressman's job is now thought to be as much administrative as political. The spirit of nonpartisan, expert administration—central to modern liberalism as it was conceived in the Progressive Era—is gradually coloring the public's view of the House of Representatives, transforming it from the most popular branch of the legislature into the highest branch of the civil service.

If this is true, the congressman's expertise is a peculiar sort, involving as it does interceding with civil servants (and appointed officials) in the spirit of personal, particularistic relations, not the spirit of impersonal rule-following associated with the civil service. Nonetheless, he is expected to keep benefits and services issuing to the district, just as a nonpartisan city manager is expected to keep the streets clean and the sewers flowing. And to the extent that ombudsmanship is a corollary of bureaucracy (as it seems to be, at least in democratic governments), his casework partakes of the spirit of administration rather than of political representation.

Hamilton's "Sordid Views"

Given the origins and nature of the problem with Congress (really with the House of Representatives, inasmuch as Senate incumbents remain beatable), it is apparent that limiting congressional terms to 12 years will do little or nothing to remedy the situation. Any new faces that are brought to Washington as the result of such an amendment will find themselves up against the same old incentives. They will still be eligible for reelection five times. How will they ensure their continued political prosperity without seeing to constituents' administrative needs? If anything, these new congressmen will find themselves confronting bureaucrats rendered more powerful by the representatives' own ignorance of the bureaucracy; for in the administrative state, knowledge is power. It is likely, therefore, that the new congressmen will initially be at a disadvantage relative to the agencies. To counter this they will seek staff members and advisers who are veterans of the Hill, and perhaps larger and more district-oriented staffs to help ward off challengers who would try to take advantage of their inexperience. Is it wise to increase the already expansive power of bureaucrats and congressional staff for the sake of a new congressman in the district every half-generation or so?

The proposed limitation on congressional terms would also have most of the disadvantages of the old schemes of rotation in office that were criticized by the Federalists. Consider these points made by Alexander Hamilton in *Federalist* No. 72 (concerning rotation in the presidency, but still relevant to rotation in Congress). In the first place, setting a limit on office-holding "would be a diminution of the inducements to good behavior." By allowing indefinite reeligibility, political men will be encouraged to make their interest coincide with their duty, and to undertake "extensive and arduous enterprises for the public benefit" because they will be around to reap the consequences. Second, term limits would be a temptation to "sordid views" and "peculation." As Gouverneur Morris put it at the Constitutional Convention, term limits say to the official, "make hay while the sun shines." Nor does a long term of eligibility (12 years in this case) remove the difficulty. No one will know better than the present incumbent how difficult it will be to defeat the future incumbent. So the limits of his career will always be visible to him, as will the temptation to "make hay" as early as possible.

A third disadvantage of term limits is that they could deprive the country of the experience and wisdom gained by an incumbent, perhaps just when that experience is needed most. This is particularly true for senators, whose terms would be limited even though Senate races are frequently quite competitive (recall 1980 and 1986), and that the Senate was precisely the branch of the legislature in which the Framers sought stability, the child of long service.

Distraction for GOP

For conservatives and Republicans, the pursuit of a constitutional amendment to limit congressional terms would act as a colossal distraction from the serious work of politics that needs to be done.

The worst effect of the incumbents' advantage in the House is to have saddled America with divided government since 1968 (excepting Jimmy Carter's administration, which was bad for other reasons). Professor Fiorina estimates that if marginal districts had not declined, the Republicans would have taken control of the House five times in the past quarter-century—in 1966, 1968, 1972, 1980, and 1984 (he did not evaluate the 1988 results). Because the marginals did decline, the Democrats, trading on the power of their incumbent members, retained control of the House throughout this period despite the succession of Republican presidents who were elected.

It would be unfair, of course, to blame the Democrats' popularity wholly on the decline in marginal districts. The GOP has not done well enough in open-seat elections to rely on the incumbency effect as the all-purpose excuse for its inability to take the House. But it is a fair conjecture that the ethos of administrative politics works to the Republicans' disadvantage even in those districts lacking a Democratic incumbent. Which is not to say that Republican incumbents don't look out for themselves; they do. But the spirit of casework and pork-barrel cuts against the grain of conservative Republican principles, and so it is hard for Republican candidates to sound like Republicans when they are preaching the gospel according to FDR and LBJ. More to the point, it is difficult for the Republican party to articulate why people ought to consider themselves Republicans and ought to vote a straight GOP ticket under these circumstances.

The attempt to limit congressional terms would do nothing to relieve Republicans of these tactical disadvantages. What is needed is not a gimmick to stir up political competition, but the prudence and courage to take on the strategic political questions dividing conservative Republicans and liberal Democrats. By (among other things) reconsidering the scope and power of the federal government, by opposing the extension of centralized administration over more and more of American life, Republicans could inaugurate robust political competition. President Reagan and the Republican party were successful at this in 1980, when the GOP gained 33 seats in the House and took control of the Senate. But they seem to have neglected those lessons in succeeding elections.

By the 1992 election, when reapportionment and redistricting have taken hold (and assuming a generous number of retirements), there could be 100 House districts without an incumbent. To win these the Republicans will require not just the better party organization they have been assiduously building, important as that is, but also a moral and political argument against what, to borrow the 18th-century vocabulary, could be called the corruption of the national legislature and of national politics generally—not corruption in the sense of criminal venality, but in the sense of insulating our legislators from the currents of national political opinion, and encouraging them, and their constituents, to subordinate the public good to their own private welfare.

In this fight, congressional term limitations would be at best a distraction. If the American people want to vote all incumbents out of office, or just those particular incumbents known as liberal Democrats, they can do so with but the flick of a lever. All they need is a good reason.

A-3. CAN THE STATES CONSTITUTIONALLY IMPOSE TERM LIMITS ON MEMBERS OF CONGRESS?: A LEGAL DEBATE

Editors' note: In 1992, the voters of Florida will be asked to vote on a term-limit initiative that will apply to members of the U.S. Congress as well as to the state legislature. In this respect, the initiative will be similar to one that Colorado voters adopted in 1990. In most cases, it will be impossible to test the constitutionality of a state limit on federal office until the limit directly affects a sitting incumbent. Until then, courts would be likely to say that a lawsuit does not yet present a "case or controversy" that is "ripe" for adjudication.

For a time at the end of 1991, however, it looked as if there might be a genuine case or controversy decided in the state of Florida. That state's constitution permits its attorney general to seek an advisory opinion from the state supreme court on proposed ballot initiatives. The attorney general did seek opinions on questions of both state and federal constitutional law. On December 19, 1991, the state court ruled that the term-limit initiative met the state's own legal requirements for appearing on the ballot. However, the court, in a divided vote, declined to decide whether the initiative would violate the federal Constitution, saying that it would be more appropriate to defer such a decision until after an initiative is adopted.

Although the Florida court did not decide the important questions of federal constitutional law, the court did receive the first full set of legal briefs prepared on that issue. The pages that follow reproduce the arguments in three of those briefs. The first, supporting the constitutionality of placing state limitations on members of Congress, was filed by Cleta Deatherage Mitchell on behalf of the Term Limits Legal Institute. The second, on the opposite side of the issue, was written by two attorneys for the U.S. House of Representatives, Steven R. Ross and Charles Tiefer, on behalf of Rep. Lawrence Smith (D-Fla.). The third selection is from a reply brief by Mitchell, in which she gives detailed responses to Ross's and Tiefer's arguments.

Citations and footnotes are omitted from these excerpts. Other omissions are indicated by ellipses.

Brief in Support of Limited
Political Terms Initiative
by Cleta Deatherage Mitchell

Proposition: Term limits do not impose additional qualifications upon federal candidates in contravention of Article II, Section 2 of the United States Constitution.

Political opponents of term limits for U.S. senators and congressmen invariably revert to their ultimate attack on the issue which is their contention that it is "unconstitutional." In fact, that is not correct. Providing for a required rotation in office is in keeping with the fundamental tenets of the United States Constitution and the principles on which the American system of government is founded. . . .

The United States Supreme Court has, through the years and through many decisions, upheld the right of the states to regulate elections, including the electoral procedures related to the candidacies of persons seeking federal office.

In *Storer v. Brown* (1974), the Court upheld a California statute which provided that candidates could not file for office as independents if they had been registered as a member of a political party within one year preceding the primary election. Certain prospective candidates for Congress challenged the state law on constitutional grounds, stating that the statute added qualifications for the office of United States Congressman, contrary to Art. I, sec. 2, cl. 2 of the United States Constitution.

The Supreme Court rejected the challenge, noting that "the States are given the initial task of determining the qualifications of voters who will elect members of Congress, Art. I, sec. 2, cl. 1. The Court went on to discuss Art. I, sec. 4, cl. 1, which authorizes the elections for senators and representatives, saying:

> . . . In any event, the States have evolved comprehensive, and in many respects, complex election codes regulating in most substantial ways, with respect to both federal and state elections, the time, place, and manner of holding primary and general elections, the registration and qualifications of voters, *and the selection and qualification of candidates.*

. . . The Supreme Court has *not* been reluctant to uphold restrictions on candidates. In various decisions, the Court has denied congressional candidates' challenges to specific state laws which kept the candidate from the ballot.

In *Jenness v. Fortson* (1971), the Court upheld a signature gathering requirement for candidates in Georgia, including federal candidates.

While striking down certain candidate filing fee requirements imposed by the state of Texas, the Court unanimously recognized that the state has a legitimate interest in regulating elections. *Bullock v. Carter* (1972).

A number of federal appellate and district courts have also ruled against congressional candidates in favor of the state's right to regulate elections, including placing restrictions on the eligibility of persons to have their names placed on the official ballots prepared by the state. In *Williams v. Tucker* (1974), an incumbent congressman filed an action seeking to have his name placed on the ballot for the general election, arguing that Pennsylvania's filing statutes created additional qualifications for the office of United States Congressman in violation of the federal Constitution. The Court disagreed, referring to Art. I, sec. 4, cl. 1 of the Constitution, authorizing the states to prescribe "the Times, Places, and Manner of Holding Elections for Senators and Representatives," stating that "the Pennsylvania Election Code merely regulates the manner of holding elections and does not add qualifications for office."

In *Signorelli v. Evans* (1980) the Court upheld a New York law which prohibited a judicial officer from filing as a candidate for Congress. (". . . a state regulation, though it functions indirectly as a requirement for congressional candidacy, may not necessarily be an unconstitutional additional qualification if it is designed to deal with a subject within traditional state authority.")

The Ninth Circuit Court of Appeals in 1983 upheld an Arizona constitutional provision which limited incumbents except in their final year of office from filing for another office, state or federal, finding that such a regulation was not an impermissible additional qualification for United States Congress (*Joyner v. Moffard*, 1983).

Brief of the *Amicus Curiae*
United States Representative Lawrence J. Smith
by Steven R. Ross and Charles Tiefer

The precedents establish that neither Congress nor the states may add to the three qualifications for holding congressional office prescribed by Article I, Sections 2 and 3.

In *Powell v. McCormack* (1969), the Supreme Court definitively determined that neither house of Congress has ". . . authority to *exclude* any person, duly elected by his constituents, who meets all the requirements for membership expressly prescribed in the Constitution." In *Powell*, the House of Representatives had attempted to add an additional qualification for membership in the House, by excluding a newly elected Representative on the basis of prior ethical transgressions. Specific ethical violations would seem a reasonably additional qualification if anything could be, and the Court acknowledged the House's authority under Art. I, sec. 5 to "be the Judge of the ... Qualifications of its own Members," but held that ". . . in judging the qualifications of its members Congress is limited to the standing qualifications prescribed in the Constitution." In other words, beyond the three standing qualifications of age, citizenship, and residency, Congress could impose no more. Since Adam Clayton Powell met those three requirements, he could not be barred from service.

The Supreme Court founded its ruling on an exhaustive review of the constitutional origins of the Qualifications Clause and practice pursuant to them. It is unnecessary to recapitulate in detail that reasoning. It suffices to note the Court's confirmation of ". . . the views of the Framers on the issue of qualifications." The Court cited James Madison's statement that "the qualifications of . . . [those who were] elected were fundamental articles in a Republican Govt. and ought to be fixed by the Constitution." Similarly, the Court cited and emphasized Alexander Hamilton's statements that *"the qualifications of the persons who may choose or be chosen, as has been remarked upon other occasions, are defined and fixed in the Constitution, and are unalterable . . ."* Madison's and Hamilton's words are thus the Supreme Court's words, stated emphatically, that the list of qualifications is "fixed" and "defined" and "unalterable."

In fact, the Framers explicitly considered, and rejected, proposals for a limit on the number of terms of service. The Articles of Confederation had included a requirement of rotation in office for congressmen, and so one of the plans at the Constitutional Convention—the Randolph Plan—had proposed that the Constitution have a rotation qualification for the House of Representatives. However, the Framers rejected any such additional qualification. . . .

A fundamental principle of our representative democracy is, in Hamilton's words, "that the people should choose whom they please to govern them." As Madison pointed out at the convention, this principle is undermined as much by limiting whom the people can select as by limiting the franchise itself. Precisely such an impermissible fourth qualification, as numerous courts have recognized, is any disqualification on the ground of prior service in office. The proposed term-limit initiative would take the list of qualifications for service in the House, "fixed" and "unalterable" as Madison and Hamilton described it and as *Powell v. McCormack* confirmed it, and make that list neither fixed nor unalterable, by adding a fourth qualification.

Of course, the Florida attorney general raised this question on page four of his petition: "The Court, therefore, may wish to consider whether the amendment would amount to a change in qualifications for the offices of United States representative and senator and whether the State of Florida has the authority to alter such qualifications." In presenting this issue, the attorney general appropriately cited the two applicable Florida cases, which concerned a Florida statute regarding resigning state offices before candidacies, *Stack v. Adams* (1970), and *State ex rel. Davis v. Adams* (1970). In *Stack v. Adams,* the court explained why Florida could not add, by "state constitutions" or statutes, any additional qualification for the United States Representatives from Florida:

> That the qualifications prescribed in the United States Constitution are exclusive and that state constitutions and laws can neither add to nor take away from them is universally accepted and recognized. The state courts, passing on the question, have, in applying it to a variety of state laws, so held with singular unanimity. . . .

From this, the court deduced a "fundamental principle": "The fundamental principle is the right of the people to elect whom they choose to elect for office."

In *State ex rel. Davis v. Adams* (1970) this court agreed with those basic standards. "The qualifications for membership in the House of Representatives are thus provided in Article I, sec. 2, United States Constitution. It is elementary that these qualifications are paramount and exclusive. State constitutions and laws can neither add to, nor take away from them." . . .

Consistent with this fundamental rule of the federal Constitution, all the various proposed additional qualifications for membership in the House akin to the term-limit qualification have been uniformly judicially invalidated. For example, numerous courts have prohibited two other suggested qualifications for membership in the House of obvious appeal: limitations against service by ex-felons and limitations against service by persons residing outside the district. Plainly, if a state cannot even bar ex-felons if voters want them, it cannot bar candidates based on their prior congressional terms of office, for the same reason: states cannot add qualifications to the three in the federal Constitution. A variety of other proposed qualifications have similarly been rejected.

Supporters of the term-limit initiative can find no comfort in cases which regulate aspects of the manner of running, such as the election methods involved in *Storer v. Brown* (1974) or *Williams v. Tucker* (1974). In *Storer,* the Supreme Court upheld a California law precluding an individual from identifying himself on the ballot as an independent candidate for Congress "if he had a registered affiliation with a qualified political party at any time within one year prior to the immediately preceding primary election." In *Williams,* a federal district court upheld a Pennsylvania statute which put to candidates the choice of skipping the primaries or accepting their outcome (i.e., did not allow candidates who ran and lost in primaries to go on the general ballot). (See also *Anderson v. Celebreeze,* 1983.)

The provisions upheld in *Storer* and *Williams* are readily distinguishable from the limitation threatened by the term-limit initiative. Those laws considered in *Storer* and *Williams* were designed to maintain ". . . the integrity of the various routes to the ballot," not to restrict individuals from holding positions in Congress. Forcing a potential candidate to choose between two alternative methods to obtain ballot status—through a party or independent of a party, but not both—bears no relation to a provision flatly prohibiting running at all. By contrast, the term-limit provision forecloses this opportunity entirely. . . .

The authoritative commentators have reached the same conclusion that the states cannot add a new qualification, such as a term limit, for members of Congress. As Justice Story explained in his celebrated treatise, "The states have just as much right, and no more, to prescribe new qualifications for a representative, as they have for a president. Each is an officer of the Union, deriving his powers and qualifications from the Constitution, and neither created by, dependent upon, nor controllable by, the states."

These commentators follow the rulings of the early House itself, whose members were contemporaries cognizant of the Framers' original intent. In 1790 the state of Maryland enacted a statute requiring that candidates for the House of Representatives have inhabited their district for a year prior to election. In 1807 the district of Baltimore elected a candidate, William McCreery, whom the House considered not to comply with the Maryland statute. The House concluded:

> [T]he States could not reserve a power to add to the qualifications of Representatives. If they could do this, any sort of dangerous qualification might be established—of property, color, creed, or political professions. . . . The Constitution had carefully prescribed in what ways the States might interfere in the elections of Congressmen. They might prescribe the "times, place, and manner" of holding elections. . . . This was all the Constitution gave to the States. . . . The qualifications of Representatives did not come within the range of powers granted. . . .

The House voted to seat McCreery, and he was seated. Such early pronouncements by Congress are deemed by the Supreme Court persuasive authority regarding the original intent of the Framers. Both the House and the Senate subsequently reaffirmed the ban against states imposing additional qualifications, relying on the authoritative commentaries subsequently prepared.

Reply Brief
by Cleta Deatherage Mitchell

There is no case law existent which has held that limiting the terms of political officials is unconstitutional or illegal.

Opponents have together filed briefs totalling 119 pages, but have cited not *one* court decision or any other precedent (of more than 150 legal authorities cited) which has held that term limits are unconstitutional or illegal. Opponents have also attempted to distinguish the case authority cited wherein courts have held that term limitations *are* constitutional, particularly the recent California Supreme Court opinion upholding term limits imposed by California voters on their elected officials.

In its decision, *Legislature of the State of California, et al. v. Eu* (October 10, 1991), the California court rejected the very arguments being offered to this court. It is noteworthy that one of the Respondents herein, NCSL, filed its *amicus curiae* brief in the California proceeding, unsuccessfully arguing to that court that the term limitation enacted by the voters of that state should be declared unconstitutional. The California Supreme Court disagreed, upholding in a 6-1 decision a lifetime ban on candidates seeking continued election to the same office:

> On balance, we conclude the interests of the state in incumbency reform outweigh any injury to incumbent office holders and those who would vote for them. . . . *no decisions of the United States Supreme Court have been found that suggest a limitation on incumbency would be unconstitutional.* Although such limitations may restrict the franchise, if we use a balancing test that weighs "the enlargement of the franchise by guaranteeing competitive primary and general elections" against "incidental disenfranchisement" of some voters, the court "must conclude that restrictive provisions on the succession of incumbents do not frustrate but rather further the policy of the Fourteenth Amendment."
>
> . . . In sum, it would be anomalous to hold that a statewide initiative measure aimed at "restor[ing] a free and democratic system of fair election" and "encourag[ing] qualified candidates to seek public office" is invalid as an unwarranted infringement of the rights to vote and to seek public office. We conclude the Legislature and compelling interests set forth in the measure outweigh the narrower interests of petitioner legislators and the constituent who wish to perpetuate their incumbency.

Opponents rely on a multitude of case law in their efforts to extrapolate some glimmer of pertinence to the issue of term limits—but the fact remains, the only case authority in which limited political terms have been squarely before a court has resulted in favorable rulings for term limits.

Insofar as the issue of a state's right to limit the terms of federal legislators, opponents rely heavily on *Powell v. McCormack* (1969). However, *Powell* does not stand for the proposition for which it is advanced by opponents. Rather, the Supreme Court in *Powell* specifically recognized that *in addition to* Mr. Powell's having met the qualifications for membership in Congress as contained in Art. I, Sec. 2 of the United States Constitution, *viz.*, age, citizenship, and inhabitancy, Mr. Powell had also been *duly elected* to the United States House of Representatives, under the election laws of the state of New York, which were enacted by that state pursuant to Art. I, Sec. 4 of the United States Constitution.

The exclusion resolution adopted by the U.S. House of Representatives at issue in *Powell* stated in the very first paragraph:

> First, Adam Clayton Powell possesses the requisite qualifications of age, citizenship and inhabitancy for membership in the House of Representatives *and holds a Certificate of election from the State of New York.*

Throughout the proceedings involving Mr. Powell, there was never any argument that his election under New York's election code had been unconstitutional nor was there ever any dispute about the authority of the state of New York to set requirements for Mr. Powell's election, including candidacy, party affiliation, ballot appearance, and the like.

In fact, a review of New York's election code then—and now—reveals that all candidates, even those for federal office from New York, are bound by strict rules regarding their candidacy, designation by a political party, nominations, and elections.

Further, the Second Circuit Court of Appeals in a 1976 opinion affirmed a lower court's ruling upholding the constitutionality of New York's election law requirements governing candidacy for the United States Senate from New York, wherein an individual had been denied the right to run as a candidate for U.S. Senate by a political party. The lower court, via a three-judge federal panel, concluded that a political party *and the state of New York have a vital interest in regulating qualification of candidates for office, including federal office.*

Opponents desperately want this court to believe that there is some law or case authority somewhere in which the limitation of incumbents' terms of office is unconstitutional. The reality is, opponents have cited no such authority, because none exists. To compound their problem, the primary case cited by opponents and relied upon by them to support their argument, namely, *Powell v. McCormack* has virtually no relevance to the issue of term limitations other than to demonstrate that the U.S. House of Representatives, the U.S. Supreme Court, and the litigants and participants in the case, all agreed that *in addition* to the qualification set forth by the Constitution in Art. I, Sec. 2, Mr. Powell had been *duly elected* to Congress pursuant to the powers conferred on the state of New York under Art. I, Sec. 4.

Opponents' recitations of constitutional history are incorrect and misleading and these proceedings are not the proper forum for an in-depth review of American constitutional and legal history.

Despite the lengths to which opponents have gone to conjure language from early American legal history which they would have this court construe as supporting a constitutional ban on term limits, the fact is that no such ban exists. Opponents have cited certain writings of James Madison and others as somehow rejecting the notion of rotation in office by the Founding Fathers.

... However, *Federalist Papers No. 53* and *62* were not addressed to the issue of rotation in office (term limits). Rather, *Federalist Paper No. 53* was an explanation of why U.S. House of Representatives' terms should be two years, rather than having annual elections. *Federalist Paper No. 62* was directed toward certain factions in 1788 who were distressed because the proposed constitution did not provide for a single legislative house, elected directly by the people. One must read the *entire* papers cited (and those immediately preceding) in order to understand that Madison's remarks were designed to explain why there should be two (2) houses of Congress, why House terms should be two (2) years, not one, and why the Senate should be elected *indirectly* by the state legislatures, rather than directly by the people themselves.

Madison would be startled to learn in 1991 that the rotation planned by the Framers (one-third of the United States Senate rotated every two years) does not occur in reality today, and that the presumed biennial rotation of members of the U.S. House of Representatives, in what was supposed to be the raucous, lively, ever dynamic people's house, is nonexistent. Instead, incumbents return there at nearly a 100% rate every two years. How would one explain to the Founding Fathers that members of Congress have devised elaborate systems to maintain their continuation in office, whereby, for example, in 1990, incumbent members of the U.S. House of Representatives collectively received $88 million from political action committee (PAC) contributions compared to challengers' receipt of less than $7 million from

PACs. And that in a year where, according to Common Cause, a non-partisan public interest group, of the 406 House incumbents seeking reelection in 1990, 79 had no major party opposition; another 158 had opponents who had raised less than $25,000 by three weeks before the election; and 124 others had opponents who had raised more than $25,000 but less than half the amount the incumbents had raised. The 102d Congress currently sitting is comprised of nearly 90% incumbents, and almost half of those have been in the same office longer than a decade.

Fact: The Constitution is silent on the issue of limiting terms of office for members of Congress, as are the Federalist Papers. The only mention of "rotation" of federal office discussed in various Federalist Papers referenced the fact that one-third of the U.S. Senate would be "rotated" every two years. Perhaps we could infer from these writings that the members of the U.S. Senate were to be limited to one term only, to assure the rotation Mr. Hamilton described.

It is not for this court to attempt in these proceedings to glean from the silence of the Constitution a sufficient directive to deny Florida voters the right to vote on limiting political terms. "In many instances we do not know whether an omission from the Constitution of 1787 represents (1) an oversight, (2) a deliberate rejection of some proposal by members of the convention, or (3) an intentional ambiguity that resulted from an expedient compromise."

The silence of the Constitution on a particular issue has never been held to be a permanent prohibition on its development. For instance, the concept of judicial review is not set forth in the language of the Constitution and yet is one of the central features of American democratic government.

Furthermore, even the explicit language of the Constitution did not act to supersede the powers of the citizenry to alter the manner in which the members of the United States Senate were elected. In a strong empirical precedent for allowing voters to limit their elected officials' terms—including federal officials—there was a long and ultimately successful struggle to eliminate indirect election of the U.S. Senate. During the period before the U.S. Constitution was amended to make uniform the direct election of all U.S. Senators, the states (particularly those with the initiative and referendum powers) acted in a grass-roots movement to do so. In 1875, Nebraska provided for a popular preferential vote on candidates for the Senate. In 1899, Nevada enacted a senatorial primary law. In 1904, Oregon, by initiative, adopted a new election law providing that the legislature could elect only members of the U.S. Senate nominated by petition of the people. The law further stated that the candidates would be selected by popular vote in a general election on a ballot which advised voters whether the candidates did or did not support the direct senatorial preference election. By 1912 twenty-nine states had senatorial primaries whereby candidates were chosen by popular vote, thus creating, over time, a U.S. Senate in which over half the members had been elected via this route, *notwithstanding the explicit language in the U.S. Constitution— and the* Federalist Papers—*to the contrary.* The Constitution specifically conferred the selection of U.S. Senators on the state legislatures, in Art. I, Sec. 3, but the people had other ideas. The precedent of history establishes that Art. I, Sec. 4, permits states to unilaterally regulate the procedure of federal election within their borders, even contrary to explicit constitutional provisions, except where those actions may be directed at wealth, race, or some other narrow, protected grounds.

Finally, let us not forget that all constitutional power is derived from the consent of the governed, and it would ill-behoove this court to interfere with the authority of the people to express themselves on the issue of term limitations based on some non-existent Constitutional prohibition, particularly when the Constitution is fundamentally an instrument of the people.

A-4. *CALIFORNIA LEGISLATURE*
V.
MARCH FONG EU, SECRETARY OF STATE
October 10, 1991

OPINION OF THE COURT (Chief Justice Lukas, joined by
Justices Panelli, Kennard, Arabian, Baxter, and George): . . .

Effect on Voting and Candidacy Rights

Petitioners [California legislature] . . . assert that the term limitations of Proposition 140 violate the First and Fourteenth Amendments
of the federal Constitution. They observe that under Proposition 140,
as previously discussed, once the prescribed maximum terms have
expired, office holders are forever barred from running for the office
they held. According to petitioners, this lifetime ban substantially
burdens two fundamental rights, namely, the right to vote and the right
to be a candidate for public office. Petitioners, urging "strict scrutiny"
of the new measure, suggest that no "compelling state interest"
supports such a lifetime ban. (See *Eu v. San Francisco Democratic
Com.*, 1989 [hereafter *Eu*].)

Respondents [March Fong Eu, secretary of state, et al.], on the
other hand, assert the measure is valid under the balancing test
announced in *Anderson v. Celebrezze* (1983), discussed below. Respondents noting certain mitigating aspects of the measure contend
that the public policy served by Proposition 140 is both rational and
compelling, having only minimal effects on voting or candidacy rights.
We first turn to the question of the proper standard for resolving
petitioners' challenge. . . .

In *Canaan v. Abdelnour* (1985) we struck down a city's blanket
prohibition against write-in voting in municipal elections. In so doing,

---

In this opinion, which is followed by a dissent, the California Supreme Court sustained
the right of the voters to impose term limitations on members of the state legislature.
(Proposition 140 did not reach members of the U.S. Congress.) On March 9, 1992, the
U.S. Supreme Court refused to hear an appeal in the case, thus upholding the state
court's decision. Citations and footnotes are omitted from these excerpts. Other
omissions are indicated by ellipses.

we applied the balancing test set forth in *Anderson v. Celebrezze,* wherein the court held unduly burdensome an Ohio law requiring independent candidates for the November 1980 presidential election to file their statements of candidacy by March of that year. The high court in *Anderson,* acknowledging that a state's regulatory interests in determining the eligibility of candidates "are generally sufficient to justify reasonable, nondiscriminatory restrictions," announced the following test:

> Constitutional challenges to specific provisions of a State's election laws ... cannot be resolved by any "litmus-paper test" that will separate valid from invalid restrictions. Instead, a court must resolve such a challenge by an analytical process that parallels its work in ordinary litigation. It must first consider the character and magnitude of the asserted injury to the rights protected by the First and Fourteenth Amendments that the plaintiff seeks to vindicate. It must then identify and evaluate the precise interests put forward by the State as justifications for the burden imposed by its rule. In passing judgment, the Court must not only determine the legitimacy and strength of each of those interests; it must also consider the extent to which those interests make it necessary to burden the plaintiff's rights. Only after weighing all these factors is the reviewing court in a position to decide whether the challenged provision is unconstitutional. The results of this evaluation will not be automatic; as we have recognized, there is "no substitute for the hard judgments that must be made."

With respect to *Anderson*'s requirement of showing the "necessity" of the particular burden imposed by the state, we must also consider whether there are any less drastic alternatives to a lifetime ban.

Thus, *Anderson v. Celebrezze, supra* requires us to consider three separate elements in ascertaining the constitutionality of state laws restricting access to the ballot: (1) the nature of the injury to the rights affected, (2) the interests asserted by the state as justifications for that injury, and (3) the necessity for imposing the particular burden affecting the plaintiff's rights, rather than some less drastic alternatives. Lacking any more specific guidance from the high court, we now apply *Anderson*'s balancing test to the challenged provisions of Proposition 140.

1. Character and Extent of Injury to Protected Rights

Two important rights are affected by Proposition 140, namely, the incumbent's right to run for public office, and the voters' right to reelect the incumbent to that office. Consequently, the "injury" to those rights resulting from the application of Proposition 140 is also twofold, namely, lifetime exclusion of the incumbent from the office previously held, and a corresponding permanent inability of the voters to return the incumbent to that office.

a. *Effect on Candidates*

As previously explained, Proposition 140 imposes a lifetime ban on legislators once they have completed the maximum number of terms. Petitioners argue, "In the long run, the term limitations permanently ban those who are arguably the most qualified candidates—incumbents with the experience and expertise in the legislative process necessary to the most effective representation of their constituencies." According to petitioners, qualified incumbents will be "purged" solely to seat "massive numbers" of inexperienced "newcomers." Petitioners predict that only a few qualified persons will be attracted to short-term public office.

Respondents, of course, dispute petitioners' premise that long-term legislators are inevitably better qualified than other candidates, and they believe that term limitations will encourage, rather than inhibit, new qualified candidates seeking short-term public service. They characterize the term limitations of Proposition 140 as additional candidacy requirements, akin to age, integrity, training, or residency, which have generally been upheld.

Respondents also stress three features of Proposition 140 that assertedly serve to mitigate the severity of its lifetime ban: First, the affected incumbent is not barred from seeking any other public office, including a seat in another legislative house or a statewide constitutional office. A former senator may seek a seat in the assembly, and vice versa. Second, the term limitations arise only after the incumbent already has had the opportunity to serve a significant period in office (i.e., eight years for a senator, and six years for a member of the assembly). Finally, the term limitations are generally applicable to persons elected or appointed on or after November 6, 1990. Except for some incumbent senators, past terms served do not count in calculating the limitation. Thus, by the time the term limitations of Proposition 140 come into play, the incumbent will have already served, and indeed may continue to serve, several terms in public office.

b. *Effect on Voters*

Petitioners also stress the impact on the voters who are prevented from casting their ballots for the particular candidate of their choice. Just as incumbent legislators are permanently barred from running for another term once they have served the prescribed number of terms, the voters are permanently barred from voting for such persons, at least for the legislative office they once held. According to petitioners, the voters thus will be denied the right to vote for those persons who arguably possess the best qualifications.

Additionally, petitioners note that because Proposition 140 was adopted on a statewide basis, "the disability [on candidates and voters] is imposed not by those who have the right to vote for the candidate, but rather by those outside the district." Petitioners thus suggest the resulting impact on or injury to the voters is aggravated or enhanced by reason of the ability of voters residing outside a particular voting district to essentially "veto" particular candidates within that district.

Respondents reply by citing federal court cases (e.g., *Burdick v. Takushi*) stating that voters have no constitutional right to vote for particular candidates. Additionally, respondents observe that the challenged measure does not fall into any of the categories of prior cases in which the right to vote was found impermissibly infringed. No identifiable groups of voters are excluded from voting or otherwise unduly burdened in the exercise of their franchise. Characterizing the term limitations of Proposition 140 as additional candidacy qualifications akin to age or residency, respondents submit that Proposition 140 does not truly impair the franchise, for the voters retain the basic fundamental right to cast their ballots for the *qualified* candidate of their choice.

Moreover, respondents observe that neither voter choice nor candidate eligibility is restricted based on the content of protected expression, political affiliation, or inherently arbitrary factors such as race, religion, or sex. The only criterion used is incumbency. Voters retain the ability to vote for any qualified candidate holding the beliefs or possessing the attributes they may desire in a public officeholder. Under these circumstances, First Amendment protection of political expression and promotion of the marketplace for ideas continue unabated.

Respondents further note that petitioners have cited no case supporting their theory that a voting restriction on "local" offices would be invalid if imposed by voters on a statewide basis. Indeed, such a rule would seemingly call in question any statewide legislation affecting the qualification of candidates for local election, such as age or residency requirements.

Finally, respondents suggest that because Proposition 140 was an initiative measure adopted by the people at a statewide election, any resulting injury to the exercise of the franchise should be deemed self-inflicted, and thus not constitutionally protected.

c. *Summary of Impact on Candidates and Voters*

In sum, although Proposition 140 does affect the rights of voters and candidates to a degree, there are several mitigating aspects, including the voters' continued right to vote for any qualified candidates, as well as the candidates' ability to run for other public offices, their entitlement to a significant period of service in office before the term limitations apply, and the "prospective" application of the limitation provision. Additionally, we should bear in mind that it is presently unclear under federal law whether and to what extent voters retain a constitutional right to vote for particular candidates such as the incumbent legislators affected by the challenged measure. Thus, the *legal* impact of Proposition 140 on the voters remains uncertain.

Having discussed the extent of the "asserted injury to the rights protected" (*Anderson v. Celebrezze*), we next analyze the "precise interests put forward by the State as justifications for the burden imposed by its rule" (*ibid.*).

2. *The Interests of the State*

Balanced against the foregoing negative impact on candidates and voters flowing from the challenged measure are the considerable state interests assertedly promoted thereby. In the words of new article IV, section 1.5, of the state constitution, term limitations are deemed necessary to restore "free, fair, and competitive elections," to "encourage qualified candidates to seek public office," and to eliminate "unfair incumbent advantages" that have resulted in an "extremely high number of incumbents" and created "a class of career politicians" instead of the "citizen representatives envisioned by the Founding Fathers."

According to respondents, the state's interests in limiting incumbency should support measures considerably stronger than a mere temporary disability from holding office. As respondents argue, the state's strong interests in protecting against an entrenched, dynastic legislative bureaucracy, and in thereby encouraging new candidates to seek public office, are both legitimate and compelling ones that support a lifetime ban from the office and outweigh any interest the incumbent legislators, or the voting public, may have in perpetuating the incumbents' positions of control.

The legitimacy of the foregoing asserted state interests in limiting incumbency are well recognized in analogous contexts. As stated by the West Virginia Supreme Court of Appeals in rejecting a similar challenge to a state constitutional amendment limiting the right of the governor to seek a third consecutive term, "Constitutional restrictions circumscribing the ability of incumbents to succeed themselves appear in over twenty state constitutions, and exist in the Twenty-second Amendment to the Constitution of the United States with regard to the presidency. The universal authority is that restriction upon the succession of incumbents serves a rational public policy and that, while restrictions may deny qualified men an opportunity to serve, as a general rule the over-all health of the body politic is enhanced by limitations on continuous tenure" (*State ex rel. Maloney v. McCartney* [W.Va., 1976]).

The *Maloney* decision continues by describing at length the substantial reasons for limiting the right of incumbents to succeed themselves. These include "the power of incumbent officeholders to develop networks of patronage and attendant capacities to deliver favorable disposed voters to the polls," "fears of an entrenched political machine which could effectively foreclose access to the political process," and the belief that regularly disrupting those "machines" "would stimulate criticism within political parties" and "ensure a meaningful, adversary, and competitive election."

In addition, *Maloney* explains that "it has long been felt that a limitation upon succession of incumbents removes the temptation to prostitute the government to the perpetuation of a particular administration. Meretricious policies which sacrifice the well-being of economic, social, racial, or geographic minorities are most likely where a political figure, political party, or political interest group can rely upon electorate inertia fostered by the hopelessness of encountering a seemingly invincible political machine."

Petitioners observe that *Maloney* involved a limitation on *consecutive* terms of a *governor*, rather than a lifetime ban on incumbent legislators. They suggest that term limitations on the executive branch are justified by the need to check the substantial concentration of power that the chief executive possesses, a consideration assertedly not applicable to the legislative branch. But we think that many, if not all, of the considerations mentioned in *Maloney* (e.g., eliminating unfair incumbent advantages, dislodging entrenched political machines, restoring open access to the political process, and stimulating electorate participation) would apply with equal force to the legislative branch.

In connection with petitioners' argument that Proposition 140's lifetime ban is unconstitutional, two other cases are instructive, though factually distinguishable. In *Clements v. Fashing* the high court upheld the validity of a Texas statute that rendered incumbent justices of the peace ineligible for the Texas legislature. The disability from office extended only during the term for which the justices were elected or appointed. A plurality of the high court took the position that barriers to a candidate's access to the ballot do not compel close scrutiny and stressed the "de minimis" nature of the restriction, noting that the act merely imposed a brief "waiting period" on current officeholders, and therefore could be sustained by a mere showing of some "rational predicate" to support it.

The *Clements v. Fashing* plurality did not affirmatively indicate that a lifetime bar to legislative service necessarily would be invalid. Significantly, unlike Proposition 140, the Texas act apparently was not aimed at limiting the powers of incumbency, but was based on the "rational predicate" that an affected justice will be less inclined to abuse his position or neglect his duties because of the justice's aspirations for higher office.

In *De Bottari v. Melendez* (1975) the court of appeal struck down a local ordinance prohibiting *recalled* council members from running for city council within a year of the recall. Although petitioners believe the case supports their position, closer scrutiny indicates otherwise. Finding the candidacy restriction too severe, the *De Bottari* court observed, "Cases in other jurisdictions upholding limitations on successive terms in office involve similar restrictions but are not authoritative here since such limitations serve totally *different governmental interests.*" *De Bottari,* using strict scrutiny, reviewed the interests that assertedly supported a temporary ban on candidacy by *recalled* candidates and found them insufficient to sustain the restriction. The court had no occasion to review the "different" interests served by general limitations on incumbency, as outlined by *Maloney.*

In sum, despite its distinguishing features, we concluded that *Maloney*'s analysis is quite pertinent to our determination whether permanent incumbency limitations are supported by legitimate and compelling considerations. We conclude they are so supported.

3. Necessity of Imposing Restrictions

We turn next to the "necessity" of imposing the restrictions of Proposition 140 on the dual rights at issue here (see *Anderson v. Celebrezze*). Petitioners contend that a lifetime ban on candidacy was unnecessary, and that other less "drastic" alternatives, such as a limitation on consecutive terms, together with additional restrictions on campaign contributions to legislators, decreased fringe and pension benefits, and additional incentives for early retirement would have been sufficient to promote and accomplish the state interests previously discussed.

As will appear, we conclude that the less drastic alternatives suggested by petitioners would have been inadequate to accomplish the declared purpose of Proposition 140 to eliminate the "class of career politicians" that assertedly had been created by virtue of the "unfair incumbent advantages" referred to in that measure.

Respondents stress the substantial advantages incumbent legislators enjoy in this state, advantages that permitted 92 percent of all incumbents to win reelection at this state's November 1990 general election. Indeed, respondents note that nine of these incumbents ran unopposed.

Respondents seem correct in this regard. Whether by reason of superior fund-raising ability, greater media coverage, larger and more experienced staffs, greater name recognition among the voters, favorably drawn voting districts, or other factors, incumbents do indeed appear to enjoy considerable advantages over other candidates. As Proposition 140's introductory statement indicates, the framers of the measure believed these substantial advantages of incumbency were unfair to other candidates and tended to create "a class of career politicians, instead of the citizen representatives envisioned by the Founding Fathers."

Petitioners suggest that a more reasonable alternative existed to the measure's lifetime ban: disqualification of the incumbent for the forthcoming term, thus "forcing the legislator to take one term off, before being eligible to run for the body." Yet, as respondents observe, the framers reasonably could conclude that a lifetime ban was necessary to assure that a former office holder could not reinvoke at least some of the advantages of incumbency to gain reelection after leaving office for a term or more.

Additionally, we believe the Framers might well have reasonably concluded that a mere ban on consecutive terms could encourage popular "career politicians" to trade terms with each other, or to attempt to arrange for a "caretaker" candidate, such as a spouse or relative, to hold office for them during the interrupted term. For example, when in 1966 George Wallace became legally ineligible to run for reelection as governor of Alabama because of state term limitations applicable to that office, his wife Lurleen successfully ran in his place, and served as governor until her death in 1968. George Wallace was reelected as governor in 1970 and again in 1974.

Realistically, only a lifetime ban could protect against various kinds of continued exploitation of the "advantages of incumbency" captured through past terms in office. The remainder of petitioners' suggested "alternatives" essentially involve narrow changes in the system of providing contributions or compensation for legislators, changes that would afford "career politicians" with independent resources little incentive to voluntarily terminate public service.

4. Conclusion

On balance, we conclude the interests of the state in incumbency reform outweigh any injury to incumbent office holders and those who would vote for them. As *Maloney* observed no decisions of the United States Supreme Court have been found that suggest a limitation on incumbency would be unconstitutional. Although such limitations may restrict the franchise (but see cases indicating voters have no right to vote for particular candidates, e.g., *Burdick v. Takushi*), if we use a balancing test that weighs "the enlargement of the franchise by guaranteeing competitive primary and general elections" against "incidental disenfranchisement" of some voters, the court "must conclude that restrictive provisions on the succession of incumbents do not frustrate but rather further the policy of the Fourteenth Amendment" (*Maloney*).

It is true, as petitioners observe, that respondents have not offered evidence to support all of the various premises on which Proposition 140 is based. But as the United States Supreme Court pointed out in *Munro v. Socialist Workers Party,* upholding state restrictions on minority party candidacy, a state need not demonstrate empirically all of the various evils that its regulations seek to combat: "Such a requirement would necessitate that a state's political system sustain some level of damage before the legislature could take corrective action. Legislatures, we think, should be permitted to respond to potential deficiencies in the electoral process with foresight rather than reactively, provided that the response is reasonable and does not significantly impinge on constitutionally protected rights." We have no reason to doubt that the high court would give similar leeway to state regulations imposed directly by the people through the initiative process.

In sum, it would be anomalous to hold that a statewide initiative measure aimed at "restor[ing] a free and democratic system of fair elections," and "encourag[ing] qualified candidates to seek public office" is invalid as an unwarranted infringement of the rights to vote and to seek public office. We conclude the legitimate and compelling interests set forth in the measure outweigh the narrower interests of petitioner legislators and the constituents who wish to perpetuate their incumbency.

CONCURRING AND DISSENTING OPINION of Justice Mosk:

I concur in the judgment insofar as it invalidates Proposition 140's purported restrictions on the retirement benefits of legislators.

Otherwise I dissent. . . .

I now turn to the question of whether Proposition 140 amounts to an unconstitutional revision.

As explained above, the initiative has as a broad purpose the transformation of the California constitution from an instrument that allows, and perhaps actually invites, the election and reelection to the legislature of "politicians," to one that prohibits such a result and in fact encourages service by "citizens."

I observe at the outset that the wisdom of Proposition 140 is of no consequence to the analysis. To be sure, the initiative may be judged foolish and impractical. But it may also be viewed otherwise. Certainly, the exercise of governmental authority by "citizens" as opposed to "politicians," including the wielding of legislative power, has long been an ideal within the Western political tradition, and sometimes even a reality. Again, however, the desirability of the measure is immaterial.

The basic governmental plan of California is established, of course, by the California constitution. The powers are the legislative, executive, and judicial. . . . The nature of the three powers and the function of the three branches have been settled since virtually the inception of our policy. In *Nougues v. Douglass* (1857), the court states:

> The three great departments are essentially different in their constitution, nature, and powers, and in the means provided for each by the Constitution, to enable each to perform its appropriate functions. These three departments are all equally necessary to the very existence of the government. The legislative power is the creative element in the government, and was exercised partly by the people in the formation of the Constitution. It is primarily [*sic*] and original, antecedent and fundamental, and must be exercised before the other departments can have anything to do. Its exercise is a condition precedent, and the exercise of the executive and judicial functions are conditions *subsequent.* The legislative power makes the laws, and after they are so made, the judiciary expounds and the executive executes them.

Manifestly, Proposition 140 amounts to an unconstitutional revision because of its significant effect on the legislature. As the discussion above reveals, the legislature is a fundamental component of the state constitutional system. It is one of the "three great departments" and is "necessary to the very existence of the government." Indeed, its power is the "creative element" in the scheme. Moreover, the legislature must be deemed fundamentally altered by any substantial change in its nature or character.

Finally, the change that would be effected by Proposition 140 would be substantial. In the state's history, only two such changes have clearly been of this sort: the movement from a full-time legislature with broad powers to a part-time body subject to narrow limitations, which was effected when the present constitution superseded the original instruction in 1879; and a movement in the opposite direction, which was accomplished under the successful proposal of the California Constitutional Revision Commission in 1966. The change here would be of similar magnitude: "Citizens" would be put in the legislature in the place of "politicians."

In *Raven v. Deukmejian,* we held that section 3 of Proposition 115 amounted to an unconstitutional revision because of its significant effect on the judiciary. The provision in question, designed to amend article I, section 24, of the California constitution, would have restricted the power of state courts to interpret certain state constitutional rights of criminal defendants. Like the legislature, the judiciary is one of the "three great departs" and is "necessary to the very existence of the government" (*Nougues v. Douglass*). Also like the legislature, it must be deemed fundamentally altered by any substantial change in its nature or character. The change threatened by section 3 of Proposition 115 would have been such.

It follows *a fortiori* that an initiative that would put laypersons into the judiciary in the place of jurists would amount to an unconstitutional revision because of its significant effect on that branch. Clearly, such a provision would go far beyond section 3 of Proposition 115 in fundamentally altering the courts by effecting a substantial change in their nature and character.

If an initiative like the foregoing would be an unconstitutional revision, so too Proposition 140. The one would improperly affect the judiciary, the other the legislature.

In sum, Proposition 140 would fundamentally alter a fundamental component of the state constitutional system by effecting a substantial change in the nature and character of the legislature. Such an alteration, of course, would be qualitatively extensive, affecting the "underlying principles upon which [the Constitution] rests" (*Livermore v. Waite*). Therefore, it would be revisory.

The majority conclude to the contrary. They reason that Proposition 140's possible future consequences for the legislature are not dispositive. I agree. They also reason that the initiative does not affect the legislature's constitutional structure or powers. Again, I agree. But as explained above, a judiciary comprising laypersons is fundamentally different from one made up of jurists—even if its structure and powers are the same. Similarly, a legislature of "citizens" is fundamentally different from one of "politicians." It is a "citizen" legislature that is the measure's object and also its necessary and inevitable effect.

The majority's claim that "the initiative process may represent the only *practical* means of achieving the kind of 'reform' of the legislature involved here" is simply immaterial. The initiative process is not a *proper* means of achieving "reforms" that are revisory. True, "our Constitution plac[es] '[a]ll political power' in the people" and recognizes their " '. . . right to alter or reform [government] when the public good may require.' " But it also restricts the wielding of that power and the exercise of that right through various provisions—among which, of course, are the requirements governing revision.

A-5. THE CALIFORNIA BALLOT PAMPHLET: THE PROS AND THE CONS OF PROPOSITION 140

November 6, 1990

Editors' note: The California Ballot Pamphlet is a document prepared by the secretary of state. Among other things, it contains summaries and full texts of proposed constitutional amendments and statutes, objective analyses prepared by the legislative analyst, and arguments on both sides of the issue. The pro and con arguments are written by leaders who are active in the political campaign on both sides. There are four sets of arguments in the pamphlet: the first is in favor of the proposition, next is a rebuttal to the argument in favor, third is an argument against term limits, and the last is a rebuttal to the arguments against. The people who prepared each set of arguments are identified, together with their organizational affiliations. The four sets of arguments are reprinted here in full.

Argument in Favor of Proposition 140

Peter F. Schabarum, *Chairman, Los Angeles County Board of Supervisors;* Lewis K. Uhler, *President, National Tax-Limitation Committee;* J. G. Ford, Jr., *President, Marin United Taxpayers Association*

Proposition 140 will for the first time ever place a limit on the number of terms a state official may serve in office.

A yes vote on Proposition 140 will reform a political system that has created a legislature of career politicians in California. It is a system that has given a tiny elite (only 120 people out of 30 million) almost limitless power over the lives of California's taxpayers and consumers.

Proposition 140 will limit state senators to two terms (8 years); will limit assembly members to three terms (6 years); and limit the governor and other elected constitutional officers to two terms (8 years).

By reducing the amount they can spend on their personal office expenses, Proposition 140 will cut back on the 3,000 political staffers who serve the legislature in Sacramento. In the first year alone, according to the legislative analyst, it will save taxpayers $60 million.

Proposition 140 will end extravagant pensions for legislators. While most Californians have to depend on Social Security and their own savings, the legislative pension system often pays more than the legislator received while in office. In fact 50 former officials receive $2,000.00 per month or more from the legislative retirement fund.

Limiting terms will create more competitive elections, so good legislators will always have the opportunity to move up the ladder. Term limitation will end the ingrown, political nature of both houses—to the benefit of every man, woman, and child in California.

Proposition 140 will remove the grip that vested interests have over the legislature and remove the huge political slush funds at the disposal of senate and assembly leaders.

Proposition 140 will put an end to the lifetime legislators, who have developed cozy relationships with special interests. We all remember the saying, "Power corrupts and absolute power corrupts absolutely." But limit the terms of legislative members, remove the Speaker's cronies, and we will also put an end to the Sacramento web of special favors and patronage.

Proposition 140 will end the reign of the legislature's powerful officers—the Assembly Speaker (first elected a quarter of a century ago) and the Senate Leader (now into his third decade in the legislature). Lobbyists and power brokers pay homage to these legislative dictators, for they control the fate of bills, parcel out money to the camp followers and hangers-on, and pull strings behind the scenes to decide election outcomes.

Incumbent legislators seldom lose. In the 1988 election, 100% of incumbent state senators and 96% of incumbent members of the assembly were reelected. The British House of Lords—even the Soviet legislature—has a higher turnover rate. Enough is Enough! It's time to put an end to a system that makes incumbents a special class of citizen and pays them a guaranteed annual wage from first election to the grave. Let's restore that form of government envisioned by our Founding Fathers—a government of citizens representing their fellow citizens.

VOTE YES ON PROPOSITION 140 TO *LIMIT STATE OFFICIALS' TERMS OF OFFICE!*

Rebuttal to Argument in Favor of Proposition 140

Ed Foglia, *President, California Teachers Association;* Dan Terry, *President, California Professional Firefighters;* Linda M. Tangren, *State Chair, California National Women's Political Caucus*

Proposition 140 is a proposal by a downtown Los Angeles politician to take away your right to choose your legislators. He has a history of taking away voting rights. He and two political cronies voted to spend $500,000.00 in tax dollars to hire a personal lawyer to defend him against Voting Rights Act violations in federal court. Newspapers call it an "outrageous back room deal."

His "Big Bucks" friends, including high-priced lobbyists, have lined his pockets with campaign contributions to help control who *you* can vote for.

- If 140 passes, lobbyists could substitute their own paid employees for the independent staff researchers of the legislature eliminated by this measure.
- 140 misleads you about the so-called "high" cost of the legislature—the cost is less than ½ penny per tax dollar.
- The biggest lie is the fact they don't tell you that 140 is a lifetime ban.

This is a blatant power grab by Los Angeles contributors and lobbyists who have been wining and dining "Mr. Downtown Los Angeles" in government for SEVEN TERMS—OVER TWENTY YEARS.

Practice what you preach, "Mr. Downtown Los Angeles," Peter Schabarum. Cut *your own* budget and limit *your own* terms. Don't be piggy and take away people's rights after you have . . . eaten at the table.

There is no need for 140. The vast majority of the legislature *already* serves less than 10 years.

That's *your* choice. Keep it. Stop Downtown Los Angeles' power grab. Vote no on 140!

Argument against Proposition 140

Dr. Regene Mitchell, *President, Consumer Federation of California;* Lucy Blake, *Executive Director, California League of Conservation Voters;* Dan Terry, *President, California Professional Firefighters*

Proposition 140 claims to mandate term limits. But in fact, it limits our voting rights.

This measure takes away the cherished constitutional right to freely cast a ballot for candidates of our choice.

We are asked to forfeit *our* right to decide who our individual representatives will be.

Proposition 140's Lifetime Ban

140 does *not* limit *consecutive* terms of office. Instead 140 says:

- After serving six years in the assembly, individuals will be constitutionally *banned for life* from ever serving in the assembly.

- After serving eight years in the senate, individuals will be constitutionally *banned for life* from ever serving in the senate.
- Similar lifetime bans will be imposed on the superintendent of public instruction and other statewide offices.

There are no exceptions—not for merit, not for statewide emergencies, not for the overwhelming will of the people.

Once banned, always banned.

Proposition 140 Is Unfair

It treats everyone—good and bad, competent and incompetent—the same.

No matter how good a job someone does in office, they will be *banned for life.*

No matter what cause they may be fighting for or how badly we, the people, want to reelect them, they will be *banned for life.*

You won't even be able to write in their names on your ballot. If you do, your vote won't count.

That's just not fair.

Limits Our Right to Choose

The backers of 140 don't trust us, the people, to choose our elected officials. So instead of promoting thoughtful reforms that help us weed out bad legislators, they impose a lifetime ban that eliminates good legislators and bad ones alike at the expense of our constitutional rights.

No eligible citizen should be *permanently banned* for life from seeking any office in a free society. And we should not be *permanently banned* from voting freely for the candidates of our choice.

Resist the rhetoric. Proposition 140 is not about restricting the powers of incumbency. It's about taking away our powers to choose.

Phony Pension Reform

Proposition 140's retirement provisions also are misdirected and counterproductive.

140 does not eliminate the real abuses: double and triple dipping—the practice of taking multiple pensions.

Instead it raises new barriers to public office by banning our future representatives from earning *any* retirement except their current social security.

140's retirement ban won't hurt rich candidates. It will hurt qualified, ordinary citizens who are not rich and have to work hard to provide economic security for themselves and their families.

Proposition 140 Goes Too Far

It upsets our system of constitutional checks and balances, forcing our representatives to become even more dependent on entrenched bureaucrats and shrewd lobbyists.

If its proponents were sincere about political reform, they wouldn't have cluttered it with so many unworkable provisions.

Vote No on Proposition 140

STOP THIS RADICAL AND DANGEROUS SCHEME! PROTECT OUR CONSTITUTIONAL RIGHTS. VOTE NO ON PROPOSITION 140'S LIFETIME BAN.

Rebuttal to Argument against Proposition 140

W. Bruce Lee, II, *Executive Director, California Business League;* Lee A. Phelps, *Chairman, Alliance of California Taxpayers;* Art Pagdan, M.D., *National 1st, V.P., Filipino-American Political Association*

Proposition 140 restores *true* democracy, gives you *real* choices of candidates, protects *your* rights to be represented by someone who knows and cares about *your* wishes. It opens up the political system so *everyone*—not just the entrenched career politicians—can participate.

Proposition 140 will bring new ideas, workable policies and fresh cleansing air to Sacramento. All are needed badly. A stench of greed and vote-selling hangs over Sacramento because lifetime-in-office incumbents think it's *their* government, not yours.

Californians polled by the state's largest newspaper say "most politicians are for sale" and "taking bribes is a relatively common practice" among lawmakers. Proposition 140 cuts the ties between corrupting special interest money and long-term legislators.

Why don't more people vote? Because incumbents have rigged the system in their favor so much, elections are meaningless. Even the worst of legislators get reelected 98% of the time. Honest, ethical, *truly* representative people who want to run for office don't stand a chance.

Do career legislators *really* earn their guaranteed salaries, extravagant pensions, limousines, air travel, and other luxury benefits? No. They use *your* money and *your* government to buy themselves power and guaranteed reelections.

Who really opposes Proposition 140? It isn't ordinary people who have to work for a living. It's incumbent legislators and their camp followers. Beware of movie stars and celebrities in million-dollar TV ads, attacking Proposition 140. They're doing the dirty work for career politicians.

VOTE "YES!" ON PROPOSITION 140. ENOUGH IS ENOUGH!

Appendix B

DOCUMENTS AND TABLES

B-1. TEXTS OF TERM-LIMIT BALLOT INITIATIVES

Editors' note: Term-limit initiatives are presented in the order in which they were adopted: Oklahoma, Colorado, and California. The fourth item in this appendix is the Washington State initiative that was defeated in 1991.

Oklahoma
Adopted, 1990

Be it enacted by the people of the state of Oklahoma that Section 17 of Article 5 of the Oklahoma constitution be amended by adding an additional paragraph numbered 17A, to read as follows:

Section 17A. Any member of the legislature who is elected to office after the effective date of this amendment shall be eligible to serve no more than 12 years in the Oklahoma state legislature. Years in legislative office need not be consecutive and years of service in both the senate and the house of representatives shall be added together and included in determining the total number of legislative years in office. The years served by any member elected or appointed to serve less than a full legislative term to fill a vacancy in office shall not be included in the 12-year limitation set forth herein; but no member who has completed 12 years in office shall thereafter be eligible to serve a partial term. Any member who is serving a legislative term in office or who has been elected or appointed to serve a term in office on the effective date hereof shall be entitled to complete his or her term and shall be eligible to serve an additional 12 years thereafter. This amendment shall be effective on the 1st day of the year following its adoption.

Colorado
Adopted, 1990

Be it enacted by the people of the state of Colorado: Section 1 of Article IV of the constitution of the state of Colorado is amended to read:

Section 1. *Officers—terms of office.*

(1) The executive department shall include the governor, lieutenant governor, secretary of state, state treasurer, and attorney general, each of whom shall hold his office for the term of four years, commencing on the second Tuesday of January in the year 1967, and each fourth year thereafter. They shall perform such duties as are prescribed by this constitution or by law.

(2) In order to broaden the opportunities for public service and to guard against excessive concentrations of power, no governor, lieutenant governor, secretary of state, state treasurer, or attorney general shall serve more than two consecutive terms of office beginning on or after January 1, 1991. Any person who succeeds to the office of governor or is appointed or elected to fill a vacancy in one of the other offices named in this section, and who serves at least one-half of a term of office, shall be considered to have served a term in that office for purposes of this subsection (2). Terms are considered consecutive unless they are at least four years apart. Section 3 of Article V of the constitution of the state of Colorado is amended to read:

Section 3. *Terms of Senators and Representatives.*

(1) Senators shall be elected for the term of four years and representatives for the term of two years.

(2) In order to broaden the opportunities for public service and to assure that the general assembly is representative of Colorado citizens, no senator shall serve more than two consecutive terms in the senate, and no representative shall serve more than four consecutive terms in the house of representatives. This limitation on the number of terms shall apply to terms of office beginning on or after January 1, 1991. any person appointed or elected to fill a vacancy in the general assembly and who serves at least one-half of a term of office shall be considered to have served a term in that office for purposes of this subsection (2). Terms are considered consecutive unless they are at least four years apart. Article XVIII of the constitution of the state of Colorado is amended by the addition of a new section to read:

Section 9. *U.S. Senators and Representatives—limitations on terms.*

(1) In order to broaden the opportunities for public service and to assure that members of the United States Congress from Colorado are representative of and responsive to Colorado citizens, no United States Senator from Colorado shall serve more than two consecutive terms in the United States Senate, and no United States Representative from Colorado shall serve more than six consecutive terms in the United States House of Representatives. This limitation on the number of terms shall apply to terms of office beginning on or after January 1, 1991. Any person appointed or elected to fill a vacancy in the United States Congress and who serves at least one half of a term of office shall

be considered to have served a term in that office for purposes of this subsection (1). Terms are considered consecutive unless they are at least four years apart.

(2) The people of Colorado hereby state their support for a nationwide limit of twelve consecutive years of service in the United States Senate or House of Representatives and instruct their public officials to use their best efforts to work for such a limit.

(3) The people of Colorado declare that the provisions of this section shall be deemed severable from the remainder of this measure and that their intention is that federal officials elected from Colorado will continue voluntarily to observe the wishes of the people as stated in this section in the event any provision thereof is held invalid.

California
Proposition 140
Adopted, 1990

Official Title and Summary:

Limits on Terms of Office, Legislators' Retirement, Legislative Operating Costs. Initiative Constitutional Amendment

- Persons elected or appointed after November 5, 1990, holding offices of governor, lieutenant governor, attorney general, controller, secretary of state, treasurer, superintendent of public instruction, Board of Equalization members, and state senators, limited to two terms; members of the assembly limited to three terms.
- Requires legislators elected or serving after November 1, 1990, to participate in federal Social Security program; precludes accrual of other pension and retirement benefits resulting from legislative service, except vested rights.
- Limits expenditures of legislature for compensation and operating costs and equipment to specified amount.

Text of Proposed Law

This initiative measure is submitted to the people in accordance with the provisions of Article II, Section 8 of the constitution.

This initiative measure expressly amends the constitution by amending and adding sections thereof; therefore, new provisions proposed to be inserted or added are printed in *italic type* to indicate that they are new.

Proposed Law

Section 1. This measure shall be known and may be cited as "The Political Reform Act of 1990."

Sec. 2. Section 1.5 is added to Article IV of the California constitution, to read:

Sec. 1.5. The people find and declare that the Founding Fathers established a system of representative government based upon free, fair, and competitive elections. The increased concentration of political power in the hands of incumbent representatives has made our electoral system less free, less competitive, and less representative.

The ability of legislators to serve unlimited number of terms, to establish their own retirement system, and to pay for staff and support services at state expense contributes heavily to the extremely high number of incumbents who are reelected. These unfair incumbent advantages discourage qualified candidates from seeking public office and create a class of career politicians, instead of the citizen representatives envisioned by the Founding Fathers. These career politicians become representatives of the bureaucracy, rather than of the people whom they are elected to represent.

To restore a free and democratic system of fair elections, and to encourage qualified candidates to seek public office, the people find and declare that the powers of incumbency must be limited. Retirement benefits must be restricted, state-financed incumbent staff and support services limited, and limitations placed upon the number of terms which may be served.

Sec. 3. Section 2 of Article IV of the California constitution is amended to read:

Sec. 2. (a) The senate has a membership of 40 senators elected for 4-year terms, 20 to begin every 2 years. *No senator may serve more than 2 terms.*

The assembly has a membership of 80 members elected for 2-year terms. *No member of the assembly may serve more than 3 terms.*

Their terms shall commence on the first Monday in December next following their election.

(b) Election of members of the assembly shall be on the first Tuesday after the first Monday in November of even-numbered years unless otherwise prescribed by the legislature. Senators shall be elected at the same time and places as members of the assembly.

(c) A person is ineligible to be a member of the legislature unless the person is an elector and has been a resident of the legislative district for one year, and a citizen of the United States and a resident of California for 3 years, immediately preceding the election.

(d) When a vacancy occurs in the legislature, the governor immediately shall call an election to fill the vacancy.

Sec. 4. Section 4.5 is added to Article IV of the California constitution, to read:

Sec. 4.5. Notwithstanding any other provision of this constitution or existing law, a person elected to or serving in the legislature on or after November 1, 1990, shall participate in the federal Social Security (Retirement, Disability, Health Insurance) program and the state shall pay only the employer's share of the contribution necessary to such participation. No other pension or retirement benefit shall accrue as a result of service in the legislature, such service not being intended as a career occupation. This Section shall not be construed to abrogate or diminish any vested pension or retirement benefit which may have accrued under an existing law to a person holding or having held office in the legislature, but upon adoption of this Act no further entitlement to nor vesting in any existing program shall accrue to any such person, other than Social Security to the extent herein provided.

Sec. 5. Section 7.5 is added to Article IV of the California constitution, to read:

Sec. 7.5. In the fiscal year immediately following the adoption of this Act, the total aggregate expenditures of the legislature for the compensation of members and employees of, and the operating expenses and equipment for, the legislature may not exceed an amount equal to nine hundred fifty thousand dollars ($950,000) per member for that fiscal year of 80 percent of the amount of money expended for those purposes in the preceding fiscal year, whichever is less. For each fiscal year thereafter, the total aggregate expenditures may not exceed an amount equal to that expended for those purposes in the preceding fiscal year, adjusted and compounded by an amount equal to the percentage increase in the appropriations limit for the state established pursuant to Article XIII B.

Sec. 6. Section 2 of Article V of the California constitution is amended to read:

Sec. 2. The governor shall be elected every fourth year at the same time and places as members of the assembly and hold office from the Monday after January 1 following the election until a successor qualifies. The governor shall be an elector who has been a citizen of the United States and a resident of this state for 5 years immediately preceding the governor's election. The governor may not hold other public office. *No governor may serve more than 2 terms.*

Sec. 7. Section 11 of Article V of the California constitution is amended to read:

Sec. 11. The lieutenant governor, attorney general, controller, secretary of state, and treasurer shall be elected at the same time and places and for the same term as the governor. *No lieutenant governor, attorney general, controller, secretary of state, or treasurer may serve in the same office for more than 2 terms.*

Sec. 8. Section 2 of Article IX of the California constitution is amended to read:

Sec. 2. A superintendent of public instruction shall be elected by the qualified electors of the state at each gubernatorial election. The superintendent of public instruction shall enter upon the duties of the office on the first Monday after the first day of January next succeeding each gubernatorial election. *No superintendent of public instruction may serve more than 2 terms.*

Sec. 9. Section 17 of Article XIII of the California constitution is amended to read:

Sec. 17. The Board of Equalization consists of 5 voting members: the controller and 4 members elected for 4-year terms at gubernatorial elections. The state shall be divided into four Board of Equalization districts with the voters of each district electing one member. *No member may serve more than 2 terms.*

Sec. 10. Section 7 is added to Article XX of the California constitution, to read:

Sec. 7. The limitations on the number of terms prescribed by Section 2 of Article IV, Sections 2 and 11 of Article V, Section 2 of Article IX, and Section 17 of Article XIII apply only to terms to which persons are elected or appointed on or after November 6, 1990, except that an incumbent senator whose office is not on the ballot for the general election on that date may serve only one additional term. Those limitations shall not apply to any unexpired term to which a person is elected or appointed if the remainder of the term is less than half of the full term.

Sec. 11. Section 11 (d) is added to Article VII of the California constitution, to read:

Sec. 11. (a) The Legislators' Retirement System shall not pay any unmodified retirement allowance or its actuarial equivalent to any person who on or after January 1, 1987, entered for the first time any state office for which membership in the Legislators' Retirement System was elective or to any beneficiary or survivor of such a person, which exceeds the higher of (1) the salary receivable by the person currently serving in the office in which the retired person served or (2) the highest salary that was received by the retired person while serving in that office.

(b) The Judges' Retirement System shall not pay any unmodified retirement allowance or its actuarial equivalent to any person who on or after January 1, 1987, entered for the first time any judicial office subject to the Judges' Retirement System or to any beneficiary or survivor of such a person, which exceeds the higher of (1) the salary receivable by the person currently serving in the judicial office in which the retired person served or (2) the highest salary that was received by the retired person while serving in that judicial office.

(c)The legislature may define the terms used in this section.

(d) If any part of this measure or the application to any person or circumstance is held invalid, the invalidity shall not affect other provisions or applications which reasonably can be given effect without the invalid provision or application.

Washington
Proposition 553
Defeated, 1991

BE ENACTED BY THE PEOPLE OF THE STATE OF WASHINGTON:

NEW SECTION. Sec. 1. A new section is added to chapter 43.01 RCW to read as follows:

A person elected to the office of governor or lieutenant governor is eligible to serve not more than two consecutive terms in each office.

NEW SECTION. Sec. 2. A new section is added to chapter 44.04 RCW to read as follows:

A person elected to the Washington State legislature is eligible to serve not more than three consecutive terms in the house of representatives and not more than two consecutive terms in the senate. In addition, no person may serve more than ten consecutive years in any combination of house and senate membership. Terms are considered consecutive unless they are at least six years apart. Therefore, elected legislators who have reached their maximum term limits are eligible for legislative office after an absence of six years from the state legislature. Persons who have already reached the maximum term of service on the effective date of this act are eligible to serve one additional term in either the state house of representatives or the senate.

NEW SECTION. Sec. 3. A new section is added to chapter 29.68 RCW to read as follows:

A person elected to the United States Congress from this state is eligible to serve not more than three consecutive terms in the United States House of Representatives and not more than two consecutive terms in the United States Senate and not more than twelve consecutive years in any combination of United States House and Senate membership. Terms are considered to be consecutive unless they are at least six years apart. Therefore, elected legislators who have reached their maximum term limits are eligible for legislative office after an absence of six years from the United States Congress. Persons who have already reached the maximum term of service on the effective date of this act are eligible to serve one additional term in either the United States House of Representatives or Senate.

NEW SECTION. Sec. 4. If any provision of this act or its application to any person or circumstance is held invalid, the remainder of the act or the application of the provision to other persons or circumstances is not affected.

TABLE B-2 Turnover and Reelection Rates in the U.S. House and Senate, 1790-1990

	House				*Senate*		
Election year	Number (and pct.) who ran for re-election	Pct. reelected of those running	Pct. of whole House who return	Class size	Number (and pct.) who ran for re-election	Pct. reelected of those running	Pct. of class who return
1790	41 (63.1)	92.7	58.5	9	7 (77.8)	71.4	55.6
1792	45 (69.2)	100.0	69.2	10	5 (50.0)	80.0	40.0
1794	68 (64.8)	97.1	62.9	10	6 (60.0)	66.7	40.0
1796	69 (65.1)	92.8	60.4	11	11 (100.0)	90.9	90.9
1798	69 (65.1)	94.2	61.3	11	7 (63.6)	85.7	54.5
1800	60 (56.6)	95.0	53.8	10	4 (40.0)	100.0	40.0
1802	74 (69.8)	94.6	66.0	11	6 (54.5)	66.7	36.4
1804	104 (73.2)	94.2	69.0	11	7 (63.6)	85.7	54.5
1806	99 (69.7)	98.0	68.3	11	8 (72.7)	100.0	72.7
1808	96 (67.6)	93.8	63.4	12	9 (75.0)	100.0	75.0
1810	90 (63.4)	93.8	59.1	11	9 (81.8)	88.9	72.7
1812	97 (67.8)	86.6	58.7	13	5 (38.5)	80.0	30.8
1814	113 (62.1)	87.6	54.4	12	6 (50.0)	100.0	50.0
1816	78 (42.7)	84.6	36.3	12	6 (50.0)	66.7	33.3
1818	111 (60.7)	91.0	55.2	14	8 (57.1)	87.5	50.0
1820	117 (62.9)	82.9	52.1	15	10 (66.7)	90.0	60.0
1822	127 (68.3)	90.5	61.8	16	14 (87.5)	85.7	75.0
1824	148 (69.5)	88.5	61.5	16	8 (50.0)	62.5	31.3
1826	152 (71.4)	89.5	63.8	16	13 (81.3)	84.6	68.8
1828	150 (70.4)	80.0	56.3	16	9 (56.3)	100.0	56.3
1830	145 (68.1)	89.7	61.0	16	8 (50.0)	62.5	31.3
1832	135 (63.4)	80.0	50.7	16	9 (56.3)	88.9	50.0
1834	176 (73.3)	80.1	58.8	16	12 (75.0)	91.7	68.8
1836	149 (61.8)	81.9	50.6	17	16 (94.1)	68.8	64.7
1838	159 (65.7)	75.5	49.6	17	9 (52.9)	100.0	52.9
1840	157 (64.9)	82.8	53.7	18	11 (61.1)	72.7	44.4
1842	90 (37.2)	64.4	24.0	17	9 (52.9)	88.9	47.1
1844	135 (60.5)	80.7	48.9	17	7 (41.2)	100.0	41.2
1846	116 (52.0)	87.1	45.3	20	14 (70.0)	57.1	40.0
1848	122 (53.0)	80.3	42.6	20	14 (70.0)	78.6	55.0
1850	130 (56.0)	74.6	41.8	21	15 (71.4)	60.0	42.9
1852	119 (51.3)	70.6	36.2	20	6 (30.0)	100.0	30.0
1854	137 (58.5)	65.0	38.0	21	10 (47.6)	70.0	33.3
1856	158 (67.5)	75.3	50.8	21	10 (47.6)	100.0	47.6
1858	156 (66.7)	75.6	50.4	21	17 (81.0)	64.7	52.4
1860	110 (63.2)	73.6	46.5	21	10 (47.6)	70.0	33.3
1862	103 (56.6)	68.0	38.5	17	11 (64.7)	90.9	58.8
1864	133 (73.1)	73.7	53.8	14	10 (71.4)	80.0	57.1

(Continued on next page)

TABLE B-2 *(Continued)*

	House				Senate		
Election year	Number (and pct.) who ran for re-election	Pct. reelected of those running	Pct. of whole House who return	Class size	Number (and pct.) who ran for re-election	Pct. reelected of those running	Pct. of class who return
1866	133 (72.7)	85.0	61.8	17	12 (70.6)	58.3	41.2
1868	146 (61.3)	84.3	51.7	22	13 (59.1)	61.5	36.4
1870	165 (67.9)	72.7	49.4	25	15 (60.0)	53.3	32.0
1872	171 (70.4)	73.7	51.8	24	9 (37.5)	88.9	33.3
1874	199 (68.1)	57.8	39.4	25	8 (32.0)	62.5	20.0
1876	213 (72.9)	72.3	52.7	24	14 (58.3)	64.3	34.6
1878	203 (69.3)	79.8	55.3	25	12 (48.0)	66.7	32.0
1880	230 (78.5)	82.2	64.5	25	17 (68.0)	52.9	36.0
1882	207 (70.6)	72.0	50.8	26	18 (69.2)	77.8	53.8
1884	247 (76.0)	76.5	58.1	25	18 (72.0)	83.3	60.0
1886	246 (75.7)	80.1	60.6	25	18 (72.0)	66.7	48.0
1888	251 (77.2)	81.3	62.8	26	23 (88.5)	91.3	80.8
1890	260 (78.5)	68.8	54.1	29	21 (72.4)	76.2	55.2
1892	264 (79.5)	78.8	62.6	29	24 (82.8)	79.2	65.5
1894	270 (75.8)	66.7	50.6	30	22 (73.3)	63.6	46.7
1896	288 (80.7)	72.9	58.8	30	18 (60.0)	66.7	40.0
1898	302 (84.6)	82.8	70.0	30	24 (80.0)	70.8	56.7
1900	303 (84.9)	88.4	75.1	30	24 (80.0)	62.5	50.0
1902	297 (83.2)	86.5	72.0	30	21 (70.0)	81.0	56.7
1904	338 (87.6)	89.6	78.5	30	20 (66.7)	95.0	63.3
1906	335 (86.8)	86.9	75.4	30	24 (80.0)	83.3	66.7
1908	354 (90.5)	87.6	79.3	31	27 (87.1)	66.7	58.1
1910	338 (86.4)	78.7	68.0	30	23 (76.7)	56.5	62.5
1912	341 (78.4)	82.1	64.4	32	24 (75.0)	58.3	43.8
1914	374 (86.0)	79.9	68.7	32	24 (75.0)	91.7	68.8
1916	400 (91.9)	87.8	80.7	32	29 (90.6)	55.2	50.0
1918	389 (89.4)	84.6	75.6	32	29 (90.6)	68.9	62.5
1920	385 (88.5)	81.6	72.2	32	30 (93.8)	60.0	56.3
1922	384 (88.3)	79.2	69.9	32	29 (90.6)	55.2	50.0
1924	401 (92.2)	89.0	82.1	32	30 (93.8)	66.7	62.5
1926	405 (93.1)	92.8	86.4	32	33 (103.1)	63.6	65.6
1928	404 (92.9)	90.1	83.7	32	32 (100.0)	78.1	78.1
1930	407 (93.6)	86.0	80.5	32	30 (93.8)	56.7	53.1
1932	392 (90.1)	69.1	62.3	32	32 (100.0)	56.2	56.3
1934	388 (89.2)	83.8	74.7	32	32 (100.0)	68.8	68.8
1936	388 (89.2)	87.6	78.2	32	27 (84.4)	77.8	65.6
1938	402 (92.4)	79.1	73.1	32	31 (96.9)	71.0	68.8
1940	407 (93.6)	88.7	83.0	32	32 (100.0)	56.2	56.3
1942	395 (90.8)	83.0	75.4	32	33 (103.1)	66.7	68.8

(Continued on next page)

TABLE B-2 *(Continued)*

	House				Senate		
Election year	Number (and pct.) who ran for re-election	Pct. reelected of those running	Pct. of whole House who return	Class size	Number (and pct.) who ran for re-election	Pct. reelected of those running	Pct. of class who return
1944	405 (93.1)	88.1	82.1	32	30 (93.8)	70.0	65.6
1946	398 (91.5)	82.4	75.4	32	29 (90.6)	52.2	50.0
1948	400 (91.9)	79.3	72.9	32	25 (78.1)	60.0	46.9
1950	400 (91.9)	90.5	84.2	32	32 (100.0)	68.8	68.8
1952	389 (88.0)	91.0	84.4	32	31 (96.9)	64.5	62.5
1954	407 (93.6)	93.1	87.1	32	32 (100.0)	75.0	75.0
1956	411 (94.3)	94.6	89.4	32	29 (90.6)	82.2	78.1
1958	396 (91.0)	89.9	81.8	32	28 (87.5)	64.3	56.3
1960	405 (92.7)	92.6	86.2	33	29 (87.9)	96.6	84.8
1962	402 (92.9)	91.5	84.6	34	35 (102.9)	82.9	85.3
1964	397 (91.3)	86.6	79.1	33	33 (100.0)	84.8	84.8
1966	411 (94.5)	88.1	83.2	33	32 (97.0)	87.5	84.8
1968	409 (94.0)	96.8	91.0	34	28 (87.5)	71.4	58.8
1970	401 (92.2)	94.5	87.1	33	31 (93.9)	77.4	72.7
1972	390 (89.7)	93.6	83.9	33	27 (81.8)	74.1	60.6
1974	391 (89.9)	87.7	78.9	34	27 (79.4)	85.2	67.6
1976	384 (88.3)	95.8	84.6	33	25 (75.8)	64.0	48.5
1978	382 (87.6)	93.7	82.3	33	25 (75.8)	60.0	45.5
1980	398 (91.5)	90.7	83.0	34	29 (85.3)	55.2	47.1
1982	393 (90.3)	90.1	81.4	33	30 (90.9)	93.3	84.8
1984	409 (94.0)	95.4	90.1	33	29 (87.9)	89.7	78.8
1986	393 (90.3)	98.0	88.5	34	28 (82.4)	75.0	61.8
1988	409 (94.0)	98.3	92.4	33	27 (81.8)	85.2	69.7
1990	407 (93.6)	96.1	89.9	35	32 (91.4)	96.9	88.6

Sources: David C. Huckabee, "Reelection Rates of House Incumbents: 1790-1988" (Washington, D.C.: Congressional Research Service, March 16, 1989); David C. Huckabee, "Reelection Rates of Senate Incumbents: 1790-1988 (Washington, D.C.: Congressional Research Service, May 15, 1990); Norman J. Ornstein, Thomas E. Mann, and Michael J. Malbin, *Vital Statistics on Congress, 1991-1992* (Washington, D.C.: CQ Press, 1992), 58-59.

TABLE B-3 Seniority of U.S. Representatives, 1953-1991

Congress	Percentage of representatives serving							Total	Mean term	Me- dian term
	1 term	2 terms	3 terms	1-3 terms	4-6 terms	7-9 terms	10+ terms			
83d (1953)										
Percent	18	14	12	44	29	16	10	100	4.9	4
Seats	78	61	53	193	127	70	42	432		
84th (1955)										
Percent	11	17	13	42	26	19	12	100	5.2	4
Seats	50	74	58	182	115	84	54	435		
85th (1957)										
Percent	9	11	16	36	31	17	16	100	5.5	5
Seats	40	46	69	155	133	74	71	433		
86th (1959)										
Percent	18	10	10	38	30	17	15	100	5.6	4
Seats	79	43	43	165	131	74	66	436		
87th (1961)										
Percent	13	15	8	36	29	18	17	100	5.8	5
Seats	55	65	35	155	126	77	74	432		
88th (1963)										
Percent	15	13	13	41	24	19	17	100	5.7	5
Seats	66	55	55	176	104	81	74	435		
89th (1965)										
Percent	19	14	11	44	22	18	17	100	5.5	4
Seats	83	60	47	190	94	78	72	434		
90th (1967)										
Percent	14	15	12	41	25	16	17	100	5.6	4
Seats	60	65	54	179	110	70	75	434		
91st (1969)										
Percent	8	15	14	37	31	15	18	100	5.7	5
Seats	36	65	58	159	132	64	76	431		
92d (1971)										
Percent	11	10	13	34	29	16	20	100	6.0	5
Seats	48	45	57	150	127	69	87	433		
93d (1973)										
Percent	16	11	10	37	30	16	18	100	5.7	5
Seats	67	49	41	157	131	67	78	433		
94th (1975)										
Percent	20	14	10	44	24	19	14	100	5.4	4
Seats	86	61	42	189	102	81	61	433		
95th (1977)										
Percent	15	21	12	48	21	17	14	100	4.6	4
Seats	64	92	54	210	90	73	60	433		

(Continued on next page)

TABLE B-3 *—Continued*

Congress	Percentage of Representatives Serving							Total	Mean term	Median term
	1 term	2 terms	3 terms	1-3 terms	4-6 terms	7-9 terms	10+ terms			
96th (1979)										
Percent	18	14	17	49	22	16	13	100	5.0	4
Seats	77	61	76	214	96	70	55	435		
97th (1981)										
Percent	17	17	13	47	28	14	11	100	4.9	4
Seats	73	75	57	205	120	60	50	435		
98th (1983)										
Percent	18	14	16	49	28	11	13	100	4.6	4
Seats	80	63	68	211	121	48	55	435		
99th (1985)										
Percent	9	19	14	41	32	13	14	100	4.7	4
Seats	39	81	60	180	141	55	59	435		
100th (1987)										
Percent	11	8	17	37	33	14	16	100	5.6	5
Seats	48	37	74	159	144	63	69	435		
101st (1989)										
Percent	8	12	8	28	38	20	14	100	5.8	5
Seats	33	54	33	120	167	86	60	433		
102d (1991)										
Percent	10	9	11	30	31	21	17	100	6.2	5
Seats	42	41	47	131	137	92	76	435		

Note: Percentages may not add to totals because of rounding.

Source: Norman J. Ornstein, Thomas E. Mann, and Michael J. Malbin, *Vital Statistics on Congress 1991-1992.* (Washington, D.C.: CQ Press, 1992), 19-20.

TABLE B-4 Seniority of U.S. Senators, 1953-1991

Congress	Number of Senators serving				Total	Mean years service	Median years service
	6 years or less	7-12 years	13-18 years	19 years or more			
83d (1953)	46 (16)	29	14	7	96	8.5	7
84th (1955)	42 (14)	37	8	9	96	8.4	7
85th (1957)	37 (10)	36	13	10	96	9.6	9
86th (1959)	42 (20)	30	14	12	98	9.4	8
87th (1961)	42 (7)	25	22	11	100	9.7	9
88th (1963)	42 (12)	26	18	14	100	9.9	7
89th (1965)	29 (8)	36	16	19	100	11.1	9
90th (1967)	28 (7)	34	19	19	100	11.6	9
91st (1969)	32 (14)	32	17	19	100	11.2	11
92d (1971)	25 (10)	24	29	22	100	11.5	11
93d (1973)	40 (13)	20	20	20	100	11.2	9
94th (1975)	35 (11)	22	23	19	99	11.5	9
95th (1977)	42 (17)	25	13	20	100	10.6	9
96th (1979)	48 (20)	24	10	18	100	9.6	7
97th (1981)	55 (18)	20	10	15	100	8.5	5
98th (1983)	43 (5)	28	16	13	100	9.6	7
99th (1985)	32 (7)	38	18	12	100	10.1	9
100th (1987)	26 (13)	44	16	14	100	9.6	8
101st (1989)	31 (10)	26	29	14	100	9.8	10
102d (1991)	30 (5)	23	28	19	100	11.1	11

Source: Norman J. Ornstein, Thomas E. Mann, and Michael J. Malbin, *Vital Statistics on Congress 1991-1992* (Washington, D.C.: CQ Press, 1992), 21.

Note: Figures in parentheses are the number of freshmen senators. Senators who are currently in their first term are listed under the "6 years or less" column.

TABLE B-6 Ten-Year Turnover by Category of Legislature, 1979-1989

Category	Senates	Houses
Red (full-time)[a]	61%	67%
White (hybrid)[b]	73	76
Blue (part-time)[c]	79	79

Source: Karl T. Kurtz, National Conference of State Legislatures

Notes:

[a] Red category: Full-time, large staff, high pay. States: California, Illinois, Massachusetts, Michigan, New Jersey, New York, Ohio, Pennsylvania, and Wisconsin.

[b] White category: In between, hybrid. States: Alabama, Alaska, Arizona, Colorado, Connecticut, Delaware, Florida, Hawaii, Indiana, Iowa, Kansas, Louisiana, Maryland, Minnesota, Missouri, Nebraska, Oklahoma, Oregon, South Carolina, Tennessee, Texas, Virginia, and Washington.

[c] Blue category: Part-time, small staff, low pay. States: Arkansas, Georgia, Idaho, Kentucky, Maine, Mississippi, Montana, Nevada, New Hampshire, New Mexico, North Carolina, North Dakota, Rhode Island, South Dakota, Utah, Vermont, West Virginia, and Wyoming.

TABLE B-7 Simulated Profile of California Senate and Assembly with Term Limits, Assuming Present Rate of Turnover

Election Year	No. of senate[a] members starting				No. of assembly[b] members starting		
	Year 1	Year 3	Year 5	Year 7	Year 1	Year 3	Year 5
1990[c]	20	20	—	—	80	—	—
1992	3	20	17	—	12	68	0
1994	3	3	17	17	12	10	58
1996	17	3	3	17	61	10	9
1998	17	17	3	3	19	52	9
2000	5	17	15	3	19	16	44
2002	5	5	15	15	50	16	14
2004	16	5	4	15	24	42	14
2006	16	16	4	4	24	20	36
2008	7	16	13	4	42	20	17
2010	7	7	13	13	27	36	17

Source: Karl T. Kurtz, National Conference of State Legislatures

Notes:

[a] The term limit in the 40-member senate is 8 years, and the reelection rate is 85%. Senators serve four-year, staggered terms; every two years one-half of senate seats are up for election.

[b] In the 80-member assembly the term limit is 6 years, and the reelection rate is 85%. All assembly seats are up for election every two years.

[c] According to California term-limit law, years of service are counted from the 1990 election.

TABLE B-8 Simulated Profile of Colorado Senate and House with Term Limits, Assuming Present Rate of Turnover

Election year	No. of senate members starting[a]				No. of house members starting[b]			
	Year 1	Year 3	Year 5	Year 7	Year 1	Year 3	Year 5	Year 7
1990[c]	17	—	—	—	65	—	—	—
1992	18	17	0	—	16	49	0	—
1994	4	18	13	—	16	12	37	0
1996	5	4	14	13	16	12	9	27
1998	14	5	3	14	37	12	9	7
2000	15	14	3	3	21	28	9	7
2002	7	15	10	3	21	16	21	7
2004	7	7	11	10	21	16	12	16
2006	12	7	5	11	28	16	12	9
2008	13	12	5	5	23	21	12	9
2010	8	13	9	5	23	17	16	9

Source: Karl T. Kurtz, National Conference of State Legislatures

Notes:

[a] Senators serve four-year, staggered terms; every two years one-half of senate seats are up for election. In both the 35-member senate and the 65-member house, the term limit is 8 years, and the reelection rate is 75%.

[b] All house seats are up for election every two years.

[c] According to Colorado term-limit law, years of service are counted from the 1990 election.

TABLE B-9 State Provisions for Initiative

Direct initiative[a]	Indirect[b] initiative	Both direct and indirect	No initiative provision
Alaska	Maine	Utah	Alabama
Arizona	Massachusetts	Washington	Connecticut
Arkansas	Michigan		Delaware
California	Nevada		Florida
Colorado			Georgia
Idaho			Hawaii
Missouri			Illinois
Montana			Indiana
Nebraska			Iowa
North Dakota			Kansas
Ohio			Kentucky
Oklahoma			Louisiana
Oregon			Maryland
South Dakota			Minnesota
Wyoming			Mississippi
			New Hampshire
			New Jersey
			New Mexico
			New York
			North Carolina
			Pennsylvania
			Rhode Island
			South Carolina
			Tennessee
			Texas
			Vermont
			Virginia
			West Virginia
			Wisconsin

Source: Harold W. Stanley and Richard G. Niemi, *Vital Statistics on American Politics* (Washington, D.C.: CQ Press, 1992), 23-24.

Notes:

[a] *Direct* means measures may be placed on the ballot with a specific number of signatures and no legislative action; requirements for number of signatures vary. An *initiative* allows proposed state laws to be placed on a ballot by citizen petition and enacted or rejected by the electorate.

[b] *Indirect* means a measure must be submitted to the legislature for consideration before it can be placed on the ballot.

SELECTED BIBLIOGRAPHY

Albert, Carl. "Limit Terms? No! Congressional Debate." *Extensions* (Carl Albert Congressional Research and Studies Center, University of Oklahoma), Spring 1991, 6-8.

Alexander, Herbert E., and Nina Bhojwani. "Term Limits and Election Reform." Paper presented at conference on legislative term limits, Focused Research Program in Public Choice, University of California, Irvine, May 31-June 1, 1991.

American Enterprise Institute. *Limiting Presidential and Congressional Terms.* Washington, D.C., 1979.

Bartlett, Charles, et al. *How Long Should They Serve?: Limiting Terms for the President and Congress.* Washington, D.C.: American Enterprise Institute, 1980.

Benjamin, Gerald. "The Diffusion of Executive Power in American State Constitutions: Tenure and Tenure Limitations." *Publius: The Journal of Federalism* 15 (Fall 1985): 71-84.

Boeckelman, Keith. "Term Limitation as a Political Movement." Paper delivered at the annual meeting of the Southern Political Science Association, Tampa, Florida, November 1991.

Cain, Bruce E. "Term Limits: Predictions about the Impact on California." Paper presented at conference on legislative term limits, Focused Research Program in Public Choice, University of California, Irvine, May 31-June 1, 1991.

California Senate Office of Research. *After the Election: Analysis of Successful Propositions on the November 1990 Ballot.* Sacramento: California Senate, Office of Research, November 1990.

Challandes, Elliot W. "To Limit or Not to Limit, This Is the Question: Implications of Congressional Term Limitations." Paper delivered at the annual meeting of the American Political Science Association, Washington, D.C., August 29-September 1, 1991.

Cohen, Linda, and Matthew Spitzer. "Term Limits." Paper presented at conference on legislative term limits, Focused Research Program in Public Choice, University of California, Irvine, May 31-June 1, 1991.

Cohen, Richard. "Letter from Albany: Coming to Terms." *National Journal,* October 19, 1991, 2555.

Colorado General Assembly. *An Analysis of 1990 Ballot Proposals.* Denver: Colorado Legislative Council, September 1990.

Connors, Tom. "No Substitute for Inexperience." *Journal of Commerce* 39, November 15, 1990, 12A.

Copeland, Gary W., and John David Rausch, Jr. "The End of Professionalism? The Dynamics of Term Limitations." Paper presented at the annual meeting of the Southwestern Political Science Association, San Antonio, March 27-30, 1991.

———. "Interest Groups and Term Limits." Paper presented at conference on legislative term limits, Focused Research Program in Public Choice, University of California, Irvine, May 31-June 1, 1991.

Corwin, Erik H. "Limits on Legislative Terms: Legal and Policy Implications," *Harvard Journal on Legislation* (June 1991).

Coyne, Jim. "Restricting Elected Officials' Number of Years in Office." *Campaign,* November 1990, 14-15.

DePauw University Center for Contemporary Media. *The Anatomy of a Controversy: A Report on the Conference on Term Limits.* February 1991.

Dick, Andrew R., and John R. Lott, Jr. "Reconciling Voters' Behavior and Legislative Term Limits." Paper presented at conference on legislative term limits, Focused Research Program in Public Choice, University of California, Irvine, May 31-June 1, 1991.

Elving, Ronald D. "Congress Braces for Fallout from State Measures." *Congressional Quarterly,* September 29, 1990, 3144-3146.

———. "Foley Helps Put the Brakes on Drive for Term Limits." *Congressional Quarterly,* November 29, 1991, 3261-3263.

———. "National Drive to Limit Terms Casts Shadow over Congress." *Congressional Quarterly,* October 26, 1991, 3101-3105.

Foundation for the Study of Presidential and Congressional Terms. *Constitutional Background and Legislative History of Proposals to Limit the Number of Years Served by Members of the House and Senate.* Washington, D.C., 1977.

Foundation for the Study of Presidential and Congressional Terms. *Presidential and Congressional Term Limitation: The Issue that Stays Alive.* Washington, D.C., 1980.

Friedman, David, and Donald Wittman. "Why Voters Vote for Incumbents but against Incumbency." Paper presented at conference on legislative term limits, Focused Research Program in Public Choice, University of California, Irvine, May 31-June 1, 1991.

Fund, John. "Term Limitation: An Idea Whose Time has Come." *Policy Analysis No. 141* (Cato Institute, Washington, D.C.), October 30, 1991.

———. "Term Limits for New York State: Expanding Democracy through a Citizen Legislature." Report issued by the Empire Foundation for Policy Research, Albany, New York, November 1991.

Glazer, Amihai, and Martin P. Wattenberg. "Promoting Legislative Work: A Case for Term Limits." Paper presented at conference on legislative term limits, Focused Research Program in Public Choice, University of California, Irvine, May 31-June 1, 1991.

Grofman, Bernard, and Neil Sutherland. "Three Kinds of Term Limits." Paper presented at conference on legislative term limits, Focused Research Program in Public Choice, University of California, Irvine, May 31-June 1, 1991.

Grover, Ronald. "The Little Word Heard Coast to Coast: No." *Business Week,* November 19, 1990, 47.

Guerra, Fernando J. "Term Limits and Minority Representation in Congress." Paper prepared for the annual meeting of the American Political Science Association, Washington, D.C., August 29-September 1, 1991.

Haas, Lawrence J. "Line Item Logic." *National Journal,* June 9, 1990, 1391-1394.

Heritage Foundation. "The Case for Limiting Congressional Terms." *The Heritage Lectures* 291 (1990).

Hertzberg, Hendrik. "Twelve is Enough: A Simple Cure for Chronic Incumbency." *The New Republic,* May 14, 1990, 22-26.

Hook, Janet. "New Drive to Limit Tenure Revives an Old Proposal." *Congressional Quarterly,* February 24, 1990, 567-569.

Independence Institute. "Limit Terms, Expand Democracy." *Independence Issue Paper* 10-90, July 18, 1990.

Jost, Kenneth. "Term Limits." *CQ Researcher,* January 10, 1992.

———. "What Does the Constitution Say?" *Congressional Quarterly,* September 29, 1990, 3145.

Kamber Group. *Modern Day Snake Oil: Term Limitations and Why They Must Be Defeated.* Los Angeles, 1991.

Katz, Jeffrey L. "The Uncharted Realm of Term Limitation." *Governing,* January 1991, 34-39.

Kernell, Samuel. "Toward Understanding 19th Century Congressional Careers: Ambition, Competition, and Rotation." *American Journal of Political Science* 21(November 1977): 669-693.

Kesler, Charles R. "Bad Housekeeping: The Case Against Congressional Term Limitations." *Policy Review* 53 (Summer 1990): 20-25.

Kinsley, Michael. "Voters in Chains." *The New Republic,* April 2, 1990.

Kurtz, Karl T. "Assessing the Potential Impacts of Term Limitations." *State Legislatures* 18 (January 1992).

———. "Let the Voters Decide." *State Legislatures* 16 (October 1990): 32.

Leo, John. "The Trouble with Self-Esteem." *U.S. News and World Report,* April 2, 1990, 16.

Martin, David L. "Racial Voting in 1990: Helms v. Gantt for U.S. Senator in North Carolina and Legislative Term Limitation in California." Paper presented at the annual meeting of the American Political Science Association, Washington, D.C., August 29-September 1, 1991.

Mitchell, Cleta Deatherage. "The Democratic Case for Term Limits." *The Mainstream Democrat,* December 1990, 21.

———. "Limit Terms? Yes! Congressional Debate." *Extensions* (Carl Albert Congressional Research and Studies Center, University of Oklahoma), Spring 1991, 3-5.

Moncrief, Gary F., and Joel A. Thompson. "The Term Limitation Movement: Assessing Consequences for Female (and Other) State Legislators." Paper presented at conference on legislative term limits, Focused Research Program in Public Choice, University of California, Irvine, May 31-June 1, 1991.

Overby, Marvin L., and Sarah Ritchie. "Mobilized Masses and Strategic Opponents: A Resource Mobilization Analysis of the Clean Air and Nuclear Freeze Movements." *Western Political Quarterly* 44 (June 1991): 329-351.

Paddock, Richard C. "Disaster or Democracy?" *State Legislatures* (July 1991): 22-27.

Payne, James L. "Limiting Government by Limiting Congressional Terms." *Public Interest* 103 (Spring 1991).

Peters, Ronald M., Jr. "Term Limits?" *Extensions* (Carl Albert Congressional Research and Studies Center, University of Oklahoma), Spring 1991, 2, 19-20.

Petracca, Mark P. "Term Limits Will Put an End to Permanent Government by Incumbents." *Public Affairs Report* 31 (November 1990).

_____. "The Poison of Professional Politics in America." Prepared for submission to the Cato Institute, February 1991.

Pitney, John J., Jr. "Appraising Congressional Term Limits." *Harvard Public Policy Review,* forthcoming.

Polsby, Nelson W. "Constitutional Mischief: What's Wrong with Term Limitations?" *The American Prospect,* Summer 1991, 40-43.

Rothstein, Paul, and John B. Gilmour. "The Impact of Term Limitation on Relative Party Strength in Legislatures." Paper prepared for conference on legislative term limits, Focused Research Program in Public Choice, University of California, Irvine, May 31-June 1, 1991.

Schneider, William, and Patrick Reddy. "Altered States: The Demographic Changes and Partisan Shifts of Four Decades (New York, California, Illinois, and Texas)." *The American Enterprise,* July-August 1990, 45.

Seligman, Daniel. "A Line on Clean Air, Conferring with the Cosmos, Incredible Shrinking Unions, and Other Matters." *Fortune,* February 26, 1990, 123.

Simmons, Charlene Wear. "Exclusion from Office." *Campaign,* November 1990, 16.

Struble, Robert, Jr. "House Turnover and the Principle of Rotation." *Political Science Quarterly* 94 (Winter 1979-1980): 649-776.

Struble, Robert, Jr., and Z. W. Jahre. "Rotation in Office: Rapid but Restricted to the House." *PS: Political Science & Politics,* March 1991, 34-37.

Time. "It's a Slap of Reality. As Draconian Funding Cuts Kick in, Mass Layoffs Shake California's Legislature and Reduce Willie Brown to Tears." *Time,* February 18, 1991, 44.

Tompkins, Mark E. "Changing the Terms: Gubernatorial Term Reform in the Modern Era." Paper prepared for the annual meeting of the

Southern Political Science Association, Tampa, Florida, November 1991.
U.S. Congress. Senate Committee on the Judiciary, Subcommittee on the Constitution. *Congressional Tenure,* Hearings on S.J. Res. 27 and S.J. Res. 28, 95th Cong., 2d Sess., 1978.
U.S. Congressional Research Service. "Congressional Terms of Office and Tenure: Historical Background and Contemporary Issues." CRS Report 91-880 GOV., Washington, D.C.: Library of Congress, 1991.
U.S. Congressional Research Service. "Re-Election Rates of House Incumbents: 1790-1988." CRS Report 89-173 GOV. Washington, D.C.: Library of Congress, 1989.
———. "Re-Election Rates of Senate Incumbents, 1790-1988." CRS Report 90-250 GOV. Washington, D.C.: Library of Congress, 1990.
———. "The Constitutionality of States Limiting Congressional Terms." CRS Report 92-19A, Washington, D.C.: Library of Congress, 1992.

CONTRIBUTORS

Gerald Benjamin is professor of political science at the State University of New York, New Paltz, and chairman of the Ulster County Legislature. He has written extensively on the subject of state and local government and worked on the staff of the New York City Charter Revision Commission (1987-89). He is the coauthor of *Rockefeller of New York* (1979) and the coeditor of *The Modern New York State Legislature* (1992).

Thad L. Beyle is professor of political science at the University of North Carolina, Chapel Hill. He is the editor of *Being Governor* (1983), the annual *State Government: CQ's Guide to Current Issues and Activities* (CQ Press, 1985—), *Gubernatorial Transitions, the 1982 Elections* (1985), *Re-electing the Governor, the 1982 Elections* (1986), and *Gubernatorial Transitions, the 1983-84 Elections* (1989).

Gary W. Copeland is associate professor of political science and associate director of the Carl Albert Congressional Research and Studies Center at the University of Oklahoma. His research on Congress, elections, and representative government has appeared in edited volumes and in such journals as the *Journal of Politics* and *Legislative Studies Quarterly*. He is the coeditor of *Congressional Budgeting* (1984).

David Everson holds a joint appointment in the Illinois Legislative Studies Center and the political studies program at Sangamon State University. He is the author of several books and articles on political parties and elections, and he is the editor of *Comparative State Politics*. He is also the author of five mystery novels about Illinois politics.

Linda L. Fowler is professor of political science at Syracuse University. Her book *Congressional Recruitment*, to be published later this year, pursues many of the research questions discussed in *Political Ambition: Who Decides to Run for Congress* (1989), which she coauthored. From 1989 to 1991 she was chair of the legislative studies section of the American Political Science Association.

Michael J. Malbin is professor of political science at the State University of New York, Albany, and director of the Center for Legislative Studies at the Rockefeller Institute of Government, SUNY's institute for public policy research. He is the author of *Unelected Representatives* (1980) and the coauthor of *Vital Statistics on Congress, 1991-92* (CQ Press, 1992). Before arriving in Albany in 1990, he worked for the Iran-Contra committee and the House Republican Conference in Congress, and as speechwriter for the secretary of defense.

David J. Olson is professor of political science at the University of Washington. He is the author of many articles on state and local politics and has written several books, including *Comparative Analysis of West Coast Ports* (1988). His articles on subnational politics have appeared as chapters in edited volumes and in journals on state and city politics.

Mark P. Petracca is assistant professor of political science at the University of California, Irvine. He is the coauthor of *The American Presidency* (1983) and is currently writing *Agenda-Building in American Democracy*. He has written many articles on constitutional reform, political consultants, democratic theory, administrative politics, interest representation, and term limitations.

Charles M. Price is professor of political science at California State University, Chico. He is the author of *California Government Today: Politics of Reform* (fourth edition, 1991) and has written many articles on state legislative politics and direct democracy.

Alan Rosenthal is professor of political science at Rutgers University and director of the Eagleton Institute of Politics. He has worked with legislatures in 35 states, and in 1990 he chaired New Jersey's Ad Hoc Commission on Legislative Ethics and Campaign Finance. His books include *The Political Life of the American States* (1984), *Governors and Legislatures* (CQ Press, 1990), and *The Third House: Lobbyists and Lobbying in the States* (CQ Press, 1992).

Stuart Rothenberg is editor and publisher of the *Rothenberg Political Report*, a Washington, D.C.-based newsletter focusing on U.S. House and Senate elections. He holds a Ph.D. in political science from the University of Connecticut and is a visiting scholar in the department of politics at the Catholic University of America.

INDEX